How to Work the Film & TV Markets

How to Work the Film & TV Markets takes independent filmmakers, television and digital content creators on a virtual tour of the entertainment industry's trade shows — the circulatory system of the entire global media landscape. This book highlights the most significant annual events around the world, details a dossier of all the players that frequent them and examines the elements that drive the market value and profitability of entertainment properties. In-the-trenches insights from our modern, real-world marketplace are contextualized into immediately implementable practical advice. Make the most of your finite investments of funds, time and creative energy to optimize your odds for success not only within the mainstream, business-to-business circuit. Learn how to select, apply and scale prudent, proven principals to complement the most promising disruptive strategies to drive your own Do-It-Yourself/Direct-to-the-Consuming-Crowd fundraising, distribution and promotional success.

Heather Hale demystifies these markets, making them less intimidating, less confusing and less overwhelming. She shows you how to navigate these events, making them far more accessible, productive — and fun!

This creative guide offers:

- An in-depth survey of the most significant film, TV and digital content trade shows around the world;
- An overview of the co-production market circuit that offers financing and development support to independent producers;
- An outline of the market-like festivals and key awards shows;
- A breakdown of who's who at all these events – and how to network with them;
- Hot Tips on how to prepare for, execute and follow up on these prime opportunities;
- Low-budget key art samples and game plans;
- A social media speed tour with a wealth of audience engagement ideas.

Heather Hale is a film and TV director, producer and screenwriter of original programming, including the indie comedy *Rolling Romance* (2018), the thriller *Absolute Killers* (2011), the Lifetime Original Movie *The Courage to Love* (2000), as well as several award-winning syndicated series and two Emmy-winning PBS series. She was the Independent Film and Television Alliance's Industry Liaison for the 2013 American Film Market as well as the Vice President of Event Programming for the National Association of Television Program Executives, where she helped design and launch the TV Producers' Boot Camp. She often serves as NATPE's official pitch prep consultant, preparing producers to pitch to financiers and distribution executives. Heather speaks and consults around the world, customizing retreats and workshops and is always writing, producing, directing and raising funds for film and television projects.

Stay up-to-date with Heather and Heather Hale Productions at **www.HeatherHale.com**

How to Work the Film & TV Markets

A Guide for Content Creators

Heather Hale

Routledge
Taylor & Francis Group

NEW YORK AND LONDON

First published 2018
by Routledge
711 Third Avenue, New York, NY 10017

and by Routledge
2 Park Square, Milton Park, Abingdon, Oxon OX14 4RN

Routledge is an imprint of the Taylor & Francis Group, an informa business

Library of Congress Cataloging-in-Publication Data
Names: Hale, Heather author.
Title: How to work the film & tv markets : a guide for content creators / Heather Hale.
Other titles: How to work the film and tv markets
Description: New York : Routledge, 2017. | Includes index.
Identifiers: LCCN 2016053011 (print) | LCCN 2017012649 (ebook) | ISBN 9781315755359
    (E-book) | ISBN 9781138680517 (hardback) | ISBN 9781138800656 (pbk.)
Subjects: LCSH: Motion pictures—Marketing. | Television programs—Marketing.
Classification: LCC PN1995.9.M29 (ebook) | LCC PN1995.9.M29 H35 2017 (print) |
    DDC 384/.80688—dc23
LC record available at https://lccn.loc.gov/2016053011

ISBN: 978-1-138-68051-7 (hbk)
ISBN: 978-1-138-80065-6 (pbk)
ISBN: 978-1-315-75535-9 (ebk)

Typeset in Palatino
by Apex CoVantage, LLC

This book is dedicated to storytellers all around the world.
And to Mom and Dad.
And Billy.

Contents

Figures

Tables

Preface

In 2013, I was coordinating all the speakers for the American Film Market as the Independent Film and Television Alliance's Industry Liaison. Emily McCloskey, the Acquisitions Editor for Focal Press/Routledge, asked me to help her source prospective subject matter experts from our many panelists and presenters who I thought might make great authors on their respective topics. After helping ensure the publisher's inventory would be as current, relevant and cutting-edge as possible from the resources we had to offer, Emily asked if I saw any remaining holes in their market-focused line-up. I answered without hesitation: "There's never been a book on *How* to *Work* the Markets — and this book was born.

As screenwriters, we're often advised to "write the movie you want to see." As an independent filmmaker and content creator, this is the book I needed to *read*. Last year. A decade ago. When I started my career. Now. Since it so perfectly aligned with the publisher's mission "to make a significant difference in the careers of independent producers by educating and informing them about the business behind the film industry": it was a "no brainer" win-win.

Thus, I put on my journalist's research cap and interviewed hundreds of entertainment industry professionals across the vast spectrum of our media business from all around the world. I relished the opportunity to ask the tough questions I really wanted to hear the truth on, from veterans who could put those answers into context. More importantly, I dared to ask the naïve questions most of us are too embarrassed to ask because they reveal the holes in our Swiss-cheese knowledge of this business that we all inevitably acquire haphazardly, in rushed bits and bytes, on the fly or on-set — often through the mistakes of others.

My unique insider/outsider perspective informs and drives this book. My experiences on these promotional circuits includes the full spectrum of sleeves rolled up behind the scenes designing and actually producing the inner workings of both film and TV markets — while helping fellow creatives make the most of the spectrum of opportunities; to enjoying some of the glamor and glitz, myself, up on stage and screen — as well as being schooled by hard knocks in the trenches.

The first time I was *(almost)* in the trades, I was delighted to read a glowing article about the 2000 Lifetime Original Movie I had speculatively written . . . only to have my smile collapse as I read the last line: crediting it all — *exclusively* — to someone I'd never even met.

For NATPE 2005, I served as the Vice President of Event Programming for the National Association of Television Program Executives where I booked all the speakers for three days on four simultaneous stages. In 2004, I helped develop their TV Producers' Boot Camp, which evolved through several iterations to the LA TV Fest. In 2015, I helped NATPE launch their Breakthrough Reality Awards and Pro Pitch. As a consultant throughout the years, have written a series of genre- and format-specific "How to Pitch TV" articles and have mentored hundreds of aspiring and veteran television producers and content creators behind the scenes to perfect their pitches, one-sheets, pitch packages, series bibles, look books and sizzle reels.

I served as a judge for NATPE's Hollywood Player Pitch Contest, the Marseille WebFest, the College Emmys, Italy's ENDAS, the Hartley-Merrill International Screenwriting Competitions as well as the Disney/ABC Writing Program. I have taught pitching to ABC Drama Executives, guest lectured at USC, Chapman and National University's MFA program, served as a volunteer for the wonderful Indie Spirit Awards and attended several Emmy Awards. When NBC Universal merged with Comcast, I was an approved independent producer vetted by IFTA to pitch television concepts directly to their broadcast network and cable buyers for their four-year agreement and annual independent development fund. I have spoken at dozens of film festivals and conferences on several continents.

I am one of just a handful to ever actually sleep at the Loews Hotel during an AFM. I was there night and day, working the event as full-time staff: facilitating the AFM Conference Series, Producers Forum, studio tour and distributors' California wine tasting. Yet my first market experience, on the front lines as an independent filmmaker, echoed my first mainstream television credit. In 2011, I walked into an exhibitor's suite at the AFM, delighted to see a full sized poster of the indie thriller I had just directed, produced and co-written on the wall — only to be heartbroken (and confused) to see all my credits had been . . . well . . . let's call it "omitted." Again. It's a tough business.

It is my sincere hope that you will learn so much about the converging and diverging businesses of the film and television industries that it'll make an immediate and significant difference in the success of your own strategies and career.

Acknowledgments

I have such abundant gratitude for all my friends, mentors, teachers, students, professional peers, clients and cast and crew members who have contributed to my professional education over the past decade and a half. I'm forever indebted to all my fantastic MasterMinders throughout the years but I'd especially like to thank those who contributed specifically to this book: Anne Marie Gillen, Jenean Atwood Baynes, Pat Quinn, Devorah Cutler-Rubenstein, Kerry David, Suzanne Lyons, Catherine Clinch, Richard "RB" Botto, Keren Green and Gina Gladwell.

An extra-special thanks goes out to all the "Market Makers," the producers of all these markets and festivals. I especially want to thank the wonderful Jérôme Paillard and Julie Bergeron, both of Le Marché du Film and Ventana Sur; the savvy, veteran Beki Probst and her perfect successor, Matthijs Wouter Knol, from the European Film Market; the keen Jean Prewitt, President and CEO of the Independent Film & Television Alliance (IFTA) and my former boss, Jonathan Wolf, "the AFM Honcho" and Managing Director of the American Film Market.

I'm literally prostrate thanking Bridget Jurgens and Jen Sparks of DOG & PONY Creative. Not only did they teach me more than I ever knew I didn't know about key art but they shared so many contacts and high-resolution image files for our communal education (making that the most visual section of this book!) but they did the brilliant cover to boot! And sweet Tui, Kiwi Jo Clark, thank you so much for your patience and endless encouragement in being my first-line reader, book doula and virtual EA. ☺ And finally, my tireless Honeyheart Billy, for all the late nights and early mornings and infinite support and love you give me every day.

So many veterans, visionaries, disrupters and trailblazers graciously contributed to this book, we had to add a whole list of contributors! I'm honored to have gotten the chance to learn from you all. Thank you.

Contributors

Colette Aguilar   CEO and Managing Director, Moonrise Pictures
Jenean Atwood Baynes   Penthouse 10 Creative Consulting
Julie Austin   Producer
Paul Bales   COO, The Asylum; Producer, *Sharknado, Z Nation*
Steven C. Beer   Entertainment Attorney
Julie Bergeron   Head of Industry Programs, Marché du Film, Festival de Cannes and Ventana Sur
Marie Bertonneau   Social Media and Marketing Coordinator, The Asylum
Eric Bonté   Marche du Film Photographer
Richard "RB" Botto   Founder, Stage 32; Screenwriter, Producer
Alexandra Boylan   Producer, *Home Sweet Home, Catching Faith, Ms. In the Biz*
Beth Braen   SVP Marketing, NATPE
Laura Brennan   *Time Tours, Inc.*
Dwight Cenac   Co-Founder, IndyOh
Catherine Clinch   Screenwriter/Blogger, Nuclear Family Films
Jerome Courshon   Film Distribution Solutions
Benjamin Craig   CannesGuide.com
Steve Creech   Vice President, Wyland Worldwide
Devorah Cutler-Rubenstein   Producer/Director, *The Substitute*
Lia Darjes   EFM/Berlinale Photographer
Kerry David   CEO, KDC & Films, IndieProducer.Net; Producer, *Agent Cody Banks, My Date with Drew*
Brooke Dooley   Executive Producer and Founder of Knox Avenue
Louise DuArt   *Up Island/Down Island*
David Duncan   *3D Cakes*
Ron Eddlemon   *21 Hours*
Ken Eisen   Programming Director, Maine Film Center
Chad Faltz   The Cross Agency
Rob Foster   *My Wife, My Fiancée & Me*
Dr. Lucas Fry   *Music Rowe*
Adam Galen   Manager, Worldwide Sales & Digital Affairs, Preferred Content
Gene George   EVP Worldwide Distribution, Starz Media
Anne Marie Gillen   The Gillen Group, *The Producers Business Handbook*; Producer, *Fried Green Tomatoes, Under Suspicion, Into Temptation*
Anthony I. Ginnane   President, IFM World Releasing, Inc.

Gina Gladwell   Screenwriter
Nicolas Gonda   Producer, *Tree of Life;* Founder, Tugg
Peter M. Graham II   Managing Member, 120dB Films
Dominique Greene   Festival Delegate, Berlinale
Elliot Grove   Founder, Raindance Film Festival and British Independent Film Awards
Sergio Guerrero   *Breaking News*
Marizta Guimet   President, Florida Media Market & GMW
E. Barry Haldeman   Entertainment Attorney
Marcy and Strath Hamilton   CEOs, TriCoast Worldwide & Studios
Mike Hatton   Executive Producer, *Ton of Hats*
Peter Himsel   EFM/Berlinale Photographer
Kevin Hoiseth   VP, International Distribution & Acquisitions, International Film Trust
Billy Holcomb   Director of Client Relations, IndyOh
Gil Holland   Producer, The Group Entertainment
Richard Hübner   EFM/Berlinale Photographer
Brian Seth Hurst   Managing Partner, StoryTech
Kevin Iwashina   Founder & CEO, Preferred Content
Bridget Jurgens   Principal/Managing Director, DOG & PONY Creative
Lloyd Kaufman   President, Troma Entertainment. Inc.
Ryan Keller   International Film Sales Agent (Founder), Instrum International
Gabrielle Kelly   Filmmaker and Educator, *Global Media Labs: The New Development Deal, Celluloid Ceiling: Women Film Directors Breaking Through*
Matthijs Wouter Knol   Director, European Film Market
Lesley Kontowicz   Screenwriter
Heidi Haddad Kozak   *The Mary Jane Girls*
Peter Bille Krogh   Managing Director, European Collection Agency
Les Lad   *Music Rowe*
Amber J. Lawson   CEO, Comedy Gives Back
Mark Litwak   Entertainment Attorney
Suzanne Lyons   Producer, Snowfall Films, Indie Film Producing; *The Calling, Undertaking Betty, Bailey's Billion$, The Chaperone*
Emily McCloskey   Editor, Focal Press/Routledge
Mariel Macia   Film Acquisitions Manager
Mikey McManus   EP, 4AM Films, Inc.; Wayfarer Entertainment
Robert Manasier   President and CEO, IFP Films/In Focus Brands
Ida Martins   CEO, Sales and Acquisitions, Media Luna New Films
Gene Massey   CEO, MediaShares.com
Carolyn Miller   *Digital Storytelling: A Creator's Guide to Interactive Entertainment*
Wendy Mitchell   Editor, *Screen International*
Kevin Moore   *Hook, Line & Sinker*
Kimberly Morgan   *Sins of the Midnight Sons*
David A. Morris   Branding and media professional
Oliver Möst   EFM/Berlinale Photographer
Bruce Nahin   Business affairs professional
Volker Otte   CEO, OnTrust Collection Agency
Jérôme Paillard   Executive Director, Marché du Film/Cinando, Ventana Sur
Stephanie Palmer   CEO, Good in a Room
Stephan Paternot   Founder, Slated
Rod Perth   President and CEO, NATPE
Janet Pierson   Head of SXSW Film Conference & Festival
Gary Polston   Screenwriter

Jean Prewitt   President and CEO, Independent Film & Television Alliance
Beki Probst   President, European Film Market
Richard Propper   Co-Founder, WESTDOC; Founder/COO, Solid Entertainment
Pat Quinn   Quinn Media Management
Orly Ravid   The Film Collaborative
Glen Reynolds   CEO, Circus Road Films
Will Robelo   Director of Acquisitions and Festivals, Spotlight Pictures
Lise Romanoff   CEO, Vision Films
Drew Rosas   Producer, *Billy Club*
Dr. Stefan Rüll   OnTrust Collection Agency
Squire Rushnell   *Up Island/Down Island*
Morris Ruskin   CEO, Shoreline Entertainment
John Salangsang   Invision for IFTA-AP Images Photographer
Steve Saleen   *21 Hours*; CEO, Saleen Automotive and SMS Signature Cars, Inc.
Jen Sall   Producer
Richard Shotwell   Invision for IFTA/AP Images Photographer
Larry Simmons   *Locked in a Room*, At Risk Entertainment
Mark and Jeanne Simon   Sell Your TV Concept More, Inc.
Sky Soleil   *The Elevator*
Jen Sparks   Principal/Creative Director, DOG & PONY Creative
Andreas Teich   EFM/Berlinale Photographer
Sara Elizabeth Timmons   Life Out Loud Films
James Ulmer   The Ulmer Report
Jeremy Walker   Independent Film Publicist
Doug Whyte   Executive Director, Hollywood Theater
Gadi Wildstrom   CEO, Freeway Entertainment
Jan Windszus   EFM/Berlinale Photographer
Jonathan Wolf   Managing Director, American Film Market
Wyland   Marine Life Artist

Introduction

The economic circulatory system of the mass media marketplace is the worldwide, annual circuit of film and television markets. The vast majority of business-to-business, country-to-country sales of entertainment properties are transacted at these international, entertainment industry trade shows. Navigating these markets and foreign territories can be daunting. Fun (but expensive) globe-trotting aside, too often, independent producers spend an inordinate amount of their hard-earned cash on airfare, hotels, market accreditations and pitch opportunities only to strike out on what they *thought* they might be able to accomplish there. Investing in exhibition space or paying sales commissions and marketing expenses raise the stakes evermore. Misunderstanding the culture, dynamics and unwritten rules of these markets has left many a great content creator wishing she could turn back the calendar for a market Mulligan.[1]

> *Please note*: To make this material as accessible as possible to readers from all around the globe (many reading this in their second or third languages), acronyms are identified and footnotes have been used to explain industry argot and define colloquial expressions.

While every aspect of our business constantly transmutes, the revolutionary advances in technology over the past couple of decades have significantly reduced the barriers to entry. They have also opened up diverse new thoroughfares towards financing, distribution and promotion, breaking wide open the frontier of possibilities for innovative risk takers. The downside is a supersaturated marketplace. The signal-to-noise ratio competing for attention, leisure time and discretionary funds is deafening. It's nearly impossible to make a blip on the radar in the din. Getting noticed (much less gaining traction) can feel overwhelming — hopeless, even.

> Our era presents an odd paradox: it has never been easier to create or distribute content — even internationally — but it has never been harder to finance or promote it.

The dotcom bubble burst. Pockets of real estate and hyped stock picks have crashed. Entire industries — countries, even — have collapsed and been forced to re-invent themselves. And while the disruptors, trailblazers and innovators have a lot to teach us about the future, the past has a great deal to teach us as well. "The more things change, the more they stay the same."[2] History tends to repeat itself. Understanding how common obstacles were overcome in the past — and why — might help us make sense of all the new opportunities on the horizon to identify those that might best serve our specific purposes.

The chasm between the "haves" (deep-pocketed financiers, finely-tuned global distribution machines, A-listers and the well-connected power players in constant orbit around them) versus the "creators" (producers and their many artistic development and production collaborators) has never been greater — or, quite frankly: more porous. Finding the sweet spot between the right combination of assets, at the perfect price point and point of entry, with the right approach strategies can feel like solving a Rubik's Cube — blind. Luck and timing inevitably play a critical role. But contemporary audio-visual digital storytellers have become increasingly shrewd: cobbling together myriad funding sources, overlapping production efficiencies and cross-collateralizing distribution and promotional methods all the while experimenting with windows.[3] **Do-It-Yourself (DIY)** variations have created wild new frontiers — and newsworthy successes and failures.

Yet, markets — and their monetizing prospects — remain a mysterious black hole to many pros in both the film and television arenas. Learning to effectively capitalize on these events throughout their annual cycle can be paramount to bottom-line profitability and long-term career trajectories. Sadly, strategies on how to prudently work the industry's elaborate calendar of events are mostly anecdotal or learned while being christened with fire (usually with slightly singed results).

For many, just stepping foot on these market floors can feel unwelcoming and intimidating. For some, the prospects of cold calling, pitching and (if you're lucky) negotiating with the labyrinth of players at each stage of a project's development can be stupefying. But these activities are part of the life cycle of most profit-aspiring projects in our ever-converging industries. These forums can prove to be career and even life changing: giving birth to fruitful partnerships, lifelong friendships, creative legacies — and sometimes windfalls.

There are those who predict the demise of these huge events or at least challenge the need for them or their continued relevance in light of the increased ease of international connectivity and the speed of media exchange of our ever-shrinking globe. But these are the precise factors that actually increase the value proposition these markets deliver. Their compressed efficiencies offer precious face-to-face interactions with thousands of proactive professionals from all around the globe, gathered together, in one place, at the same time, with the same shared synergistic focus of buying and selling (developing, financing, marketing, distributing, promoting and monetizing) content. In spite of all the wonderful access, speed, conveniences and resources modern technology affords, it still cannot replicate the power of the in-person, first impression to ascertain initial interpersonal chemistry. Not to mention, the power of breaking bread or clinking glasses or mugs to nurture camaraderie with new and old business associates.

THIS GUIDEBOOK = ORIENTATION + COMPENDIUM + ALMANAC + "HOW-TO" MANUAL

No one could possibly be an expert in every element of this expansive material. Not to mention: it is constantly changing. Encompassing the entire global marketplace of the converging industries of film, television and Internet media into one book is an ambitious undertaking. Add to that that reference books, by their very nature (especially in today's nanosecond world), begin to stale-date upon being published. Yet, unlike current event blogs, books, as a literary form, offer the space and time to do deep dives on specific topics while contextualizing the big picture. Thus, this guidebook is intended as part orientation and overview, part compendium and almanac and part "How-To" manual. While these events are moving targets, a ballpark Annual Calendar of the key industry events has been created as a quick reference (see Table I.1).

Another at-a-glance guide that might prove useful to put all these pieces into perspective is the numbers matrix juxtaposing some of the key statistics of the major markets (see Table I.2).

These two tools will be actively hyperlinked to a global map with current event links, interviews and case studies and kept as up-to-date[4] as possible on the book's complementary website: www.HowtoWorktheFilmandTVMarkets.com.

WHO THIS BOOK IS FOR

This book is not just for neophytes entering our business. Though it was certainly designed to be accessible and empowering to aspirants, it should prove equally as practical to veterans exploring new opportunities on the other side of their format fence. As all these sibling industries collide, the fault lines break open opportunities for actors and seasoned below-the-line veterans to ascend the above-the-line ladder just as savvy business people, academics and technicians from overlapping fields apply their extensive transferable expertise as they move laterally into entertainment industry careers. Thus, this book is for everyone who has a story to tell (and wants to get their story out there) — and all those who love the collaborative craft of storytelling!

THE GOAL OF THIS BOOK

"Hollywood" can be an opaque and convoluted marketplace. Behind-the-scenes, from-the-trenches glimpses reveal how historic business models have traditionally functioned as an invaluable frame of reference for how they are being revolutionized. Written in simple layman's terms as if I were facilitating a fun, interactive, peer-to-peer workshop — or just trading insights with comrades, I wanted to divulge not only "how the sausage gets made" (i.e., how film and television properties are actually conveyed through the stages of development, financing, production, screening, and promotion around the world) but also to unveil the wizards behind the tiers of curtains.

Our business is as collaborative as our art. Meeting and staying connected face-to-face are invaluable — especially with prospective partners from the other side of the world, from other cultures, speaking different native languages and navigating business through very different cultural prisms. It's hard to beat the ways markets facilitate these interactions. This annual injection of inspiration, education, fresh information, and camaraderie — not to mention the catalyzing force (for the creative class, especially) of arbitrary and cyclical deadlines for deliverables and milestones — cannot be underestimated.

This book will help you create a default flight plan that you can customize for each new approach and make navigating this round robin circuit something you can look forward to, pilot with facility, economy, and effectiveness — and hopefully: benefit and profit from (or at least have more fun in these milieus). Or — if you choose to circumvent this whole scene altogether: how to proficiently and prudently apply their most proven strategies outside their perimeters.

Table I.1 Annual Industry Calendar

FILM MARKETS	CO-PRODUCTION MARKETS	FESTIVALS (Film)	FESTIVALS (TV)	TV MARKETS	AWARDS	Other
JANUARY						
	CineMart & Rotterdam Lab	IFF Rotterdam		NATPE	Breakthrough Reality Awards	
					Brandon Tartikoff Legacy Awards	
		Sundance FF		Realscreen Summit	Golden Globes	
		Palm Springs IFF		DISCOP Dubai	People's Choice	
			FIPA		PGA Awards	
					SAG Awards	
						CES
FEBRUARY						
EFM	Berlinale Co-Pro Market	Berlinale IFF		World Content (Prague)	Oscars (Academy Awards)	
			aTVfest	Kidscreen Summit	BAFTAs	
					Film Independent Spirit Awards	
					DGA Awards	
					WGA Awards	
					Razzies	
MARCH						
	Sofia Meetings/Balkan Screenings	SXSW			Spanish Film Awards (Goya)	
		Sofia IFF				CinemaCon
			FESCPACO			PromaxBDA
			Celtic Media			
Hong Kong FILMART	HAF	Hong Kong IFF		Hong Kong FILMART	Asian Film Awards	
					Hong Kong Film Awards	
						Entertainment Expo Hong Kong
APRIL						
		Tribeca FF		MIP-TV (MIPDocs & MIPFormats)	MTV Movie Awards	
	Frontières	Brussels IFF			TV Land Awards	Entertainment Expo Hong Kong
		Hong Kong IFF				
	Beijing Film Market	Beijing IFF				NAB
		Buenos Aires IFF				
MAY						
Marche Du Film		Festival de Cannes				LA Screenings
						Upfronts
JUNE						
	DISCOPRO			DISCOP Abidjan		Digital Content NewFronts
						INTX
London Screenings		Los Angeles FF		NATPE Europe		
		Palm Springs ShortFest		Stream Market	German Film Awards (Lola)	Midem

Annual Calendar of Industry Events

JULY

- Real Screen Awards
- Real Screen West
- Munich FF
- Monte-Carlo TV
- BANFF World Media
- ATX TV Fest
- SeriesFest
- Paris Co-Pro Village
- Champs-Élysées FF
- Moscow Business Square
- Moscow IFF
- Frontières
- Fantasia IFF

AUGUST

- Bogota Audiovisual Market
- Comic-Con
- CineLink Co-Pro Market
- Sarajevo FF
- DISCOPRO
- Kalasha
- DISCOP Nairobi

SEPTEMBER

- Emmy Awards
- Streamy Awards
- Toronto IFF
- Telluride FF
- Venice Production Bridge
- Venice IFF
- Raindance IFF
- Europe-Latin America Co-Pro Forum
- San Sebastian FF
- Holland Film Meeting
- Netherlands FF
- IFP No Borders Int'l Co-Pro
- FesTVal Spain
- ITVFest

OCTOBER

- Britannia Awards
- MIPCOM (& MIPJr)
- TIFFCOM
- World Content (St Petersburg)
- Realscreen London
- NYTVF
- VerCiência Brazil
- Asian Film Market
- TIFFCOM
- Busan IFF
- Tokyo IFF
- Austin FF
- Boat Meeting
- Kyiv Molodist IFF

NOVEMBER

- World Animation & VFX Summit
- US–China Film Summit
- World Content (Moscow)
- My Content
- DISCOP Joburg
- MIP Cancun/Lantam Summit
- AFI
- AFM
- New York IFF
- DISCOPRO
- BANFF
- CPH:FORUM
- Copenhagen IDFF
- TorinoFilmLab
- IDFA Forum
- IDF Amsterdam
- Frontières Int'l Co-Pro Market

DECEMBER

- Asian Television Awards
- Asia TV Summit
- Ventana Sur
- Arc 1950 Co-Production Village
- Les Arcs European FF
- Singapore IFF

For the most up-to-date, hyperlinked version of this Annual Calendar of Industry Events, please visit: www.HeatherHale.com/AnnualCalendar

Table I.2 Major Markets Number Matrix

MONTH	MARKET	LOCATION	MAJOR MARKET NUMBERS														
			ATTENDEES	COUNTRIES	BUYERS/AGENTS	COMPANIES	EXHIBITORS	EXHIBITING COUNTRIES	BOOTHS/PAVILIONS	THEATRICAL DISTRIBUTORS	SALES AGENTS	PROGRAMMERS	PRODUCERS	FILMS	SCREENINGS	PREMIERES	FOUNDED
Jan	NATPE	Florida	7,000	46	1,113	300+											
Jan	REALSCREEN SUMMIT	Washington	2,600+	28	50												
Feb	EFM	Berlin	8,628	98	1,499		487		183					748	1,109	574	1973
Mar	HONG KONG FILMART	Hong Kong		60	7,300		800	30							400	80	1997
Apr	MIPTV	Cannes	11,083	100+	3,915	1,700	1,632		25								
Apr	MIPFORMAT	Cannes	992	67	327												
Apr	MIPDOC	Cannes	850	58	400	560						1,600			27,097		
May	MARCHE DU FILM	Cannes	11,900	120	1,834	5,055	644		410	2,300	1,500	790	4,000	3,450	1,426	790	1959
Jun	NATPE EUROPE	Prague	700	47	350	152											

Jun	REALSCREEN WEST	California	1,137	15	200+								
Sep	REALSCREEN LONDON	London	400+										
Oct	ASIAN FILM MARKET	South Korea	1,572	16	208					74	60		
Oct	MIPJUNIOR	Cannes	1,400	65	590	785			976	35,470			
Oct	MIPCOM	Cannes	13,700	112	4,800	4,623	2,019	46					
Nov	AFM	California	8,000	80	1,670	794	2,825	40	400	1,000	700	437	1981

These were the most current statistics provided when we went to print (May, 2017). Not all events track or share the same statistics or calculate them the same way.

Please feel free to visit www.HeatherHale.com/MarketsNumbersMatrix for the most up-to-date, hyperlinked stats available. Send updates to: Author@HeatherHale.com

Read this before you attend a market. Before you shoot. Before you even write. Improve your premise and literary development. Enhance your insights into the psychographics of your audience, your key art, fundraising and packaging efforts all the way through principal photography and post-production to all the deals you make along the way, through to the strategies you employ for marketing and distribution. Whether you want to find your most profitable and productive place within this ever-changing ecosystem or machete your own, iconoclastic new path through our communal obstacle course, it's good to know what the rules are (*or at least were*) and who the players on the game board are (and how they're evolving). I hope this book empowers you to do both and has an immediate, practical and constructive impact on the skills and strategies of the creative class — the digital storytellers of our new millennium.

The world needs all our stories.

NOTES

1 A second chance; a golf term meaning a "do over."
2 A French adage: "plus ça change, plus c'est la même chose."
3 "Windows" refers to the time-periods content is distributed via various formats (i.e. a film's theatrical release, when content is made available via cable, pay TV, DVD, VOD, etc.)
4 Feel free to send updates to: Author@HeatherHale.com.

Part I
The Markets

What Is a Market?

Film and television markets are the entertainment industry's trade shows and like everything else in show business, they tend to be more glamorous, faster paced and much more intimidating than most other business sectors. Following a competitive, annual globe-trotting circuit akin to that of pro golfers, anglers or race car drivers, content providers continent-hop to meet, pitch to and hopefully negotiate face-to-face with financiers, sales agents, distributors and exhibitors from every culture and platform. Whether just initiating the development of a new concept, keeping tabs on active sales campaigns or periodically touching base with relationships solidified over decades, these markets are where fruitful, long-term relationships are born and enriched.

Entire cottage industries have popped up around these mass migrations. Elements of the full spectrum of the industry emerge locally or follow the flock to where the action is. Software vendors, legal and financial service providers, locations luring production and publicists enticing attention to their clients or clients' projects all come in droves. Reporters stalk the market floor for industry scoops while critics pan the symbiotic and often concurrent festival circuit silt for gold. Of course, as with any industry, all of this heat and activity also attracts a whole host of posers, players, scam artists, sharks, wannabes and someday-might-bes who flock to the markets too, crowding the many proactive independent producers trying to navigate the whole hectic scene to find their productive place in it. But everyone shares the same goal: *to do some business.*

MARKET ESTABLISHING SHOT

Exhibition Space

Exhibitors rent out booths or stands on the market floors, in the pavilions or venue hotel rooms. As an example, in the case of the American Film Market, every bed is removed from the beachfront Loews Hotel in Santa Monica and each hotel room is converted into office suites and temporary meeting and screening rooms as per each company's schematic. Over at the annual conference of the National Association of Television Program Executives (NATPE), the market floor at the Fontainebleau in Miami, Florida is augmented by its four towers, poolside cabanas and suite overflow at the adjacent Eden Rock Hotel — all customized into showcase spaces.

Source: © NATPE.

Source: © NATPE. Courtesy SWPix and NATPE.

Source: © NATPE.

The day before each market opens, exhibiting company representatives line the walls of their suites or booths with posters. They load display stands with catalogs and one sheets, hook up flat screen TVs and set up iPads to show off trailers, sizzle reels, completed scenes and episodes. DVDs and flash drives are pre-loaded with screeners at the ready as tradeshow giveaways to qualified leads.

Screenings

Screenings vary from theaters that are booked well in advance for highly publicized red-carpet gala events, complete with stars and paparazzi; to small group viewings booked for first thing on a weekday morning in converted hotel rooms; to spontaneous, one-on-one tablet screenings while standing at lounge tables during the many happy-hour gatherings. It is not uncommon for prospective buyers to have already viewed all of the inventory they are interested in acquiring prior to attending the market via secure viewing databases like Cinando.[1] Instead of traveling halfway around the world to stare at screens non-stop during the market, they focus their precious limited time on building rapport face-to-face and closing deals with professionals they've come to meet in person.

> Ask any exhibitor, at any trade show, in any industry: "Who do you want walking around the market floor?" Their answer will be unanimous: "qualified buyers." Anything else is distracting clutter to their primary purpose of investing their time, energy and company resources,

explains Jonathan Wolf, Managing Director of the **American Film Market** (AFM). "For the first fifteen years, that's all it was." But things change . . .

Educational and Networking Opportunities

Since the turn of the millennium, the markets have begun to diversify their reach to encompass the independent, creative producing class. In addition to the sales foci of their market floors, every show now offers educational conferences, panels, pitching and networking opportunities. "Like a super tanker out in the ocean, these events change slowly," Jonathan continues. "Attendees who haven't been in a long time are often surprised at how different the show is in its tenor or tone. The Filmmaker's Lounge, for example, was unheard of 15 years ago."

Many events strive to facilitate matchmaking opportunities like co-production marketplaces, topic-specific roundtables and invite-only cocktails, meals or niche educational and networking forums. Cannes led the pack with their Producers Network and Producers Workshop. Virtually all the other events have followed suit with customized educational tracts and private cocktail parties enabling qualified and emerging professionals the opportunity to interact with their accredited tribes.

All of the events are experimenting with matchmaking services. Jenean Atwood Baynes led the charge when she was the Director of Buyer Initiatives for NATPE, aggressively experimenting with various iterations of the NATPE Navigator, offering a white glove treatment to participating exhibitors by providing meeting concierge services as well as testing a myriad different speed-dating-like pitching opportunities for vetted and prepped-in-advance professional producers.

Many badges (but rarely day passes) come with year-round access to connectivity databases similar to LinkedIn for each specific market. As examples: Cinando, MYAFM and myNATPE enable attendees to do advance research and follow-up for a year after each event. Most venues also have ever-improving and usually free mobile apps that dramatically increase your on-site productivity.

WHAT'S THE DIFFERENCE BETWEEN A MARKET AND A FESTIVAL?

This is not meant to be overly simplistic. Quite the contrary: it is incredibly common even for industry professionals of all ranks and longevity to lump these events together and crisscross their references synonymously in conversation. When referencing "Cannes," a seasoned veteran might be referring to Le Marché du Film (the Cannes Film Market), the Festival de Cannes (the Cannes Film Festival), MIPCOM or MIPTV (television markets) or even MIDEM (a market for the music industry's ecosystem) — all different events, held at different times throughout the year — but at the same facilities in the same beautiful eponymous French city. These blurred lines become all the more muddled to the uninitiated as the film market and festival collide on the Croisette (the beach front promenade), where the crush of red-carpet premiere crowds can make it difficult for dealmakers to hustle from meeting to meeting.

Confusion Abounds

Berlinale (the Berlin International Film Festival) is inextricably integrated with its concurrent and adjacent European Film Market (EFM). Is TIFF in September or October? Well, the Toronto International Film Festival is in September but the *Tokyo* International Film Festival is the very next month, in October. Are there two AFMs? Well, the American Film Market is in Santa Monica in November, separate and distinct — and a whole world away from — the *Asian* Film Market in Korea, the month before, in October, which is held in conjunction with the Busan International Film Festival. "Toronto" is often talked about as if it were a market, as is Sundance, because so many sales and such great industry buzz results from these fine Tier 1 *festivals*. Although neither have market floors, suites or pavilions, they both enjoy robust market-like activity and have many market-like elements.[2]

    In some cases, it's hard to know which event you're attending. Many attendees are blissfully oblivious to these distinctions — and that's fine if you're there for fun — but if you're investing your money with intention, it's important to be able to delineate between these events and their purposes. Far too many chagrined filmmakers have mistakenly bought a pass to a festival when they meant to get a badge for its market. Or worse: they committed thousands of dollars in airfare, hotels and registrations, only to find themselves on the other side of the globe — during the wrong week — at its sibling event they confused it with, making it nearly impossible for them to achieve their initial intentions. These "learning opportunities" can, of course, result in a lot of edifying experiences but far better for you to clearly understand their disparities in advance in order to more effectively pursue your goals — and enjoy them both for what they offer.

Festivals Versus Markets

Festivals are curated. They are subject to the festival director's taste or the gatekeepers passing judgment on quality. There are no "prizes" given at markets. Nor is there any kind of a selection or vetting process. The size and scope of the material presented at the markets represents essentially the entire spectrum of that year's (or the past few years' worth of) inventory. To put this in perspective: the 21 films *in competition* at the 2016 Cannes Film *Festival* were dwarfed by the 3,350 films that were presented at its concurrent Cannes Film *Market*.

    Festivals are typically about the art, honoring the craft and audience enjoyment. They are about community. And while many attract international filmmakers, they tend to be more locally based or sometimes genre-focused. Festivals are usually open to the public whereas markets are typically restricted to accredited industry professionals for the purposes of sales (to then turn around and sell those same products to the wider, public audience — sometimes even via the promotional platform of festivals).

> Festivals = Show
> Markets = Business

Typically, the panelists at film markets are producers, distributors, sales agents and attorneys revealing the inner workings of the business of show with a unified focus on sales, sales and more sales. The same is true at the TV markets, but here, where episodic or serial content is king, you are more likely to see panels of Show Runners and Writer-Producers (as Creative Executives) as well, with an educational focus on future trends.

Directors don't typically attend markets unless they are coming wearing one of their other multi-hyphenate hats (attending instead as a *writer*-director or *producer*-director), trying to set up projects or transact deals. Their domain tends to remain over on the festival circuit where directors are king and art is their queen. On panels at festivals, directors, actors and department heads share "in the trenches" stories about their creative collaborative processes: origin stories of their creative concepts, what it was like to work together, production challenges and creative solutions.

Festival screenings are for audiences to enjoy, to build a project's pedigree and fan base. Festival parties are for fun and celebration (and, of course, PR — with an eye to driving sales later). Critics don't critique market product (that is, until it is ready to hit the marketplace — and thus relevant to filmgoers). As a matter of fact, in the case of the American Film Market at least, press is actually excluded from all screenings (though, they are welcome to cover the educational conferences and rest of the event's business). A rough-hewn oversimplification of press activity, then, might be that critics review the art at festivals while reporters cover the business from the market floors.

Many distributors scout festivals not so much to watch the films but rather to watch the audience's reactions to those films they are prospecting. Setting aside their own personal, subjective opinions, if a distributor likes the audience's reception to what's playing and thinks she might be able to sell it, she might duck out into the lobby — even just fifteen minutes into a promising screening — to make a pre-emptive bid.

Kevin Iwashina, Managing Partner of Preferred Content, a film, television, and digital sales, finance and advisory company, explains:

> Film festivals offer already curated product, so the artistic reviews, critical response, publicity representation and consumer press are the most important parts of that process. In a market environment, it's a different kind of awareness, more focused on trade publications.

Festivals are sponsored by local film groups, independent theater chains, online platforms, and local non-profits. They are often funded by ticket sales and sometimes grants or public funds. Markets, on the other hand, are paid for by sponsors targeting the industry players; the players themselves, exhibiting their wares to peers, platforms and other territories, not to mention the badge fees of the many attendees hoping to buy access to key decision makers, information and education.

Both markets and festivals tend to have conference components such as panels, workshops, keynote addresses, breakout roundtable discussions, pitch fests, and so on. In addition to the structured educational opportunities offered, real-world epiphanies abound in every elevator and bar. I learned more in a few minutes from an inadvertently overheard snippet of conversation between a veteran sales agent teaching her wet-behind-the-ears-peer "negotiating strategies" than in my entire four-year bachelor's degree! It's unfiltered, "boots on the ground" information. This first-hand input is magnified exponentially by professional comrades sharing their own war stories of what (and who) to avoid and what to try next (or how to do it better next time). Enjoying the luxury of down time, breaking bread and toasting a glass or mug with prospects, creatives and entrepreneurs alike — even those already living in key media metropolises — often come away reinvigorated by emerging opportunities and fresh, new approaches of getting it right.

Festivals can be more glamorous with their red-carpet premieres, parties and paparazzi but markets also boast huge stars gracing opulent black-tie events. With increasing overlap between events and industries, many of these gala events are seamlessly integrated. But bear in mind: a local garage marathon — a simple compilation of student films — can qualify as a festival, even if none of the projects are ever sold or even seen outside that venue. Equally, a calendar or art house theater's monthly promotion of a series of niche or classic films can be *branded* as a "festival" even if there's no actual competition and it's just a *marketing strategy* to get local butts in the seats.

All of these scenarios are opportunities to celebrate elements of the craft, engage with your community and often to promote you and your projects — but markets can't be replicated quite as easily. Not just because of their scope and scale but because they require the *attendance and participation of so many key decision makers*. Perhaps the most important distinction between festivals and markets is the pure density and intensity of *buyers* at markets. At film festival parties and premieres, you are often relying on pure chance to randomly run into ambiguous prospects. At the markets, the directories, suites, signage, maps and online tools not only enhance your identifying, accessing and doing advance due diligence on distributors, financiers and sales agents, but exponentially increase your odds of securing professional pitch opportunities to a much more expansive and better vetted pool of legitimate candidates. Even considering festivals increasingly adding formal pitch opportunities to their schedules, their program might afford one to even five wonderful opportunities over a four-day festival — which you could accomplish in an hour at a market. It's economy of scale — and logistics. While markets and festivals — like everything else in the entertainment industry — are all about promotion (and perception), it all ultimately comes down to relationships — and the markets are the lifeblood of the entertainment's *industry*.

SHOULD YOU GO TO EITHER? BOTH? WHY?

In my opinion, every filmmaker or content creator should go to at least one market. Ideally, as early in your career as possible. Your head will explode with what you'll learn. Actually, if money is no object (*but when isn't it?*), hit as many as you can. If it is (usually), figure out a way to volunteer, network, joint venture, co-op, couch surf, roommate or road trip your way to as wide a variety of both markets and festivals as you can over the course of your career. Even if you don't accomplish the goals you set out to (or aren't even sure why you're going in the first place!), just immersing yourself in these milieus is a bit like living in another land to learn a foreign language. Each journey will forevermore change the way you look at everything you're doing — even if only to further validate and empower your own DIY strategies.

Our business is constantly transmuting. So are these markets. In an ideal world, you could hit them all, all the time (but then, you might want to consider becoming a sales agent!). Most of us can't hit them all (unless our core business is sales). Rare is the producer who has pockets deep enough or the luxury of free time or infinite resources (or even interest) to stretch that far, that often, to attend and effectively present at every market, every year. Thus, you must carefully select and budget these forays and/or your partners who will promote your projects for you. It's a bit like succession planting, an organic gardening strategy where you vary where and when you plant your seeds to extend your growing (selling) season to increase the fruits (profits) of your labor and ensure your farmland remains fertile season after season.

There is typically a 75 percent churn rate among the producers that attend many of these events. Even among the exhibitors or vendors who are there, year after year, for decades: about a third of them vary from market to market, year to year, too. So, while your current resources might dictate which market you attend now, if "worked" effectively, your attendance at any of these events can be capitalized into a greater return on your investment by amortizing it across all your future projects because all of your inventory and efforts will benefit as your knowledge matures and your network expands.

The cyclical and roving nature of these events also offers prime point-of-entry opportunities for content creators to commence conversations about future projects in their development pipelines: to solicit financing, vet the current market value of contemplated talent attachments and to seek potential co-production joint ventures and distribution deals. Targeting and strategizing these traction-creating conversations effectively is the crux of this book.

Thus, be ever alert for opportunities to hit these events when and as you can. Seeing this part of the industry up close and personal might make you adjust your projects or focus — or even reroute your entire career path. Or, it might shift your DIY gears with renewed vigor and insights, stimulating wonderful brainstorms of entirely new hybrid paths that open up new models for all of us.

That's the beauty of the collision of input: the sensory overload these chaotic events offer might trigger your perception of connections you might not otherwise have synthesized. Regardless, you will come away with your ax sharpened. And you will have some fun. Hopefully, you'll even make some new friends. And ideally, you'll have put some gas in the tank and generated some traction. In a world where international business can increasingly be conducted via email and videoconferencing, cultivating these business connections periodically, with consistent, in-person touchpoints, has become all the more important to staying on the right people's radars, keeping your relationships on the rails and project pipelines moving forward.

Q: But . . . Does My Sales Agent Even Want Me There?
A: Yes. And no.
(The universal answer to all things Hollywood = "It depends . . .")

In an ideal world, you won't actually have time to hit the market because you'll already be funded and busy producing your next project.

But . . . *what if you're not?*

"In the old days" producers didn't typically attend these markets. In the twentieth century, pioneering independent filmmakers and content creators might have been underfoot at these markets. But now the markets increasingly program entire tracts and forums specifically for Content Creators.

Allow the people you've signed contracts with do the job you're paying them to do: sell your existing "in the can" product now. But rarely is there a better time to network at a market than when you have something being sold there. It's so easy to establish your credibility in an instant by just pointing to your poster on the wall or opening the catalog to your screening times. This is when you *should* be looking for financing, distribution and co-production opportunities for your *next* project.

Hitting a market where your product is being represented[3] can be simultaneously exhilarating and profoundly humbling. You might feel validated: you've finally "made it!" But a sympathy epiphany will engulf you: your tiny, little indie film or solitary television format must compete in this insane cacophony for shelf, wall or screen space and ADHD[4] eyeballs?! But this is nothing compared to its rivals for attention in the open mass audience marketplace. Nothing more viscerally drives home the reality of how important your high concept, perfect title, clever logline, sharp, concise pitch and brilliant key art are to your project ever getting noticed in the midst of this orchestrated chaos.

AREN'T FILM AND TELEVISION TOTALLY DIFFERENT INDUSTRIES?

Film and television have historically been discrete businesses segments with very different development, financing, distribution and marketing models that rarely overlapped. But, as the types and forms of entertainment morph and converge more each day, the traversing players bring not only their trusted teams — but also their familiar methods of operation — right along with them.

Successful independent filmmakers and television and Internet content creators are rethinking every aspect of our overlapping businesses — especially pre-conceived notions like a television show has to be either 22 or 44 minutes long, with 22 episodes in each season — *or even on TV.*

This increasing blending far outweighs the distinctions between these two arenas but the full spectrum of both worlds will be addressed in this book. The platforms and means of distribution continue to vary and evolve but to independent content creators (i.e. audio-visual storytellers for mass and/or niche audiences), how this material is consumed (i.e. paid for or received) is perhaps less important to us than how it is financed and created, discovered and curated. Thus, the dreams we share for our independent labors of love vary only slightly based on the medium.

THE INDEPENDENT FILMMAKER'S FANTASY

Your brilliant script attracts a couple of A-list stars who are willing to attach without a pay or play offer. They even agree to work, partially deferred, for SAG's Low-Budget Scale. You will produce your directorial debut. Of course, not a soul challenges

THE TV OR DIGITAL CONTENT CREATOR'S DREAM

Your sizzle reel, one sheet, series bible, pilot and sample script attracts A-list talent that all the broadcast and cable nets want to be in business with — but you're also being courted by Over-the-Top-Television (OTT) platforms who are game to fund you as a rookie at the helm. You attract a high-profile, trustworthy, joy-to-work-with co-producing partner who comes on board to competently and ethically take all the financial, logistical and legal headaches off your plate. You are liberated to exercise your auteur muscles during an extended period of prep, which includes rehearsals that cast and crew alike are all excited to participate in, that the budget can comfortably accommodate. You over-prepare (not that that's possible) but are delighted by the miracles and lucky breaks that surprise you throughout your principal photography and post-production.

You premiere at a top-tier international film festival, win the festival's top prize as well as the audience award. You're the critics' darling. The most respected mini-majors in the business get into a highly publicized bidding war and the winner sells out all the worldwide territories in a flurry, recouping all the investors' capital with a nice 20 percent bump prior to theatrical release. You're even the buzz as a breakout dark horse for award season. You win an Indie Spirit Award. Your next two projects get funded with advance distribution commitments. You buy a beautiful beachfront Malibu home (but only as a second home crash pad for the AFM or studio meetings when you're not in Tuscany) and you move on to your next labor-of-love project in your slate.

your whole first season and give you complete creative control. A short list of Show Runners are lined up *to court you*. While you hit it off with all of them (for future projects, of course), the one who really gets this project has a personal connection to it and really wants to mentor you and let you stay involved in the creative elements while she'll clear all the logistical and legal headaches off your plate.

Forget that 100th episode! The show is a breakout success and gets syndicated on competing nets by year three (thank you, *Modern Family*!). You get a studio deal that comes with a courtyard cottage on the studio lot with a few reserved parking spaces. You get to wave at the tourists as the tram passes by (which includes your high-school nemesis on day one). You buy a sky-high penthouse in the Florida Keys (but only as a second home crash pad for NATPE when you're not in Barcelona) and you move on to your next cherry-picked labor-of-love project in your slate.

(This book is about the reality for the rest of us.)

While I wish those Cinderella dreams for all of you (and covet them myself), being discovered at a top-tier film festival and achieving landmark per-screen averages, an impressive theatrical run length and enviable investor ROIs[5] — or going viral on

YouTube and creating new viewing ratings benchmarks — are newsworthy stories precisely because they are, indeed: *rare*. We cheer because they are the *breakout* survivors of our own Hollywood *Hunger Games*.

The rest of us have to cleverly and resourcefully "work the system." Which is what this book is all about: to help you get as many at bats as possible to help you get on base — maybe even loading the bases — all the while hoping (and training) for that elusive homerun. Consider this your Spring Training Playbook. I hope it becomes dog-eared and drenched in highlight and that you refer to it again and again with each new try-out.

> This business is an ultra marathon. Consider these markets your Aid Stations.

YOU MIGHT BE AN INDEPENDENT IF . . .

Odds are: if you're reading this book, you're an independent.
And you know it.

(Clap your hands.)

But let's define independent films and television programming as those properties that are financed without the involvement of the "Big Six" US studios. Period.

The "Big Six"[6] studios have been the household name brands of the movie and television businesses for decades. They typically produce film and television within their own corporate divisions and distribute them via their subsidiaries all around the world. The rest of the films and TV projects financed, produced and/or distributed outside this vertically integrated structure are considered independent. Thus, anything and everything that is *not* a Hollywood studio film, broadcast network or cable series (even if it ultimately ends up being distributed by one of the studio machines) is typically considered "independent."

Thus, from art-house docs to *The Hunger Games* (Lionsgate) to *Divergent* (Summit), independent producers create more than 500 films and countless hours of television programming each year, generating more than $4 billion in annual revenues. Responsible for more than 70 percent of film production in the United States alone, these independent productions create considerably more worldwide job opportunities than the majors. And certainly, engage a more diversified talent base and tell a wider spectrum of stories.

Of the 94,000 businesses that make up the US film and television industry, 85 percent are small businesses, employing less than 10 people each. It's truly Main Street. Mom & Pop Shops. Single Shingles. Clusters of collaborating entrepreneurs driven by their creative and intellectual passion. These are most of the content creators pitching at the markets. That's us. That's the "who" this book is for: independent storytellers and content creators around the world — or those aspiring to tell their stories. The challenge for us is to figure out which of the magic formulas might get our stories funded, produced and screened throughout the world — or at least profitably launched on the smaller screens.

An economic highway, these markets provide the carpool lane for independent producers to meet and greet the Mini Major production companies, distributors and independent film sales companies[7] who draw upon their pre-established relationships with local distributors in each international territory to release and monetize intellectual property. And, of course, we're all — always — looking to meet independent equity financiers. Investors. People who can underwrite our dreams. Most independent market attendees are looking to discover new financing, production and distribution sources or solutions that might not only help them gain momentum — but maybe even hold onto a bigger piece of the pie or better control and monitor their assets. Sometimes, the best strategy can be to align yourself with larger, more powerful independent production companies who can help you in a myriad of ways to take it to the next level. Sometimes not.

We'll explore all your exponentially increasing options so that you'll recognize the best opportunities you can drum up — and which strategy might be the most prudent and realistic for which project, when — and how to do it.

Let's roll . . .

NOTES

1 See more on Cinando in Chapter 4 Le Marché du Film (The Cannes Film Market).
2 See Part VIII Important Annual Ancillary Events for more information on working the film festival circuit.
3 Hopefully, your rep is only charging you your fair pro-rata share of their marketing expenses.
4 **Attention Deficit Hyperactive Disorder**
5 **Return on Investment**
6 See Chapter 2 Hollywood's Oligopoly: The Big Six.
7 Explained in Chapter 3 The Players on the Film Market Stage.

Part II
The Global Film Industry

The worldwide entertainment and media industry encompasses film, TV, music, Internet, video games, print and outdoor advertising. Valued at over $2.1 trillion (US$), with digital formats surpassing TV and print, these amalgamated industries are forecasted to pass the $2.3 trillion mark by just 2020. Considered the cornerstone and driving force of the broader entertainment sector, the film industry enjoyed its biggest year in box office history in 2015 with $39.3 billion.[1] PricewaterhouseCoopers[2] predicts global theatrical revenue will hit $49.3 billion by 2020.[3]

Over 100 countries contribute to the approximately 6,500 films every year that earn theatrical global box office on the more than 125,000 screens in 25,000 theaters around the world. North America (the US and Canada) typically account for about a third of the worldwide box office. This "territory" hauled in $11 billion in 2015. The world's second largest box office region is the Asia Pacific, driven largely by China, which is growing exponentially, nearing the $7 billion dollar threshold all by itself and is projected to overtake North America for the first time ever in 2017. Next in line, EMEA (Europe, the Middle East and Africa) accounts for about $10.6 billion, with Latin America following with $3 billion, driven largely by Brazil, Mexico and Argentina (although Brazil is often broken out and grouped with the "BRIC" block of countries: Brazil, the Russian Federation, India and China).

Film production has exploded and matured all around the globe. As "film nations" continue to emerge, each culture exports its artistic sensibilities and values to the rest of the world. With an environmental impact of next to nil for this entire business sector (give or take isolated and temporary noise or traffic impact of a few hours to days), our economic and artistic output not only raises awareness of and (hopefully) breaks down religious, political, socioeconomic and ethnic barriers, but it also serves to connect each country's eclectic diasporas with their respective homelands.

To Hollywood, Bollywood, Nollywood — and Beyond!

HOLLYWOOD

While the birthplace of film can be debated from France to Australia, there is little debate that Hollywood was the birthplace of the movie *business*. California is the eighth largest economy in the world. By itself. As a state. Its entertainment industry exports and the subsequent ripple effect they have had on so many ancillary businesses are indisputable drivers of this nation's success.

Today, the production of motion pictures and television programs is distributed across many of these United States, supporting almost two million jobs, paying out over $133 billion in wages, with the average salary being 42 percent higher than the national average. With American studios controlling the lion's share of global distribution and well over a quarter of the globe's movie screens, "Hollywood" remains the world's movie capital. *For now.*

BOLLYWOOD

With over a 100-year history, the term "Bollywood" originally applied only to Hindi films, stereotypically vibrantly colorful, musical romances made in Bombay. But since the city's name change to Mumbai in 1990, "Bollywood" has become an umbrella nickname for all cinema originating in India.

A dynamic film region, $3.3 billion cinema tickets are sold annually with Hollywood movies accounting for less than 5 percent of those box office sales. The Mumbai-based film center has its own unique challenges — which, of course, always offer incredible opportunities to those paying attention.

Less than 4 percent of India's 1.2 billion residents regularly attend movies. India's middle class is estimated to be at least 300 million people but currently, only about 45 million of them are regular cinemagoers. This must be at least partially due to the fact that India has less than 13,000 theaters compared to the over three times that (almost 40,000) in the US — a country with one quarter their population. Not to mention, there were 780–900 languages spoken in India at one point — almost a new language and culture every 300 miles. The official[4] number of languages now is 122 (though many estimate it's still probably as high as 300). Regardless of what the actual number is, it's obviously an economically and logistically unrealistic number to translate or subtitle.

The average Bollywood film costs about $1.5 million to make versus $47.7 million for the "average" Hollywood movie. But, to be fair, that's a wildly skewed US figure, ignoring the barbell-shaped distinction between Hollywood studio films and the mode[5] independent film budget, which would put the majority of American independent films made today much closer to India's average. That said, India's low per capita income, poorer infrastructure, significantly lower marketing costs and ticket prices make comparisons to Hollywood's reported profit and revenue figures disproportional at best.

But, as everywhere else in the world, things are changing. The year 2000 brought bank financing to India's production communities and two large Indian studios are listed on London's stock market. Bollywood plotlines are becoming increasingly realistic and (for better or for worse) their sex, violence and language have become grittier as well.

NOLLYWOOD

Nigeria's $800 million dollar movie industry is fondly referred to as "Nollywood." Not an actual place, Nollywood's business center is the crowded, chaotic Alaba Market in Lagos. Newly representing 1.4 percent of the country's GDP, the decades-younger Nigerian film industry is valued at approximately 853.9 NGN billion (~$5.1 billion US) — and growing. The second largest employer after the government, this sector generates more revenue on a per capita basis than Bollywood (but again, the population variances skews the comparative relevance of these figures).

Nigeria has over 500 languages spoken, the peak estimated to be 521.[6] Neck and neck with Bollywood in terms of the number of annual productions (around 1,000 each), most Nigerian films are of an artisanal nature, made in about ten days, for around $15,000 US and they rarely see a theatrical release. With two-thirds of its population living on less than a dollar a day, Nigeria doesn't have very many cinemas, though the number of theaters are expected to double over the next few years. Thus, the Nollywood films that do see a commercial release are usually direct-to-DVD and sold via the 200,000 "video parlors" across the country. Unfortunately (as elsewhere), piracy is widespread and dramatically impacts Nigerian filmmakers' profits. They must scramble to maximize their profit in the initial two-week window before counterfeit copies flood their marketplace.

As in Bollywood, love stories are popular but so are action films. Nollywood productions are often partially funded by the church, which can result in consistent themes glorifying the moral poor over the corrupt rich. As with any nationality, whether in their home country or expatriated, Nigerians gravitate to and respond to familiar faces on screen. Malawians and Kenyans likely identify more with native idols Genevieve Nnaji or Ramsey Nouah than Hollywood's latest A-list flavor of the month.

Everyone wants their story told. We seek catharsis by vicariously identifying with the images we see on screen, looking for resonance in the themes. But presently, just 7 percent of the countries with consistent film activity account for 55 percent of global production, with the top ten countries representing about 75 percent of the world's box office. This funnel is perhaps sharpest in the US where just the top ten studio blockbusters claimed 34.5 percent of 2015's $11 billion in record-breaking box office.

India, the US, China, Japan, the Russian Federation, France and the United Kingdom (in descending order) typically distribute over 200 films each every year onto the worldwide stage while Germany, Spain, the Republic of Korea, Italy, Argentina, Mexico, Brazil and Bangladesh (also in approximate descending order) each distribute between 80–199 films each year.

With 1.3 billion potential ticket buyers — and an exponentially growing middle class — China is projected to pass the United States next year. But China institutes quotas

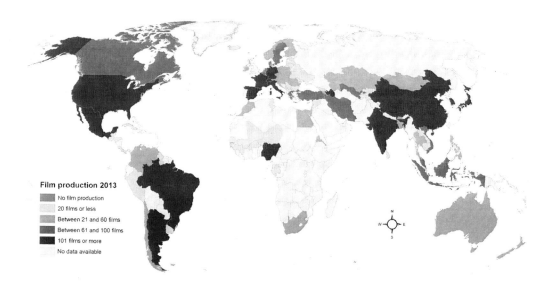

Source: © UNESCO 2013[7].

🔥 HOT TIP!

Participation in the Beijing International Film Festival has proven to be a welcome strategy to grease the wheels for entrée past the dragon gatekeeper.

and restrictions on the foreign films allowed to be released within its borders. Recent negotiations with Russia may result in quotas specifically for Russian films, giving them a leg up over its other imported competitors.

HOLLYWOOD'S OLIGOPOLY

Hollywood is an oligopoly, which means that media power in North America (as in many other places) is consolidated between a handful of players. Like it or not, Hollywood studios dominate worldwide distribution. Very few movies from any country secure significant global penetration outside their own borders without some assistance from the Hollywood studios' distribution machines.

The Big Six

Traditionally referred to as "The Big Six," the major US studios and their vertically integrated parent conglomerates, control about 80 percent of the box office and ancillary market shares. But less than just a decade ago, they controlled 90 percent — so their hold is slipping, somewhat, to independent and international competition. Their rankings jockey year by year, but as an example, this was their 2015 year-end stance.

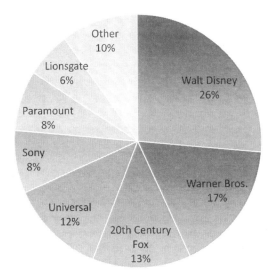

It is nearly impossible to compete with "The Big Six" in terms of mass market projects — especially those targeting children or youth, graphic novel or bestseller adaptations, animation and CGI-intensive projects. Disney has a near corner on the kids market with the highest per-film average revenue in the United States and the most academy awards (26). But these behemoths are shifting their feature efforts away from production (save for the big tent pole blockbusters, prequels, sequels, franchises and remakes, where

STUDIO BLOCKBUSTER HITS AND FRANCHISES

Warner Bros.: *The Dark Knight, Harry Potter, American Sniper, The Hobbit, Inception, Man of Steel, The Matrix, The Hangover, Gravity, The LEGO Movie, I Am Legend, The Blind Side.*

Disney: *Marvel's The Avengers, Pirates of the Caribbean, Toy Story, Iron Man, Frozen, Finding Nemo, Alice in Wonderland, Guardians of the Galaxies, The Lion King, The Sixth Sense, Up.*

Universal Studios: *Despicable Me, E.T.: The Extra-Terrestrial, Jurassic Park, Meet the Fockers, How the Grinch Stole Christmas, Jaws, Bruce Almighty, Fast and the Furious, the Bourne series.*

Sony/Columbia Pictures: *Spider-Man, James Bond, Men in Black, Ghostbusters, Hancock, The Da Vinci Code, Terminator, 22 Jump Street, Hitch, Tootsie, The Karate Kid.*

20th Century Fox: *Avatar, Star Wars, Independence Day, Home Alone, Night at the Museum, X-Men, Cast Away, Alvin and the Chipmunks, Mrs. Doubtfire, Planet of the Apes, Ice Age.*

Paramount Pictures: *Titanic, Transformers, Forrest Gump, Shrek, Iron Man, Raiders of the Lost Ark, Star Trek, Beverly Hills Cop, War of the Worlds, Ghost, How to Train Your Dragon.*

they increasingly diversify their risk among one another on the huge budget films) to leading the pack as the global marketing and distribution powerhouses they have proven to be.

The "Big Six" don't "need" the film or TV markets. But their various divisions or affiliated companies are consistently represented on these circuits. In addition, most studios have "independent arms," branded shingles looking for new talent or to sell their smaller scale niche material.

STUDIO "INDIE" SHINGLES

- Focus Features
- Fox Searchlight
- Miramax
- Sony Pictures Classics

Unless you've written a brilliant, high-concept, original spec screenplay that's getting all sorts of industry heat; or you have locked down the rights to a *New York Times* best seller or a "ripped-from-the-headlines," worldwide, pop-culture sensation (or you're an A-lister,[8] yourself), the studios don't "need" you (or any of the rest of us, for that matter) — which leaves all of us independent producers full-court pressing the mini-majors.

The Mini Majors

These are the independent power players in the industry (usually without an actual physical studio lot) who can be just as difficult to access but who most often get up to bat with original titles. Thus, they are the more realistic targets for those of us without "studio material" or comparable resources.

Aligning yourself with these production companies and distributors can be the key to your success in the independent filmmaking or content creation arenas. High-profile production companies (those that are star-driven, helmed by A-list producers, directors, writers or even former studio execs) enjoy at least the *perception* of excellent industry relationships or access to incredibly deep pockets.

It used to be common for many of these firms to have housekeeping, first-look, overhead or distribution deals with the Big Six studios. A win for both parties, the studio got first right of refusal on all the intellectual property that these smaller entities could acquire in exchange for fronting some of their overhead and development costs — all the while holding out the carrot of a solid distribution (and ostensibly marketing) commitment. Many of these deals were wiped out by the Writer's Guild strike of 2008 (not to mention the constricting economy) but also by the studios significantly streamlining their output.

A good resource to get annually updated information on these affiliations is to Google for Variety's most recent Facts on Pacts.[9] The most current available (March 21, 2016) at the time of our publishing shows 135 established firms with deals with the Big Six studios — that's less than half the Y2K heyday of 292. The chart also reveals a dozen of the mini majors' production pacts with talent that can be a very helpful insight when considering attachment strategies.

DISNEY

Boxing Cat Films
Tim Allen

Buenos Aires Prods.
Mario Iscovich

Infinitum Nihil
Johnny Depp,
Christi Dembrowski

Junction Ent.
Jon Turteltaub

Lucamar Prods.
John DeLuca,
Rob Marshall

Mandeville Films
David Hoberman,
Todd Lieberman

Mayhem Pictures
Gordon Gray

Secret Machine
Justin Springer

**Taylor Made
Film Prods.**
Brigham Taylor

Whitaker Ent.
Jim Whitaker

FOX

**Bad Hat Harry
Prods.**
Bryan Singer

Boom! Studios
Ross Richie,
Stephen Christy

Chernin Ent.
Peter Chernin

Davis Ent.
John Davis

**DreamWorks
Animation**
(distribution only)

Epic Magazine
Josh Bearman,
Josh Davis

Feigco
Paul Feig

Film Rites
Steve Zaillian

Flitcraft
Scott Frank

Genre Films
Simon Kinberg

**Noah Hawley,
John Cameron***

Lightstorm
James Cameron

New Regency
Arnon Milchan
(equity partner with
all Fox divisions)

**Oddball
Entertainment***
Wes Ball

Hutch Parker Ent.
Hutch Parker

Scott Free
Ridley Scott

6th & Idaho
Matt Reeves

Temple Hill Ent.
Wyck Godfrey,
Marty Bowen

21 Laps
Shawn Levy

Walden Media
(co-financing)

FOX SEARCHLIGHT

Court 13
Benh Zeitlin

Decibel Films
Danny Boyle

FOX 2000

Color Force
Nina Jacobson

Holden Glass*
John Green

The Jackal Group
Gail Berman

**State Street
Pictures**
George L. Tillman Jr.,
Robert Teitel

**Sunswept
Entertainment**
Karen Rosenfelt

PARAMOUNT

Bad Robot
J.J. Abrams

Broadway Video
Lorne Michaels

**Jerry Bruckheimer
Films**
Jerry Bruckheimer

Ian Bryce Prods.
Ian Bryce

**Di Bonaventura
Pictures**
Lorenzo di
Bonaventura

**Dichotomy
Creative Group***
Adam Goodman

Disruption Ent.
Mary Parent

Robert Evans Co.
Robert Evans

Hasbro*
Brian Goldner,
Stephen Davis

Hello Junior
Johnny Knoxville

Platinum Dunes
Michael Bay,
Brad Fuller,
Andrew Form

Saw Mill Prods.*
Josh Appelbaum,
Andre Nemec

Sikelia Prods.
Martin Scorsese

Skydance
David Ellison, Dana
Goldberg (includes
co-financing)

SONY

Arad Prods.
Avi Arad

Elizabeth Cantillon

Escape Artists
Todd Black,
Jason Blumenthal,
Steve Tisch

DeVon Franklin

Free Association
Channing Tatum,
Reid Carolin

Ghost Corps*
Dan Aykroyd,
Ivan Reitman

Happy Madison
Adam Sandler
(includes animation)

Immersive Pictures
Josh Bratman

T.D. Jakes

Kevin James

**Laurence Mark
Prods.**
Laurence Mark

Mosaic
Jimmy Miller

Olive Bridge Ent.
Will Gluck

Original Film
Neal Moritz

Overbrook Ent.
Will Smith,
James Lassiter

Amy Pascal

Scott Rudin Prods.
Scott Rudin

**Joe and Anthony
Russo**

Safehouse
Joby Harold,
Tory Tunnell

Smoke House
George Clooney,
Grant Heslov

Studio 8
Jeff Robinov
(distribution only)

Matt Tolmach

SONY PICTURES ANIMATION

Frederator
Fred Seibert
(includes consulting)

**Michelle Raimo
Kouyate**

**Genndy
Tartakovsky**

UNIVERSAL

Aggregate Films
Jason Bateman

Apatow Prods.
Judd Apatow

Bluegrass Films
Scott Stuber,
Dylan Clark

Blumhouse Prods.
Jason Blum

Brownstone Prods.
Elizabeth Banks,
Max Handelman

**Captivate
Entertainment**
Jeffrey Weiner,
Ben Smith

**Michael De Luca
Prods.***
Michael De Luca

Fake Empire
Josh Schwartz,
Stephanie Savage

**Gold Circle
Entertainment**
Paul Brooks

**Illumination
Entertainment**
Chris Meledandri

ImageMovers
Robert Zemeckis,
Jack Rapke,
Steve Starkey

**Imagine
Entertainment**
Ron Howard,
Brian Grazer

Legendary
Thomas Tull
(includes co-
financing/
distribution)

Little Stranger Inc.*
Tina Fey

Chris Morgan Prods.
Chris Morgan

One Race Films
Vin Diesel,
Samantha Vincent

Will Packer Prods.
Will Packer

Penguin
Random House
Peter Gethers

Marc Platt Prods.
Marc Platt

Scholastic*

Secret Hideout
Alex Kurtzman

Silvertongue Films*
Deborah Forte

**Skybound
Entertainment***
Robert Kirkman,
David Alpert

Working Title Films
Tim Bevan,
Eric Fellner

WARNER BROS.

Alcon Ent.
Andrew Kosove,
Broderick Johnson
(distribution only)

Appian Way
Leonardo DiCaprio

Berlanti Prods.
Greg Berlanti

**Block
Entertainment***
(Bill Block)

**Cruel and
Unusual**
Zack Snyder,
Deborah Snyder

De Line Pictures
Donald De Line

Di Novi Pictures
Denise Di Novi

Executive Options
Tom Hardy

Gerber Pictures
Bill Gerber

Getaway Pictures
Rob Lorenz

Gulfstream
Mike Karz,
Bill Bindley
(co-financier)

Heyday
David Heyman

Langley Park
Kevin McCormick

Life's Too Short
Chuck Lorre

Lin Pictures
Dan Lin

Mad Chance
Andrew Lazar

Malpaso
Clint Eastwood

Chris McKay

Pearl Street
Ben Affleck,
Matt Damon

Phantom Four Films
David Goyer

**Todd Phillips-
Bradley Cooper**

Polymorphic
Polly Johnsen

Rat-Pac Ent.
Brett Ratner
(includes
co-financing
with Rat-Pac
Dune Ent.)

**Guy Ritchie,
Lionel Wigram**

Roserock Films
Hunt Lowry

Team Downey
Robert Downey Jr.,
Susan Downey

Vertigo
Roy Lee

Village Roadshow
Bruce Berman
(co-financier only)

Weed Road
Akiva Goldsman

Wychwood
David Yates

NEW LINE

Atomic Monster
James Wan

Benderspink
Chris Bender,
JC Spink

Flynn Picture Co.
Beau Flynn

Spring Hill Prods.*
LeBron James,
Maverick Carter

Wrigley Pictures
John Rickard

ALCON

Kira Davis

Denis Villeneuve

AMBLIN PARTNERS

Kennedy/Marshall
Kathleen Kennedy,
Frank Marshall

BOLD FILMS

Nine Stories*
Jake Gyllenhaal

Red Hour Films*
Ben Stiller

BROAD GREEN

Matt Alvarez*
(exclusive
production deal)

Storyscape*
Bob Cooper,
Richard Saperstein

LIONSGATE

**Allison Shearmur
Prods.**
Allison Shearmur

MGM

**Caryn
Mandabach***

Whalerock
Lloyd Braun

NEW REGENCY

Blind Wink Prods.
Gore Verbinski

David Fincher

**Plan B
Entertainment**
Brad Pitt,
Dede Gardner,
Jeremy Kleiner

Protozoa Pictures
Darren Aronofsky

SKYDANCE

**Laeta Kalogridis,
Patrick Lussier**

Marti Noxon*

*INDICATES NEW DEAL SINCE
THE 2015 EDITION. UNLESS
NOTED, THE DEALS ARE
FIRST LOOK

FIERCE FILM COMPETITION

I don't want to belabor film statistics but . . . just as a refresher: 7,000 movies get made every year.

Every.

Year.

These 7,000 just completed films flood a marketplace already bookended by at least a year or more of back inventory clogging up the existing pipeline and competing for attention with the buzz-worthy pregnant projects looming on the horizon as future inventory. All of this compresses the bandwidth of industry focus. Of that annual number: less than 10 percent (about 600) actually get out there to make any kind of a blip on the radar; about 125 secure significant studio distribution; and only a couple dozen are nominated for key awards.

But, if you think the competition in development, packaging and soft prep for financiers, cast and distribution is fierce (which it is — it's insane!) — wait 'til you're competing for the public's eyeballs, leisure time and discretionary dollars! A truly humbling experience. The fact that many independent films take a decade to even reach this point should give you an appreciation of the perseverance and dedication of the people and projects you're "competing" with.

NOTES

1 According to comScore (formerly Rentrak).
2 www.pwc.com/gx/en/industries/entertainment-media/outlook.html.
3 www.statista.com/statistics/259987/global-box-office-revenue/.
4 According to a recent four-year study: http://peopleslinguisticsurvey.org/.
5 The most common value.
6 http://en.wikipedia.org/wiki/Languages_of_Nigeria#/media/File:Niger-Congo_speakers. png.
7 Feature film provisional data as of June 2015.
8 Call me. ;-) *Please.*
9 The most recent version available will always be linked on this book's website www.Howto WorktheFilmandTVMarkets.com/FactsonPacts.

The Players on the Film Market Stage

3

Now let's pan our camera across the cast of characters you're likely to meet on the film market floors . . .

It can be confusing for first-time film market attendees to anticipate who they might encounter at these markets or figure out who they need to actually network with, partly because "buyers" are typically at the markets as "sellers." Additionally, "exhibitors" can refer to a wide swath of market vendors who have rented market floor space whereas, in the reel world, "exhibitors" usually refers to theater chains and local cinemas that, in some cases, may also be "distributors." No wonder rookie attendees get confused!

Jonathan Wolf, Managing Director of the AFM, explains:

> It's just like Fashion Week, where all the industry buyers show up to see all the new lines from all the clothing manufacturers. Just as Bloomingdales is a buyer there, they then turn around and become a seller as a retailer. You're talking about the same individual, it just depends on which hat are they wearing, wherever they are at that moment. Buyers look to acquire while they're at the AFM but as soon as they get back home, they're sellers again. As an example: Fox Searchlight is a Buyer on our campus but as soon as they get back to the Fox lot, they're a distributor.

Most sellers at any given market begin their transition back to buyer mode in the last few days of each event — and this is the prime time for independent producers to pitch to them.

Entertainment industry professionals go to markets for all sorts of reasons: to network, stay up-to-date on market trends, keep tabs on their business partners, reconnect with old friends and, of course, to party (it *is* the *entertainment* business, after all!). But before signing on any dotted lines, it's prudent for independent filmmakers to meet prospective partners face-to-face. You might be working with these people — with your intellectual property inextricably tied up with them — legally and financially — for years to come. You want to get a sense of who these strangers are who might hold the financial future of your project (or even your career) for a few years in their hands. Ideally, you want to convert them from prospects to fans, champions, allies — and partners.

You might be looking to ascertain first impressions on distributors for current projects or to do due diligence on the credibility of financiers for future ones. You might be checking out sales agents, interviewing producers' reps, getting the latest updates on location incentives, updating current underwriting guidelines for reputable financial institutions willing to fill in the gaps by loaning against the collateral of the pieces you've managed to secure. Sometimes, just the generous knowledge-sharing of your peers can shave years of mistakes off your plan. And the camaraderie can be priceless in the grueling decathlon that the independent journey can often be. I hope the following cast breakdowns help disambiguate some of the overlapping terminology to clarify who the players are.

FILM DISTRIBUTORS

As the name implies, these individuals and companies distribute films. They license material for the period of time negotiated in your distribution contract, then market and sell those films directly to the public or to other distributors or exhibitors (theater chains) in various geographic territories.

Depending on the terms of your deal, the rights you have licensed to them and the breadth and depth of their contacts and expertise, distributors will likely try to monetize your product via every platform possible: broadcast and cable networks, subscription, transactional and/or ad supported **Video On Demand** (VOD), online and ancillary outlets such as: airlines, hotels, cruise ships, military, schools and retail stores.

Typically, the "buyers" that most independent filmmakers solicit at the film markets have spent a great deal of money to exhibit and screen their own pre-existing inventory and are thus (understandably) far more focused on selling their own catalog to foreign territories than listening to you pitch them your prospective one-off. Most of the best distributors are in pure selling mode during most of each market. Their proactive independent film-buying mode is often reserved for when they're on the prestigious film festival circuit, seeking pedigree and audience response. But, in the final days of most markets, they have freed up the bandwidth to be a little more receptive to considering what to invest their marketing monies and efforts in next. And that's where you can come in — hopefully not pitching cold — but having done some advance warm-up homework.

EXAMPLES OF FILM DISTRIBUTORS

- The "Big Six" studios and their indie arms
- A24
- Cinedigm
- FilmBuff
- K5 International
- Lionsgate
- Oscilloscope
- Roadside Attractions
- Studio Canal
- Summit Entertainment
- The Weinstein Company

In the world of theatrical distribution, film distributors do their best to acquire all rights to all territories and platforms, then get their films into as many cinemas (and other outlets) around the world as they have the relationships and resources to secure.

Signed contracts with these entities will usually take all responsibility (and rights) away from the film's creator/owner and empower the distributor to make all decisions as to how to market and release each product to the public. Often this includes creating (or redoing) all the key art, the trailer — and sometimes even further editing the film (depending on the terms of the contract) — all of which, of course, are charged back from future revenues.

They are also usually in charge of the books. And all cash flow. So, be very wary of fly-by-night operations but be just as diligent with established firms. Film distributors always retain a percentage of the revenues they generate, the theatrical gross of which is almost always cut in half prior to receipt by the exhibitors (i.e. theaters, see below) taking their share. Film distributors used to typically offer established producers advances and minimum guarantees, though that is increasingly rare for independent producers in today's tighter economy.

> NOTE: While television "Distributors" increasingly attend film markets (and vice versa), for simplicity and clarity; they are covered separately in 3.3 "The Players on the TV Market Stage."

INTERNATIONAL (FILM) SALES AGENTS (ISAS)

Film sales agents negotiate certain rights from filmmakers and then pitch these sets of distribution rights to prospective domestic and international distributors — sometimes even directly to exhibitors. They earn a commission in exchange for each sale they broker.

Some sales agents are affiliated with production companies and/or domestic distributors. A few sales agents function only domestically (often called Producer's Reps, see below) while others just sell to domestic television outlets (broadcast, cable and **Pay Per View**). But most are international (often called foreign sales companies) and focus on maximizing a film's monetization by licensing the film's rights to as many different territories as possible outside the film's country of origin. Since well over 50 percent (to 70+ percent) of a film's revenue typically comes from abroad, a reputable and competent company or individual in this capacity can be a vital component to your film's success.

For completed films (or those nearing completion), sales agents will often create (or outsource) both the physical and electronic marketing materials and various technical, digital exploitation deliverables. They may have the film dubbed or subtitled into different languages. Of course, they will charge you for each of these expenses, usually out of the film's revenue, usually with their overhead administration charged on top. They are "middlemen," to be sure, and while some of this can be done without them on much smaller, slower scales, if you truly want to maximize your film's worldwide sales potential (without the help of a studio performing these same functions), utilizing the services of a film sales agent can be the key stepping stone to that success.

Sales agents formulate film festival strategies and film market promotional campaigns to best position their projects for export to the worldwide markets (whereas film distributors dictate the local advertising campaigns in their respective territories). ISAs will likely draft each territory or platform's distribution agreement, deliver the film's assets to each distributor, collect the revenue and pay you your percentage (after deducting their commission and expenses). They also typically control the books and revenue flow. Thus: choose your partners wisely.

Many sales agents will forecast the film's value in the various foreign territories. For projects in development or pre-production, they might even share precious casting knowledge to refine attachment wish lists or even offer script development notes regarding cultural nuances. For especially worthy projects in development and/or based on good, long-term relationships, many sales agents will even serve a proactive role in connecting filmmakers with prospective finance and co-production partners.

AGGREGATORS

A new breed of sales agents has emerged to facilitate the new media arena. Aggregators specialize in acquiring digital rights to sell to Internet platforms and the digital space (i.e. VOD, OTT and satellite outlets), often grouping packages of genre films into blocks that can be marketed together. As film and television content distribution further merge, this specialty is likely to be obsolesced as it becomes a core skill set of the major players.

PRODUCER'S REPRESENTATIVES

A Producer's Rep is typically a domestic-only agent who works with you for a short period of time, often selling your film to just one distributor. Like lawyers and mechanics, there can be a wide spectrum in the quality, knowledge, and value they bring. Some can be priceless. Others can be charlatans out to make a quick buck off wannabes with stars in their eyes — hijacking their momentum and derailing their confidence — two of the greatest disservices of all. The cream of the crop can be especially valuable hired during a festival run to help a filmmaker build momentum and buzz to capitalize on a top tier film festival acceptance, award or as a critical team member on a key contained campaign strategy.[1]

COLLECTION AGENTS

Not surprisingly, firms that watchdog the layers of middlemen and various tiered players have popped up the globe over. This might prove cost-prohibitive on lower budgeted projects (say, under $2 million US), but when there is a lot of money at stake — or tiers of partners with layers of legalese — it can be quite complicated as to who gets what, when, in what order of priority or percentages, and based on whose definition. These firms can offer much needed third party oversight confidence to equity investors. Couple that with the high-end bookkeeping services provided, bringing in a collection account manager as a bonded, impartial party to securely and transparently receive and disburse everyone's allocations can provide prudent peace of mind for all parties on complicated, crowded, riskier transactions.

Analogous to the film's financial policeman, they can ensure your entire participation pool is awarded their pro-rata share of the production's revenues — with everyone staying in their right lanes (i.e. gross receipts or sales) — and at the correct intervals as detailed in the waterfall. This way, each investor, production partner, and above-the-line, profit-sharing or deferred talent is also provided prompt and accurate financial reporting.

COLLECTION AGENCY EXAMPLES

- Compact Collections
- European Collecting Agency
- Film & Media Collecting Agency
- Fintage House/Protocol International
- Freeway Entertainment Group
- OnTrust Collection Agency
- Scandinavian Film Collect
- SOGESOFICA

Chasing distributors for payment used to fall squarely at the feet of foreign sales agents or even business affairs executives following up on contracts they negotiated. Increasingly active in this arena, collection account managers are proving far more cost-effective for independent producers than trying to collect from far-flung territories (or even their own distributors) on their own.

The typical fee is 1 percent of revenues and since it comes out of the receipts collected, it doesn't have to be factored into the film's production budget (except for maybe the set-up charge). These firms can collect deposits on pre-sales if they are conditions to bank loans and, of course, delivery payments, first-cycle theatrical payments all the way through library catalog sales. They also track royalty reporting from broadcasters and distributors all over the world — for years to come — so they can be great assets to your team if your predicted revenues warrant their services.

EXHIBITORS

"Exhibitors" in the world of theatrical film distribution typically refer to theaters and cinemas. At markets, however, just like with other industries' trade shows, "exhibitors," in this context, simply means those companies or individuals who have rented (or bartered) a suite or space to "exhibit" their wares: be it their catalog of films, their shooting location, industry software, membership, consulting, legal or financial services. So, any of the wide swath of support businesses that keep the media industries moving could be an "exhibitor" on a show floor — in addition to distributors screening movies available to license.

Many markets require exhibition space in order to host market screenings. Many film sales agents or large, well-funded production companies will have booths while smaller companies have been known to cooperatively share space either by splitting a booth or suite or taking a small stand or even just a table in some kind of pavilion grouped by region or format, often organized by the event host.

MARKET MAKERS

While this is a Wall Street term,[2] I thought I'd hijack the title for our purposes herein to indicate the hosts, organizations and event coordinators who "make" these markets happen. Having been one these myself in several capacities over the past couple of decades, I cannot emphasize enough how important it is to remember that these people, be they high-profile presidents and directors all the way "down" to the full-time staff, part-time volunteers and even student interns, can be some of your best resources at these events. They know their way around. They have insider information, cultural knowledge and historical perspective. They likely know which events will be lackluster sponsored sales pitches versus the hidden gems of ahead-of-the-curve talent and ideas. They can help you apply the best discount codes. They know the finest, cheapest, most convenient or best value hotels, restaurants, travel, badge and service deals at their events. No one navigates their websites or apps faster — or knows who's confirmed or cancelled sooner. Trust them. Get to know them. Befriend them. Just like any other gate-keeper in "Hollywood" — or our global media marketplace — support staff can change your life.

NOTES

1 More on this in Part VIII Important Ancillary Events.
2 Firms who stand at the ready to consistently buy or sell stock at the publicly quoted price.

The Film Markets

Ranking the annual, global film markets into any kind of priority is a dicey, politically charged proposition at best. Like everything else in our industry (and our world): importance, relevance, size, vitality and prominence ebb and flow over time. The significance of any one of these events varies upon what criteria you are using. Not to mention your own perspective and own personal experience. Your country of origin, languages spoken, cultural references and geographic vicinity are bound to be factors as are your format interests, genres and target audiences. Where you are at in your career and where your project is at in its life cycle in correlation to the timing of the various points of entry and promotional opportunities in the annual landscape are all critical variables impacting your choice of forays, motivation, goals and, of course, determining success. While any benchmark is imperfect, these are generally accepted as the three most important film markets in the world:

1. Marché du Film (Cannes) in May in France.
2. European Film Market (EFM) in February in Germany.
3. American Film Market (AFM) in November in California.

Highlighting these three most significant events provides a framework for film markets in general.

Le Marché du Film (The Cannes Film Market)

4

Deservedly the "Grande Dame" of film markets, Le Marché du Film (The Cannes Film Market) is nearing her sixtieth birthday. What started out in 1959 as just a few dozen professionals viewing films on fabric screens stretched across the top of the old Palais Croisette has

MARCHÉ DU FILM

grown into the world's premiere film market. Held annually for ten days in May on the French Riviera (tough to beat!), the market runs concurrently with her prestigious sister event, the most famous film festival in the world: the Festival de Cannes, inaugurated in 1946. Every year, their overlapping yacht parties and tuxedo-required night screenings inspire emerging independents by reminding us that not everyone in the biz is a struggling artist.

INTERNATIONAL PROFILE

Source: © Le Marché du Film.

Almost 12,000 attendees from about 120 countries come to see almost 800 world premieres at Le Marché du Film. Almost 2,000 buyers, 2,300 theatrical distributors, 1,500 sales agents and 800 festival programmers come to consider the 3,350 completed titles available. Almost 4,000 producers attended in 2016. Americans account for about 18 percent of the Marché's international attendance, followed closely by Europeans (approximately 15 percent from France, 10 percent from the UK and 5 percent from Germany). Cannes instituted their first

China Summit in 2015 and, in 2016, almost 500 Chinese attended. Significant attendance comes from Brazil, India, Italy, South Africa and South Korea. Recent inaugural appearances have included: Afghanistan, Bahrain, Brunei, Burma, Cambodia, Iraq, Kurdistan, Kyrgyzstan, Laos, Madagascar, Mauritius, Nepal, Paraguay, Syria and Uganda.

Source: © Le Marché du Film.

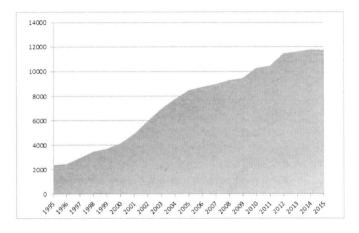

Source: © Le Marché du Film.

By far the most famous, most glamorous, most star-studded market of all, Le Marché du Film is also the most paparazzi- and tourist-crowded. Notorious for its intersection with its adjacent and concurrent film festival's many red-carpet premieres, market professionals from all around the world must navigate pedestrian traffic jams to get to their business meetings.

Source: Photo courtesy of www.cannesguide.com.

Jérôme Paillard, the Executive Director of Le Marché du Film, explains:

Sometimes our strengths can also be our difficulties. With 30,000 professionals (between the market and festival), it's not necessarily easy to find the right people — especially if you are coming to Cannes for the 1st time or with very little experience.

Thus, the Marché strives to contrive scenarios that provide structured networking environments and subtle matchmaking for credentialed attendees. These opportunities are helpful to everyone but especially market newcomers and foreign professionals visiting from well over a hundred countries.

"Every year, about a third of the Marché du Film registrants are first-time attendees," explains Julie Bergeron, Manager, Industry Programs. "It's important to us that they feel welcome in our community."

🔥 HOT TIP!

Le Marché du Film's website (www.marchedufilm.com) offers a downloadable First Timer's Kit and two introductory videos that can be very helpful to watch to get a feel for this market.

THE PRODUCERS WORKSHOP

Without a doubt, producers attending their first (or second or third) Marché should sign up for the Producers Workshop. Instituted in 2011, the Producers Workshop was designed to orient emerging producers new to the international scene or who have little or no prior experience at the Marché. The first program of its kind, the Producers Workshop continues to set the bar for all other markets to aspire to.

After orienting new producers with a tour of the Cannes campus and the optimum use of Cinando (see below), this custom four-day program offers additional workshops, seminars, group coaching, networking opportunities and speed-dating-style sessions to catch-up with invited co-production initiatives[1] — all in addition to the full suite of Marché du Film events, programs, screenings and access. Designed to better enable you to initiate and accelerate international business dealings, experts teach the producers how to navigate Cannes, work with sales agents and illuminate everything from the role of the producer, the inner-workings of international co-productions and finance to pitching, marketing, distribution and sales.

The Producers Workshop focuses on training and peer-to-peer networking. Julie clarifies: "The networking is really more between the participants themselves and less with sales agents." The distinct badges help you identify one another among the throngs in the open marketplace. There is also an online networking forum where you can connect in advance as well as follow-up after the event. 2016 saw a record 404 producers participate in this program. Effectively capitalized on, this would exponentially enhance your professional network.

Source: © Le Marché du Film.

Jérôme agrees it's prudent for the majority of attendees to launch their Cannes market experience with the Producers Workshop. "It's a full course, ten to twelve sessions," he explains. "It's an excellent first step to get the most out of the following days." This broad-based educational tract sets the tone and establishes a common framework for the market — and the film year — to come. "We cover all the themes," Jérôme shares: "international sales, deals, financing, marketing, strategies and present sales."

Julie explains:

> We accept producers, directors and scriptwriters. We connect them with the experts they most need to meet. It is designed for one- (maybe two-) time attendance. Although it is essentially the same curriculum every year, some attendees do actually request to come back through the program a second time (especially if a few years have lapsed since their first market). We cover the same standard topics but the experts do rotate and the information is always current.

Source: © Le Marché du Film.

The Producers Workshop also offers small group roundtables and mentoring. "It's very specific, very practical," Jérôme explains. As an example of the types of questions workshop attendees might ask in their small group coaching sessions, he offers:

How would you recommend we break the ice with a German producer? How should we start that relationship? We cover legal questions on issues such as copyrights. There are big differences between the different countries' authors' rights systems and many producers are afraid to share their projects.

These breakout sessions include just a dozen or so producers each, so they are quite intimate and responsive. Ultimately far more affordable than trying to meet all of these individuals around the world one-by-one and far more efficient than trying to learn all this material from books and videos on your own time — even if you tracked them down in their suites or pavilions, it's unlikely you'd enjoy this kind of dynamic interaction. In a relaxed but focused environment, the Producers Workshop facilitates introductions to these receptive and contributory veterans who have agreed in advance to mentor new producers via this format.

This program comes at an additional fee, of course, but it will exponentially increase the value of your market experience. And, as with almost all the programs at all the markets, the economics of your value proposition is dramatically enhanced if you take advantage of the bundled packages and early bird discounts.

🔥 HOT TIP!

> While admission is a relatively easy process, the Producers Workshop is limited and sells out early, so make sure this is one of the first things you check off your "Cannes To Do" list!

THE PRODUCERS NETWORK

Whereas the Producers *Workshop* is all about freshman training, the Producers *Network* could be analogized as the sophomore class all the way through to graduation. Allowing you to put your workshop training into action, the Network is all about transacting business.

A vetted program, the Network is limited to producers who qualify with a theatrically released feature film within the past three years. Julie explains:

> We validate each registration with our criteria. We're very stringent: it's the individual's — not just their company's — credit that matters. Some are newcomers. Others are veterans who come back every year when they have a new film that gets them back in to the program. It is an important time of their year. We make it possible for them to interact with executives that are difficult to meet at the market.

Obviously, this isn't something everyone can take advantage of every year — and that's by design. So, when this window of opportunity is available to you, it's foolhardy not to capitalize on it. Not to mention, everyone you interact with will be an active, productive player in the marketplace — right now — and that's rare air to breathe, indeed. It ensures your relaxed networking is with the movers and shakers in the business. It also keeps the forum constantly relevant. The size of this group varies, 2016 was a record-breaking year again with 579 producers participating in the program.

Jérôme shares: "We organize a big breakfast every day of more than two hundred people." Julie continues: "We have sixteen tables, with a different guest at each table, over seven days. The Producers get to pick the table which is most relevant to them." Jérôme explains:

> Each table has a guest and a moderator. They each share their experiences around the table, whether they organize film festivals or arrange financing. It's a select group of people, all of whom have achieved a certain level of expertise by having produced films in their respective countries.

Source: © Le Marché du Film.

Source: © Le Marché du Film.

In addition to the series of seven breakfast meetings that feature high-profile experts sharing their insights, the Producers Network also includes exclusive, daily happy hours. Both lively atmospheres offer the opportunity to network with film funds active in international co-production. "Without a doubt, if you are looking to meet the maximum number of people at the market," Julie closes, "the Producers Workshop and Producers Network add so much value. They give you a place to go every day to meet other producers and industry execs."

"GOES TO CANNES" WORKS IN PROGRESS SCREENINGS

Sometimes a project's timing is off from what would be ideal for the markets or festivals you've prioritized. The buying and selling professionals who attend these markets appreciate this and are accustomed to seeing works in all stages. They recognize potential when they see it. You may have been advised not to share your film "until it's ready" and this advice is prudent when it's in reference to entering your film to be *judged* in a *festival* or being subjected to critical or public reviews but within a business-to-business "work-in-progress" context, especially when being revealed to sales agents versus distributors, it's an entirely different arena. This is their job: to discover films they can sell.

Thus, in a continuing effort to be of service to the burgeoning creative class, the Marché partners with renowned festivals to screen their selected works-in-progress.

RECENT "GOES TO CANNES" (WORKS IN PROGRESS) FESTIVAL PARTNERS

- Annecy International Animation Film Festival and its Market (MIFA)
- Buenos Aires Festival Internacional De Cine Independiente (BAFICI)
- Dubai International Film Festival (DIFF) and the Dubai Film Market (DFM)
- Fantasia International Film Festival and Frontières Co-Production Market
- Festival Internacional de Cine en Guadalajara
- Festival Internacional de Cine Panamá
- Fondation Liban Cinema
- Los Cabos International Film Festival
- National Film Development Corporation Malaysia (FINAS).

These screening opportunities empower producers to capitalize on the convergence of international prospects with what they have ready by the time the market rolls around. It also enables sales agents and festivals to track projects and people of interest through their development, production and post-production processes through the convenience of these integrated outlets. "It's difficult to get as many buyers anywhere else in one place, at the same time, as you can at Cannes." Jérôme explains. "The latter part of the market is the perfect time for sales agents to screen these films."

"We want to support visibility," Jérôme explains further, "to create events that allow them to interact with their peers." Ironically, even the Executive Director of Le Marché du Film blurs the line between his market and its sibling festival's offerings. So intertwined are they, he references L'Atelier, a wonderful Directors' program that the Festival offers concurrently (which is covered below in the Festival de Cannes section) as evidence of their joint efforts to inspire and encourage independent filmmakers from around the world.

CANNES INVESTORS CLUB

Film financing is one of the greatest hurdles for independent filmmakers — but it's a challenge for equity investors as well. With this in mind, in 2015, the Marché du Film launched the Cannes Investors Club for a select group of high net worth individuals new to film. In addition to enjoying the festival, the investors were provided with almost 40 hours of keynote presentations, case study analyses and roundtable discussions delivered by 20 experts on the fundamentals of profitable film-financing, risk mitigation strategies and the elements of successful distribution.

The first market-specific private investors club of its kind, this initiative hopes to inspire a year-round think tank that will innovate high-profile financing structures and enhance investment in our industry looking not only at bottom-line ROI, but also seeking to promote socially responsible projects.

THE VILLAGE INTERNATIONAL

Source: © Le Marché du Film.

Originally launched in 2000, the Village International offers film commissions, national institutions and funding entities promotional exposure for their shooting locations and services. Almost like an Epcot Center for the film landscape, you can go on a virtual tour of the entire global film industry right in this pavilion. Co-production entities use the Village as their headquarters. With delegations from Algeria to the UK, the Marché is not only the biggest industry gathering of the year but also the most global and diversified. In 2016, the Marché welcomed first-time exhibitors: Israel, Catalonia, Egypt and Sri-Lanka; 2015 attracted Albania, Finland, Iran and Japan; and 2014's new entrants included: Denmark, Ecuador, the Philippines and Marseille.

Jérôme explains: "Most of our planning logic comes down to smaller worlds within the larger world." "It enables you to network with everyone from a given territory all at once. The outside terrace is all about networking and parties."

Source: © Le Marché du Film.

NEXT PAVILION

Source: © Le Marché du Film.

Located in the heart of the Village International Pantiero, the NEXT Pavilion is a relatively new initiative that provides an incubator for literally: *what's next?* As the boundaries of cinema become increasingly diffuse, NEXT offers an observatory and lab for alternative economic and storytelling models. Debating and demonstrating everything from virtual reality to crowdfunding, crowdsourcing and crowdticketing to Theatrical on Demand, cross-media, multi-platform and multi-territory distribution, this brand new venue allows you the chance to pitch your concepts and participate in expert workshops exploring cutting-edge industry mutations. A new 85-seat conference room was added in 2016 to facilitate the enhanced demand of the innovators and explorers of the future of cinema for this type of content.

Source: © Eric Bonté 2015.

MARCHÉ MIXERS

Another relatively new addition to the Cannes Market line-up is a series of three, invite-only, cocktail meet-and-greets that group professionals together by genre, region, sector or other special interest, giving them a chance to relax and get to know one another within their expertise. The 400–500 themed mixer guests are selected and invited by the market organizers.

Every year, these mixers respond to new trends, helping the trailblazers mix it up with their tribe. 2016 hosted Festivals and Sales Agents, Doc Lovers and "Fantastic Fanatics" (professionals who specialize or excel in horror and fantasy material). One of 2015's mixers was "Europe Sails with Latin America" while the year prior focused on those doing business with Asia. 2014 also celebrated the tenth anniversary of Cinando (their successful database and VOD platform covered below).

DOC CORNER

Source: © Le Marché du Film.

With documentaries making up a significant 16 percent of the market's titles, and in keeping with their catering to market segmentation, the Marché's Doc Corner gives market badge holders the opportunity to upload documentaries completed in the past year at no additional charge. This video library offers more than 300 (70 minutes plus) docs available for view and issues daily screenings reports to the respective rights holders.

Private tables can be booked in the Doc Corner, providing sales agents a dedicated space to use as home base, which includes a hostess who will greet visitors, take messages and help schedule meetings. Similar to the Producers Workshop and Producers Network, in their effort to stimulate community, Le Marché programs roundtables with documentary experts for a special peer brunch gathering a select group of 200 guests from the documentary community.

CINANDO

The incomparable Cinando was originally launched by Le Marché du Film in 2003 as a complete database of all the Cannes attendees. It has since grown and morphed to provide a secure viewing portal for full feature screeners, attendee contact databases and access as well as schedules for several major film markets and key festivals.

Rather than re-create the wheel, markets like the AFM, the EFM, Hong Kong FILMART and, of course, Cannes' sibling event in Latin America, Ventana Sur, as well as major festivals with market-like elements such as Sundance and Toronto, have partnered with Cinando to enable their attendees to use this same platform to prepare for their events throughout the year.

Source: © Le Marché du Film.

Companies and projects can be presented via Cinando. The profiles of producers, distributors and sales agents from around the world can be accessed and you can easily interact with other event participants. Analogous to a cross between an industry database like IMDBPro or Variety Insight and a Vimeo or Interdubs screening platform, Cinando takes all that a step further by ensuring streaming security to vetted distributors and festival programmers only. The online screening rooms provide reports not only of who watched your film, but for how long, when and where they stopped, if and when they resumed, providing rich granularity for sales analysis.

As its intention was never to be a historical reference resource for old films, it is an inventory of what's actively in development or recently completed and on the marketplace (or really, since Cinando's inception). It's a current and forward-looking market tool. All Marché badges come with a one-year access to Cinando and it is currently available in English, Spanish and Mandarin Chinese.

NOTE

1 Such as: Rotterdam's Cinemart, the Berlinale Co-Production Market, No Borders (IFP), San Sebastian's Europe-Latin America Coproduction Forum, etc.

The European Film Market (EFM)

The first major film market of the year, the European Film Market launches the industry's annual trade circuit in early to mid February when industry players from all around the globe convene in Berlin, Germany for nine days. Almost inextricable from its concurrent and exceedingly well-integrated sibling event, Berlinale (the Berlin International Film Festival), the EFM was birthed by the festival's programmers to do more for their films in the marketplace. To further assist their films in development, the Berlinale Co-

EUROPEAN
FILM MARKET
efm

Source: www.efm-berlinale.de

Production Market is yet another distinct but thoroughly embedded and overlapping event. Enhanced by the symbiosis of this trifecta, the EFM launches the year of international film rights and audio-visual content trade and serves as a great barometer for the film year to come.

Right behind Cannes, the EFM has a sincere commitment to quality content from around the world. The market is always looking to expand their networking, access opportunities, and educational initiatives to promote relevant conversations, effective collaborations and provide platforms for projects in development. Not surprising, given its artistic provenance, one of the things the EFM prides itself on is discovering new and emerging talent. "That's been our mantra over the years," explains Beki Probst, the President of the EFM. "We try to get attention for the small films and offer them a place in the sun."

> "Any good film will do well at the EFM.
>   A bad film won't do well anywhere."
>   ~Beki Probst, President, European Film Market

Ms. Probst has been involved with the market since 1981. She was the Director of the EFM from 1988 until just recently when, in 2014, she stepped over to serve as President and allow her able successor, Matthijs Wouter Knol, previously the Program Manager of the Berlinale Talents for six years, to helm the EFM, nurturing the legacy of this prestigious event while bringing new ideas and energy.

Mr. Knol explains:

> One of the biggest differences between the AFM, Cannes and the EFM is that the AFM is just a market — with no festival attached — while Cannes is a private festival — for the industry (you practically have to bribe a concierge or a hairdresser to get tickets!). Whereas the EFM is connected to a city festival (Berlinale) — that's open to the public. That's a huge difference. It's all about the art.

Ms. Probst adds:

> The colder climate — February in Berlin — makes for a little more serious, more intimate event than at the beaches [i.e. the French Riviera and Santa Monica, California]. The near freezing weather makes being comfortable inside a cozy cinema more alluring than competing with the bright sunny beaches at the other events.

The annual sales cycle kicks off in earnest at the EFM. International Sales Agents and other buyers armed with fresh new annual budgets scout for and screen new titles to add to their catalogs. Offering both commercial and art house fare as well as a platform for both finished films as well as films still in development, the market enjoys a significant presence from film boards from across Europe and parts of South America.

VENUES

Source: Jan Windszus © Berlinale 2013.

Being so focused on the art of film, it's appropriate that, in 2006, the EFM made its main home one of Berlin's premiere art museums, the spectacular renaissance building: Martin-Gropius-Bau. With over 70,000 visits during the nine days of the market, the Martin-Gropius-Bau is host to nearly 400 exhibiting companies. Their flexible and efficient market stands are arranged in and around the Central Hall and on all three floors and the Gallery. This site also features a fully equipped 200-seat HD/DCP compatible cinema, cafés, a lounge area, Internet stations and a business service center.

In 2009, the EFM expanded into a second beautiful location, the modern Marriott Hotel, centrally located at Potsdamer Platz (see below). This premier secondary venue offers exhibitors an excellent infrastructure, customized exhibition space and three fully equipped screening rooms. The Ritz-Carlton and Hyatt handle some overflow while the many Berlinale partner hotels — spread across central Berlin, ranging from

Source: Lia Darjes © Berlinale/EFM 2015.

one to five stars — set aside a limited number of rooms at special prices for accredited professional guests. The EFM has a total of 39 screens, the five newest of which are in the newly refurbished Zoo Palast, with its state-of-the-art cinema technology. The EFM provides free continuous shuttle service between all its cinemas although almost all of the screening venues are walking distance from Potsdamer Platz.

Source: Lia Darjes © Berlinale/EFM 2015.

Potsdamer Platz

Potsdamer Platz was the heart of Old Berlin. It was home to the first traffic light on the continent and used to be one of the busiest intersections in all of Europe. Nearly destroyed during the war, this former city center was intersected by the Berlin Wall, separating East and West Berlin. It wasted away, almost forgotten, for decades. After the wall came down in 1989, Berlin had a unique opportunity to revitalize a "European City" right in the center of a historic district — which they have done — beautifully. This renovated public square in the center of Berlin stands as testament to honoring the past yet moving forward into the future. What was once separate and dilapidated is now reunified and reinvigorated.

FIRST TIMERS

On the first day of the Market, the EFM offers an introductory session that orients first-time EFM participants to the European Film Market, the Berlinale Co-Production Market, the Berlinale Talents and the World Cinema Fund, as well as the current Berlinale Festival offerings.

🎵 HOT TIP!

The EFM makes all three of their buyers, exhibitors and participant lists publicly available on the EFM website (but the contact information is only available to paid market badge registrants, logged into their online accounts):

www.efm-berlinale.de/en/people/participants-list/participants-list.html.

EFM INDUSTRY DEBATES

The Hollywood Reporter, *Screen International* and *Variety* each host a high-profile panel discussion with the initiative's official partner, IFA, consumer electronics unlimited. Admission to the one-hour EFM Industry Debates (and the subsequent networking cocktails) is free of charge for EFM participants with a market badge as well as accredited festival visitors, though advance online registration is required.

Celebrating its tenth year in 2017, this extensive program of discussions focuses on current developments and trends relevant to international film and media. Top experts from all areas of the entertainment industry offer their in-depth insights to spark the debates that shape our business. Recent EFM Industry Debates' topics have included: "India's Big Chance," "China's Online Video Revolutionaries," "High-End Drama Series Made in Germany," "Cross-Atlantic Series Success: (Re)Making TV for Europe and the World," "Producers as Entrepreneurs" and "Joys and Challenges of Alternative Distribution."

🎵 HOT TIP!

EFM badge holders can stream the EFM Industry Debates for up to a year after the event at: www.efm-berlinale.de | Match & Meet | EFM Industry Debates.

⚡ HOT TIP!

Hot Tip! Check out www.berlinale.de | Professionals | Berlinale Residency for more information on the three month Berlinale Residency program and stipend for writers and/or directors from around the world (who qualify).

EFM DRAMA SERIES DAYS

The EFM has historically been a theatrical market. Although DVD distributors (i.e. buyers) increasingly attend the EFM, it has not traditionally been a venue for television programming. However, in keeping with the ever-converging film and television arenas and the integration of these three concurrent, adjacent events, a brand new joint initiative between the EFM, the Berlinale Co-Production Market and the Berlinale Talents & Festival was launched in 2015: Drama Series Days. This new tract is a logical evolution as so many market attendees work in both film and television, but also: Germany is not only the biggest TV market in Europe — it's one of the biggest TV markets in the world.

"These new initiatives at the EFM acknowledge the fact that serial stories have become an integral part of our audio-visual culture," Matthijs explains.

> Moreover, we want to improve how we accommodate the needs of our visitors for such projects in the years to come. Serving as a platform for broadcasters and series producers, and buyers and distributors to network and conduct business, this new initiative includes two panel discussions with key commissioning and acquisition executives as well as market screenings illustrating trends from around the world but focused on Europe. The highlighted series came from Germany, Scandinavia, the UK and North America.

AMERICAN INDEPENDENTS IN BERLIN

American Independents in Berlin is an initiative organized in conjunction with the Independent Filmmaker Project (IFP) and the Sundance Institute. Two screening series, "IFP Selects" and "Sundance at EFM," showcase around 50 of the United States' best new independent films to the 1,500 international buyers, distributors and festival programmers. Networking mixers are open to all EFM attendees to highlight the American creative and business landscape. The American Independents in Berlin's stand and dedicated lounge on the second floor of the Martin-Gropius-Bau provides a fully staffed support services hub and a convenient meeting place for American filmmakers, companies and organizations.

CREATIVE EUROPE MEDIA (MEDIA-STANDS.EU)

Like Cannes and the AFM, the EFM is always looking for ways to expand its services to better meet the needs of producers attending its market. Unlike America, many

European markets enjoy government support of the arts and related industries. From Iceland to the Balkans, Creative Europe MEDIA financially supports the audio-visual industries, culture and media sectors by funding the development, distribution and promotion of feature films, animation and documentaries and nurturing video games and VOD.

Media-stands.eu is an umbrella stand that provides free consultancy at the EFM (Le Marché and the Cannes television markets[1]) to more than 100 selected independent European audio-visual professionals who meet the eligibility requirements. They are introduced to new financing and distribution strategies advisors who can mentor them on new marketing and distribution models, crowdfunding, current trends in financing and new European opportunities, global licensing and licensing packages by regions.

EFM ASIA

Launched in 2014, "Bridging the Dragon" was a three-year co-production platform that enabled European and Chinese producers to build stronger connections between their two territories. The EFM partnered with the Berlin-based Sino-European networking platform, "Bridging the Dragon," to strengthen the links between Asia and Europe during this one-day home base for workshops, case studies, roundtable discussions, panels and matchmaking services. Topics ranged from what works in China (and why), understanding the Chinese audience, co-producing challenges and opportunities. In 2015, the day was capped off with the evening's EFM Industry Debate analyzing China's growth from an essentially illegal, disc-based black marketplace just a few years ago, through China's relatively low per capita cinema visits, to being a leader on the cutting-edge of online video. The EFM Goes East day culminated in a networking cocktail party sponsored by *Variety*.

LOLA AT BERLINALE

Highlighting the best in compatriot features and documentaries, LOLA at Berlinale is a joint effort between the EFM and Berlinale (the Berlin International Film Festival) along with the German Film Academy (which awards the German Film Awards, aka Lola[2]) and German Films (a national company that promotes German movies). Much like the Oscar or Indie Spirit Awards screenings in the US, which are open to accredited voting members, the critically acclaimed German films and/or those that were successful at the box office and might be contenders for Lolas are screened with their Directors in attendance. These viewings are open to all accredited market professionals in addition to the German Film Academy members who are eligible to vote and might prefer to see the long-listed potential nominee candidates in a cinema with an audience.

EFM STARTUPS

Berlin is a startup metropolis with an excellent international reputation. For the first time, in 2015, the EFM opened its doors to the innovative Berlin creative industries, offering ten successful startup entrepreneurs the opportunity to network with the international film and media industries. Organized in collaboration with Startup Germany, a Berlin-based key organization connecting startups with established investors and industry players, the initiative is backed by Medienboard Berlin-Brandenburg. It will be exciting to see what new business models this synergy is bound to produce as the technical know-how to implement new production, distribution or marketing strategies is explored through this synergistic matchmaking.

MEET THE DOCS

Meet the Docs is just like its title implies: it's an environment and slate of programming that promotes networking and exchange among buyers, sellers, directors and producers of documentaries. In collaboration with the European Documentary Network (EDN), an organization of over 1,000 European members, the EFM facilitates networking via daily sessions offering leading documentary distributors the opportunity to introduce themselves, present their company profiles and (most importantly) share the kinds of documentaries they seek.

Source: Oliver Most © Berlinale 2015.

Source: Oliver Most © Berlinale 2015.

MEET THE FESTIVALS

Again, self-explanatory. At the "Meet the Docs" stand on the second floor of the MGB, "Meet the Festivals" gives you direct access via one-on-one matchmaking opportunities to book short meetings with the top documentary festival programmers and market representatives to discuss your projects. A variety of panel conversations are curated and organized in collaboration with these international doc festival partners to spotlight current issues in the documentary filmmaking industry.

NOTES

1 See Chapter 11 The MIPs, in the TV Markets section.
2 See the Chapter 32 on Awards Shows.

Source: © AFM.

AMERICAN FILM MARKET
& CONFERENCES

Source: © AFM.

With more than $1 billion worth of deals sealed every year, the American Film Market is the one pure market focused exclusively on commerce. The "AFM" (as it is referred to in the industry) has screened more than 15,000 films during its 35-year history. Some 8,000 professionals from all around the globe enjoy eight sunny days (usually the first week in November, Wednesday to Wednesday) on the AFM campus overlooking the world-famous beaches of Santa Monica. And they come to do business.

Truly a global marketplace, industry professionals come from 80 countries, over half of which exhibit, largely from the US, the UK, France and Japan — with Latin America and Asia recently significantly increasing their presence.

Almost everything ultimately seen in theaters and on television around the world has a moment in the sun at the American Film Market: from major studios' big budget blockbusters to high-profile independent films being marketed by the mini majors (such as *Divergent* and *The Hunger Games*); to lower budgeted art-house films that have earned an international film festival pedigree (such as *Dallas Buyers Club*[1] and *Her*[2]);

Source: © John Salangsang-Inivision for IFTA-AP Images.

Source: © Lobby John Salangsang/Invision for IFTA/AP Images.

to the full spectrum of ultra-low-budget genre films ranging from horror to found footage to whatever is hot at the moment in the latest cycle of vampires, werewolves or
zombies — to musicals and westerns — and everything in between.

Right in the hub of the motion picture business capital of the world (Los Angeles
County is home to more film industry companies than any other region of the world),

the AFM is a convenient market for studio executives to visit but it also attracts international sales agents, theatrical distributors, DVD and VOD buyers from all around the globe. Also in attendance are fleets of attorneys, bankers and financiers, film commissioners and festival programmers, post-production vendors and independent studio facilities. The highest and best use of everyone's time here is undeniably when you've got something to sell — a polished, finished film, ready to be monetized worldwide.

But indie producers at the script stage often come to the AFM seeking financing, packaging, co-production opportunities, distribution commitments and pre-sales as well. When Warner Bros. passed on George Clooney's *The Ides of March* (2011), he and his writing partner personally pre-sold sufficient territories at the AFM to raise the $12.5 million necessary to make their movie. Stephen Sommers and his partner, famous, best-selling author Dean Koontz, raised $27 million in two days at the AFM for *Odd Thomas* (2013). QED raised the money at the AFM for Peter Jackson's independent film *District 9* (2009), which was distributed around the world by Sony. Of course, marquee value names and profitable track records help, immeasurably (as does marketable material).

"You don't usually bump into equity financiers at festivals," explains Jonathan Wolf, Managing Director of the American Film Market.

> If you're looking for pre-sales or banks that will lend against them, production subsidies, soft money, packaging agents — that's who you'll meet at the American Film Market. That's the whole point: to get you face time with people who can make a difference for your project.

Unlike the convention halls or tent pavilions of many of the other markets, the bulk of the American Film Market takes place between two primary hotels. Home base is the beautiful Loews Santa Monica Beach Hotel where registration holds court in the atrium open to floor after floor of exhibitor tradeshow suites above. Every bed is removed from the hotel and all the rooms are converted into office showcases. Most badges come with free WiFi throughout the Loews hotel for two devices.

Right next door, Le Merigot hosts the Filmmakers Lounge and several more exhibitor sales offices. The AFM Conference Series is held over at the Fairmont, a lovely mile walk overlooking the Pacific Ocean or a quick hop on the frequent and free AFM shuttles that stop at many of the hotels and all the theaters in Santa Monica enlisted for market screenings. Jonathan describes: "With two new multiplexes, we have more commercial theaters than any other market. 95 percent of our films have not been seen anywhere else commercially (that's one of the reasons we don't allow press to the screenings)." With almost 700 screenings of more than 400 films, 29 new films are screened every two hours during the event.

"The AFM is the only market run by the content providers," explains Jonathan. "We're a non-profit trade organization made up of sales companies and distributors." The AFM is owned by IFTA, the Independent Film and Television Alliance (more on IFTA below). They work diligently to make their event increasingly relevant and functional to their member businesses. "Like a super tanker out in the ocean," Jonathan explains, "these events turn slowly. The Filmmakers Lounge, as an example [see below], was unheard of 15 years ago. People who haven't attended in awhile are always surprised at the changes in our tenor and tone."

AFM CONFERENCE SERIES

Its crown jewel, the AFM Conferences attract audiences of 700 attendees daily. Adhering annually to an ordered sequence of topics, the series kicks off on Friday with the Finance Conference. Not surprisingly, since this information is not only critical to each professional at the market but seems to be in constant flux, this is always the most popular of the conference mornings. Pitching, a far more universal and evergreen topic, kicks off the weekend and Industry Plus Pass (see Hot Tip! box below), followed by Production, Festivals and Distribution, Sunday through Tuesday, respectively.

Source: © Richard Shotwell/Invision for IFTA/AP Images.

🎬 HOT TIP!

Best Badge Value For an Independent Producer
Register Early (by the first week in October) and Buy:

> **The Industry Pass Plus**
> (Four days: Saturday–Tuesday)
>
> +
>
> **A one-day à la cart pass**
> (for Friday's Finance Conference)

Roundtables

The AFM Roundtables are in-depth, interactive discussions about specialized areas of film production and distribution that take place in the AFM Studio on the lobby level of the Loews Hotel. Access varies depending on the session but most audiences are under a hundred guests. Some are invite-only, such as 2013's faith-based panel on programming family values in a commercial world, kicked off with a keynote by Producer Mark Burnett (*The Bible*, *Survivor*). Other topics might be by group, such as the International Documentary Association (IDA) hosting a panel on monetizing and distributing documentaries. If the demand exceeds the room's capacity or, for particularly high-profile, general interest guests, huge plasma screens stream some sessions live to the lobby atrium.

MyAFM

In its continued efforts to be accessible and facilitate year-round interaction, the American Film Market has created an app and an online community that enables attendees to connect with one another before, during and after the market. This streamlines queries, appointment requests, social media interaction, project promotion and even social get-togethers. You can upload your marketing collateral (trailers, key art, pitch decks, links) for prospects to review and share your social media profiles (Twitter, Facebook, LinkedIn, Stage 32, Slated, etc.). You can also use this tool to maintain your market schedule, refer to the map and shuttle routes on the run and use MyAFM throughout the year to maintain new relationships and send private messages to connect with attendees you might have missed. It's also a great resource for you to stay connected during the years you cannot attend (you can buy annual access with or without a market badge).

Source: © AFM.

To support your due diligence preparation — even months in advance (or follow-up months after) — you can search both the attendee and exhibitor directories. The attendee directory links to their profiles while the exhibitor list (see below) connects to The Film Catalogue (see below). You can reach out to all of these participants directly, maintain notes on them and add them to your tracking list.

Jonathan explains part of the motivation for creating the app: "The whole purpose is to enhance the value of the face time. Film is a collaborative business and art but technology has not yet made it possible to ascertain chemistry without connecting." This resource is yet another reason to pay attention to badges and suite numbers. If you don't get an attendee's or exhibitor's business card, you can quickly glance at their badge and track them down later via these online tools.

AFM SOCIAL MEDIA

- www.americanfilmmarket.com
- www.facebook.com/AmericanFilmMarket
- www.linkedin.com/company/american-film-market
- www.twitter.com/AFMOfficial

EXHIBITORS

Exhibitors pay to promote their product, so they are easily the most visible and accessible both online and in person. They want to be found. *By buyers.* In addition to being searchable and accessible on the AFM's main website and MyAFM, the exhibitor list ultimately links back to The Film Catalogue, where all the product they are screening or pitching at all the major film markets are posted with key art, trailers, production status, genre, language(s), budget, director, cast, company, title, etc. Their AFM suite numbers are also listed so you can tag and track your favorites and stumble upon new prospects. Only films represented by exhibiting companies may purchase screening times at AFM screening venues. AFM Offices start at about $4,000 for an AFM Mini-booth (52 sq. ft.).

🎬 HOT TIP!

The AFM **Exhibitor** List is public:
http://americanfilmmarket.com/exhibitor-list
The AFM **Attendee** List is available to all MyAFM subscribers.
The AFM **Buyers** List is an exclusive benefit for AFM Exhibitors.

THE FILM CATALOGUE

The Film Catalogue is a free service provided by IFTA to the independent film and television marketplace. This online resource houses background information on 7,000

Source: © IFTA.

motion pictures and thousands of trailers. Any company "actively engaged in distribution" may list their projects and films in The Film Catalogue. IFTA defines this as companies that attend (as a licensor) at least two of the major film markets (AFM, Cannes, EFM or Hong Kong FilmArt).

THE FILM CATALOGUE IS AVAILABLE IN

- English
- French
- German
- Italian
- Japanese
- Korean
- Mandarin
- Portuguese
- Spanish

The day before the market (Tuesday), all the exhibitors set up their offices. This casual load-in day is popularly accented by complimentary hamburgers made fresh from convenient In-N-Out Burger trucks that park at the back of the Loews.

Source: © AFM.

BUYERS

Buyers are typically the most elusive players at the market, as they don't usually have a set location (unless they are also exhibiting, which is sometimes the case). They are usually mobile, perusing the hallways, going from exhibitor pitch meeting to screening to cocktail parties and lunch and dinner meetings. The buyers have access to private buyers breakfasts and a buyers' lounge where they can negotiate deals — or just get off their feet for some quiet downtime.

For the purposes of the AFM, a "buyer" is defined as any company that has contracted with one or more members of the Independent Film & Television Alliance (IFTA) to distribute (or sub-distribute, i.e. re-license) at least three motion pictures or television programs in at least one audio-visual medium over the past three years. All buyers must be pre-accredited (by the first week in October). No accreditations are done during the AFM.

THE INDEPENDENT FILM & TELEVISION ALLIANCE® (IFTA)

IFTA is the global trade association of the independent motion picture and television industry. Serving as a voice and advocate for independents worldwide, IFTA represents more than 150 member companies in 23 countries made up of the world's foremost independent production and distribution entities, sales agents and institutions engaged in film finance.

Collectively, IFTA's members produce more than 400 independent films and countless hours of television programming every year, generating more than $4 billion in annual sales revenue. For more than 30 years, IFTA members have produced, distributed and financed many of the world's most prominent films, 20 of which have won the Academy Award® for "Best Picture." Recent productions include: *The Artist* (Wild Bunch and The Weinstein Company), *The King's Speech* (The Weinstein Company), *The Hurt Locker* (Voltage Pictures and Summit Entertainment) and *Slumdog Millionaire* (Pathé).

In addition to hosting the American Film Market and maintaining The Film Catalogue, IFTA actively speaks out and lobbies US and international government officials on critical matters directly affecting Independents and their business such as media consolidation, net neutrality, the elimination of trade barriers, new technology, anti-piracy, copyright protection and the need to foster broad-based global growth of the industry. IFTA is aggressively working to solidify solutions on these and many other crucial issues impacting our business.

DON'T BE A LOBBY LIZARD

In the past, one of the major criticisms of the AFM was that the lobby and pool areas were notoriously crammed with "lobby lizards": people who crashed the event without a badge, pilfering all the free trades and "taking meetings" all day, every day, just to be seen "in the activity" out by the pool or in the lobby bar. This caused many of the legit market attendees to avoid the lobby or the pool area — essentially never coming out of the security-controlled areas.

But a couple of years ago, the AFM designated the pool area as a badge-controlled market site. The result was remarkable and instantaneous. Wonderful, healthy, affordable fresh lunch options became available — along with fresh air, sunshine and the spectacular view. Even the lobby became infinitely less packed, too — with more room for the paying attendees to relax, mingle and run into one another — one of the best benefits of these events. People who hadn't attended for a few years barely recognized the event, it raised the caliber of connections and ease of movement so markedly.

Source: © John Salangsang/Invision for IFTA/AP Images.

Shockingly, there are authors and speakers out there who encourage actors, writers, directors, composers, etc. to camp out in the lobby to "pick up business." Loitering without a badge isn't a wildly productive strategy for most (and frowned on by many) — but the instinct to capitalize on this mass convergence and logistical convenience is a resourceful one. There are parties every night that you can often get invited to or attend as the guest of a badge holder. If you can schedule a legit meeting with an exhibitor, they can invite you to their suite literally via a temporary "hall pass." These passes need to be returned for their next guest but some exhibitors may even offer extra full-day passes to their partners or promising prospects, which would enable you to stroll the halls. And swinging through the lobby to pick up the bumper issues of the trades is always a prudent cost-saving measure to keep you up-to-date on the business. Double duty might be to time your breeze-through when a session of interest might be simulcast on the lobby screens. Or just go enjoy the beach and read through the trades to catch up on what's happening at the market.

Source: © John Salangsang/Invision for IFTA/AP Images.

AFM DATES THROUGH 2025

- November 1–8, 2017
- October 31–November 7, 2018
- November 6–13, 2019
- November 4–11, 2020
- November 3–10, 2021
- November 2–9, 2022
- November 1–8, 2023
- November 6–13, 2024
- November 5–12, 2025

Source: © AFM.

NOTES

1 $5 million budget, premiered at the 2013 Toronto International Film Festival.
2 $23 million budget, its premiere closed the 2013 New York Film Festival.

Regional Film Markets

7

HONG KONG FILMART

The Hong Kong International Film & TV Market "FILMART" is the largest entertainment market in Asia. During this event's 20-year history, China's box office has exploded from less than $100 milion annually to nearing #1 in the world. Thus, this Chinese transmedia hub has evolved exponentially as well: from a nice post-EFM/pre-Cannes Hong Kong networking opportunity to the primary East–West distribution deal making platform and co-production gateway.

A four-day event held at the Hong Kong Convention and Exhibition Center, their twentieth anniversary in 2016 attracted 7,300 buyers and 800 exhibitors from more than 30 countries and regions for over 70 events, including seminars, press conferences and networking activities and more than 400 screenings, 80 of which were world premieres, almost half being Asian films from the Hong Kong Film Festival.

Regional pavilions often include America (with nearly 40 US companies), Canada, the Chinese mainland (Beijing, Shanghai, Shandong, Sichuan, Guangdong, Hangzhou and, most recently, Chongqing), France, India, Indonesia, Israel, Italy, Japan, South Korea, Malaysia, the Philippines, Singapore, Taiwan, the United Kingdom, Russia and, most recently, Cambodia, Macau and the Middle East. Their "Locations World" provides a platform for film commissions from all over the globe to promote the benefits and incentives of their regions as shooting locations. Recent presenters have included: Cambodia, France, Japan, Malta, Malaysia, South Africa, South Korea, Thailand and the Philippines.

Hong Kong-Asia Film Financing Forum

Held concurrently with FILMART and organized by the **Hong Kong Trade Development Council (HKTDC)**, the **Hong Kong International Film Festival Society (HKIFFS)** and the Hong Kong Motion Picture Industry Association, the **Hong Kong-Asia Film Financing Forum (HAF)** serves as a three-day matchmaking platform for the film industry.

Source: © Hong Kong FILMART.

🔥 HOT TIP!

In the years when the EFM conflicts with the Chinese New Year, attending FILMART can be one of the most fertile ways to connect with Asian professionals who might have missed the European launch of the film and television commercial year.

Helping commercially viable and promising film projects in Hong Kong and Asia locate financial and business support through co-productions or joint ventures, HAF attracts about 1,155 filmmakers and financiers from at least 35 countries and regions looking for co-production ventures with top financiers, producers, bankers, distributors and buyers. 750 private business meetings are typically facilitated for the 30 projects selected for the opportunity.

Source: © HAF.

The false starts between Hollywood and China have been painful and well publicized but it seems that the early foragers have worked out some of the cultural/commerce kinks over the past couple of years through the first few high-profile negotiations. The inability to extract profits or move capital internationally (due partly to China's restricted currency) and the culture clashes over the timing, meaning, length and content of contracts seem to be abating as the obvious need for cooperation drives more genuine and effective collaboration.

Source: © Hong Kong FILMART.

Business of IP (BIP) Zone

The trade aspects of intellectual property (IP) are always a hot topic. FILMART's Business of Intellectual Property Zone (BIP Zone) provides *free onsite consultations* with a dozen IP lawyers and experts who conducted more than 80 meetings covering specific issues ranging from buying and selling, monetization and licensing IP for the film, TV and digital entertainment industries. IP protection service providers cover issues of IP infringement, facilitation of copyright trading and licensing worldwide as well as IP protection and enforcement services.

Expo Hong Kong

FILMART and the HAF are two of ten annual events now rolled into the twelfth annual "Expo Hong Kong" facilitated by the HKTDC. Their three-week agenda encompasses animation and digital entertainment (games), music, equipment, post-production services, short and microfilms. The other eight core events are: the Hong Kong International Film Festival (HKIFF),[1] the Hong Kong Film Awards (HKFA),[2] the Hong Kong Asian-Pop Music Festival (HKAMF), the IFPI Hong Kong Top Sales Music Award, ifva (Incubator for Film & Visual Media in Asia Festival), the Asian VFX and Digital Cinema Summit, the Digital Entertainment Summit and the TV World International Forum.[3] It seems March–April has become the perfect time to explore East–West, multi-platform/multi-media collaborations.

ASIAN FILM MARKET

Established in 2006 and embedded in the Busan International Film Festival[4] in South Korea, the Asian Film Market is growing at a robust rate. A major platform for Asian film projects and creative talents, in particular, this AFM promotes Korean blockbusters, encouraging cross-border Asian casting decisions and European film fund co-productions. The Busan International Film Commission & Industry Showcase (BIFCOM) is hosted concurrently in the same exhibition hall by the Busan Film Commission along with the Asian Project Market.[5]

Korean Blockbusters

Since the introduction of multiplex cinemas in Korea in 1998, in a country with a population of 50 million, a handful of films have crossed the 10 million-admission mark — an impressive 20 percent of the entire population. Kang Woosuk produced and directed *Silmido*, the first local picture to cross that threshold in 2003, and more recently, Kim Hanmin produced the 2014 box-office hit, *The Admiral: Roaring Currents*. The Korean Film Council (KOFIC) proactively solicits international Ko-Productions.

HALLYU — THE FLOW OF KOREA

In 1999, Beijing journalists first started reporting on the popularity of South Korean cultural exports, dubbed "Hallyu" (roughly translated as the "flow of Korea"). As recently as August 2014, *The Economist* magazine identified Korean pop culture as "Asia's foremost trendsetter." In the past couple of decades, Korean celebrities have enjoyed popularity across Asia and beyond, even inspiring a K-pop museum in Los Angeles.

TOKYO INTERNATIONAL FILM FESTIVAL CONTENT MARKET (TIFFCOM)

Source: © TIFFCOM.

Part of a multi-content event called the "Japan Content Showcase" that includes the Tokyo International Music Market (TIMM) and the Tokyo International Anime Festival (TIAF), TIFFCOM is the film and television marketplace affiliated with the Tokyo International Film Festival (TIFF)[6] held in October. TIFFCOM 2015 attracted 347 exhibitors from 24 countries and regions to exhibit to the 1,433 registered buyers from 50 territories. The National Pavilions typically include exhibitors from the Republic of Korea, Taiwan, the United Kingdom, Hong Kong, Cambodia, Vietnam, Canada, Indonesia, Korea, Malaysia, Spain, Taiwan, Thailand, and most recent first-time exhibitors from Colombia, Cote d'Ivoire and Estonia.

With a uniquely Japanese flair, promotional marketing efforts range from Samurai with fake swords and open barrels of sake to kimono-clad women to cos-playing teens. The local Japanese broadcasting networks bring the standing sets from their popular local TV programs.

Source: © TIFFCOM.

VENTANA SUR

In 2009, the Marché du Film/Festival de Cannes teamed up with Argentina's Film Institute, INCAA, and with the support of the European Commission, Creative Europe formed what has become the major Latin American film market. A pure market for completed films, Ventana Sur is all about Latin American movies. Most of the business taps into the lucrative US Latino market for US distribution deals. Latin American pay TV and Spanish distribution feature heavily in the market's deals as well as international deals for more art-house titles and festival fare.

2015 saw 2,797 accredited delegates, including over 300 buyers and sellers from across the five continents. Some 167 theatre screenings were held in eight theaters. At the end of each day, the distributors of each film receive a list of the accredited delegates who attended each screening. While most buyers prefer to see films in a theater with an audience, 410 of the most recent Argentinean and Latin American films were also made available in the video library with 40 quiet and comfortable individual viewing stalls. The rest of the film market follows a fairly traditional structure including the Producers Network, run by Julie Bergeron, who also runs the original one at Cannes.

LONDON SCREENINGS

London Screenings is not a traditional market: it is exclusively an export event designed to promote British films and talent to the international marketplace. About 50 or so new UK films are shown strictly by invitation-only. Represented by UK sales companies, they are screened for approximately 120 buyers, representing all the world's territories. This four-day exclusive industry event is an intimate, relaxed and contained environment where buyers can negotiate international distribution deals with over 60 British sales companies. Their breakthrough category showcases completed feature films from emerging British filmmakers seeking sales representation. This segmentation also provides sales companies, buyers and film festival directors from around the globe the chance to monitor upcoming British talent. The event is presented by Film London in association with the BFI and supported by the Mayor of London, Film Export UK and UK Trade and Investment.

NOTES

1 See Part VIII Important Annual Ancillary Events for more information on working the film festival circuit.
2 See Chapter 32 Award Shows.
3 For more: see Hong Kong FILMART in Chapter 14.
4 See Part VIII Important Annual Ancillary Events for more information on working the film festival circuit.
5 See Asian Project Market in Chapter 17 Other Major Co-Production Markets.
6 See Part VIII Important Annual Ancillary Events for more information on working the film festival circuit.

Part III
The Worldwide Television and Digital Media Business

Mise en Scène[1]

8

There are books and blogs galore on the television industry (and independent film business) but before we delve specifically into the world of TV markets (and the professionals who frequent them), let's first do a quick, armchair location/tech scout of the worldwide television landscape. Undeniably as cursory as a rock skipping across a river, hopefully this speedy viewfinding orientation will provide us with a shared base camp from which to venture.

> The only constant in life is change.
>
> ~attributed to Heraclitus c.500 BC

THE UK AND THE US

There's an incredible amount of programming being shown on the estimated 15,000 television channels around the world. The largest broadcasting corporation on earth is the **B**ritish **B**roadcasting **C**orporation (BBC). A public service broadcaster, the BBC operates multiple regional and local networks. Through public and commercial broadcasters, satellite and cable, the United Kingdom has access to hundreds of television stations from all around the globe.

In the US, there are an estimated 3,788[2] broadcast television stations and 628 broadcast networks, 50 of which are nationwide. The big five American commercial networks (NBC, CBS, ABC, FOX and The CW, in ballpark order as of 2015) have between 204 to 229 full power affiliates each, reaching 95–97 percent of US households. In 2015, that amounted to over 116.3 million households (of those estimated to have a television set). Programming in America is delivered via terrestrial television stations, cable or satellite services and over the Internet through a myriad of branded outlets ranging from Spanish language, genre-based, news, sports, lifestyle, religious and shopping networks. Private grants and public donations fund public stations in America.

GERMANY

Germany is the biggest television market in Europe. Their national and regional public broadcasters compete with nearly 400 privately owned stations, 90 pay TV channels and 9 public stations — reaching 75 percent of their population every day. More than 92 percent of German households have cable or satellite television and watch, on average, almost four hours[3] of television a day. Their exports currently reach 82 countries.

THE BRIC BLOCK

Brazil

Brazil's pay TV market is the largest in Latin America, with revenues expected to top $10.32 billion by 2018. Though there is still considerable room for growth, there is significant pressure from the over three-dozen OTT[4] platforms (Brazil is Netflix's largest Latin American territory). Brazil's 100+ channels are mostly privately owned, though media ownership is highly concentrated (as it is elsewhere). Still, some restrictions on foreign investments and telcos were recently lifted in 2011, allowing providers like AT&T to secure a foothold in the market.

Russia

Some 74 percent of the population of Russia routinely watches their six national channels, three of which reach 90 percent of the country. Two-thirds of the approximately 3,300 regional and local television stations are owned or controlled by the federal government. Over 100 million homes have access to more than 700 TV channels through cable and satellite television and 60 VOD services license content in Russia.

About 600 Russian companies produce content, 90 percent of which are located in Moscow, with acquisition budgets favoring local productions. Russian President Putin and China's Paramount Leader Xi Jinping[5] have aggressively pursued Sino-Russian media, culture, history and language exchange. Three Chinese channels are currently broadcast in Russia (in Chinese, Russian and English) and international versions of *RTR Planeta* and *Russia Today* currently air in China in English, and the Russian channel Kultura is set to broadcast in China soon.

India

India's television industry has been growing steadily, averaging close to 15 percent a year for the past few years and is expected to reach $15.2 billion by 2019. With a total television viewership of 415 million (168 million TV households), they are the second largest TV market in the world, behind China. Their public television network, Doordarshan, operates about 20 national, regional and local services. There are an increasing number of privately owned TV stations, and 823 cable and satellite stations, 184 of which are pay channels.

China

In China, there are no privately owned television stations. All broadcast media is owned by or affiliated with the Communist Party of China or a governmental agency. The state-run Chinese Central TV (CCTV) is China's largest media company, controlling more than 2,000 of the 3,300 local, regional and national TV channels, dominantly delivered via broadband by telecom powerhouses China Telecom and China

Unicom. Most provincial TV is delivered via satellite but receiving satellite TV signals without permission is against the law in Mainland China. Of the 400 million TV households, 210 million subscribe to cable **TV** (CATV), which is how most pay TV is offered. Of these cable subscribers, 140 million receive digital service; a tiny 5.64 million subscribers receive high-speed Internet service while the rest are still on analog systems, a one-way network limiting the interactivity and growth of on-demand services. 89 percent of online Chinese have access to the Internet via a smartphone.

A total of 15,000 episodes of indigenous TV series were produced in China in 2015. Employment in the film and television industries provide 90 percent better wages than the average job in China. Content can be censored (i.e. the negative coverage of the Beijing Olympics, the Tiananmen Square protests, Dalai Lama, etc.). The Central Propaganda Department lists subjects that are off-limits to domestic broadcast media and the government maintains the authority to approve all programming. Actors who use drugs or break the law (i.e., visit prostitutes) are not allowed to appear on television, movies or any other forms of broadcast (radio or advertisement). Foreign-made television programming must be approved prior to broadcast.

🎵 HOT TIP!

The New MINT

Jim O'Neill, former chief economist at Goldman Sachs, who coined the acronym BRIC[6] (for **B**razil, **R**ussia, **I**ndia and **C**hina) has recently popularized the new moniker "MINT" for **M**exico, **I**ndonesia, **N**igeria and **T**urkey as the most populous "frontier markets" with favorable demographics and economic prospects forecasted to be among the "Next Eleven[7]" largest economies in the world over the next two decades.

TURKEY

Perhaps surprisingly, the second largest TV *industry* in the world is Turkey. According to the Turkish Exporters Assembly, they have experienced a two-thousandfold increase in the past decade when their international sales were hovering just below $100,000. In 2015, with 15 of their indigenous programs being exported to 70 countries, they crossed the $250 million US threshold — this from just $10,000 US in exports in 2004. A fiercely competitive market at the crossroads of Europe and the Middle East, it is tough to get on — and stay on — Turkey's eight free-to-air channels. With a population of 76 million (18 million households) — half of which is under 30 (making for a robust labor force of 28 million), this newly industrialized country is one of the world's fastest growing emerging economies.

AFRICA

And finally, Africa: the huge continent with over 1.2 billion people, with a median age of 19.5, living in 54 disparate countries with a dozen official languages. While the middle class is burgeoning and infrastructure is improving, less than 30 percent of the population has access to analog, digital or satellite TV and many of those that do are still reliant on free-to-air channels. Its nationwide digital switchover/analog switch-off is still in process but pay TV and VOD revenues are growing exponentially, with some projecting $6.2 billion coming from sub-Saharan Africa by 2020, the same year mobile broadband users are estimated to reach 1 billion.

Africa's wholesale television content business has doubled since 2010, now worth almost $500 million US in annual revenues, 95 percent of which is traded at DISCOP Africa (see below). Almost 80 percent of 2015's business was in the dominant English-speaking markets of South Africa, Kenya and Nigeria. The country's production industry has grown over the last two decades from 4,000 to 30,000 employees.

NOTES

1 A French term that originated in the theater and translates literally as "put in the scene." In filmic parlance, it means "everything in the frame" (from composition to the movement of characters); the articulation of cinematic space.
2 According to the FCC as of December 31, 2014.
3 This figure is 223 minutes to be exact — and increasing.
4 OTT is defined in Chapter 10 Players on the TV Market Stage, p. 89.
5 The General Secretary of the Communist Party of China, the President of the People's Republic of China and the Chairman of China's Central Military Commission.
6 In 2010, South Africa was added to make the acronym BRICS.
7 The "Next 11" include: Bangladesh, Egypt, Indonesia, Iran, Mexico, Nigeria, Pakistan, the Philippines, Turkey, South Korea and Vietnam.

The Studio Scene
LA Screenings, the Upfronts (and NewFronts)

While the TV markets are home turf for the independents, a quick survey of the studio scene is in order before we canvas that terrain, just to put the mammoth pieces of the industry pie into perspective. Hollywood studios don't "need" the film and TV markets — although many of their subsidiaries and independent shingles may attend. As distribution and marketing powerhouses, with the longest-standing international relationships and reputations, they have their own unique ecosystem. Two of the most critical events in the studios' annual television buying and selling (i.e. financing and distributing) cycle are the LA Screenings and the Upfronts.

THE LA SCREENINGS

Originally, American broadcast television networks loosely coordinated the annual studio screenings of their new pilots. This series organically evolved into the "LA Screenings," which now attracts 1,500 international television distributors from 70 countries to Century City Plaza Hotel (near Beverly Hills, California) to secure the international broadcast and/or distribution licensing rights for these shows. An estimated 60 percent of the studios' annual television revenues are generated from just this handful of days in mid-May.

THE UPFRONTS

Advertising funds most North American broadcast and ad-supported cable shows and the bulk of television ad sales in the US are negotiated "up in front of" the traditional Fall season by the handful of media agency holding companies who represent close to three-quarters of the commercial time bought. When the Nielsen's "sweeps" ratings are aggregated and reported, these agencies, major advertisers and the press gather in New York for the third week in May to watch the networks' annual pitches of their fall primetime line-ups in grand marketing spectacles at high-profile venues like Carnegie Hall, Lincoln Center and Radio City Music Hall. Stars from their new or most popular shows appear in musical and comedic performances while trailers or sizzle reels show off the new programming in hopes of attracting ad dollar commitments.

Most of these agencies and their advertisers vie for the coveted 18–49-year-old audience, often looking to select ten shows that have the potential of attracting 10 million viewers per show, ideally heavily weighted in that key demographic. Thursday night is often one of the most appealing time slots for retail brands wishing to reach consumers who they expect will shop over the weekend.

Canada has similar upfronts, the last week in May or first week of June, where broadcast and cable channels sell ads for both Canadian and licensed American shows. Australia recently started holding upfronts, too, between October and December, kicking off the Southern hemisphere's summer.

THE NEWFRONTS

While not technically part of the studio system, a few studios do attend the Digital Content **NewFronts**, a nine-day event in May in New York hosted by the Interactive **A**dvertising **B**ureau (IAB) that highlights digital publishers' content and cross-platform partnerships soliciting interactive advertising dollars. National Geographic Partners (a joint venture with 21st Century Fox) and Disney's Maker Studios both made presentations at the 2016 NewFronts, along with the usual suspects: dominant online platforms like YouTube, Hulu, Yahoo! and AOL as well as major online publishers like Condé Naste Entertainment, Bloomberg Media, the *New York Times*, Playboy, *The Economist*, Mashable, BuzzFeed and Hearst Magazines Digital Media — topped off with a live performance by Channing Tatum and his *Magic Mike Live* Vegas review.

STAGGERING ODDS OF SCRIPTED TV

In the US, at least: 90 percent of scripted television shows fail. Forget the thousands of spec pilots and bibles that get written every year — of which only about 500 ever actually secure the coveted, legitimate summer pitch meetings to the "Powers That Be" (financing and distribution entities). These meetings result in somewhere between 100 and 160 drama and comedy pilot script orders. This is followed by a flurry of spec[1] pilots submitted by agents across town, adding to the nets' reading stacks.

Each network commissions one to two dozen pilots with an ensuing talent sweep akin to an NFL draft, with every outlet competing in a flurry for the same above-the-line talent in a ridiculously compressed time period. Of all these totally subjective at bats, only about five to a dozen per outlet get commissioned to series. Of which, two per network will likely make it as 65 percent of the network shows that premiere are cancelled in their first season. Another third of these survivors will be culled during their second season. It's such a huge gamble, sportsbooks take real money bets on which TV shows will make it!

Broadcasters tend to focus group their buffet of selections, refining and readying the most viable options for their upfront presentations to their advertisers. Whereas cablers, independent of the ad-based calendar and its symptomatic talent black hole, internally develop made-to-order programs for their subscriber bases at a much more reasonable pace, resulting in infinitely less creative waste. Cable shows have twice the likelihood of a second season as network shows. So, if you're lucky enough to have a choice of gauntlets to run, the cable route does have 50 percent better odds of survival once you're released out of the slalom chute.

Add in the explosive growth from Over the Top TV outlets like Netflix and Hulu, which went from producing no original programming to 15 shows total between them in 2012, to 44 in 2015. There are currently 409[2] original television series on broadcast

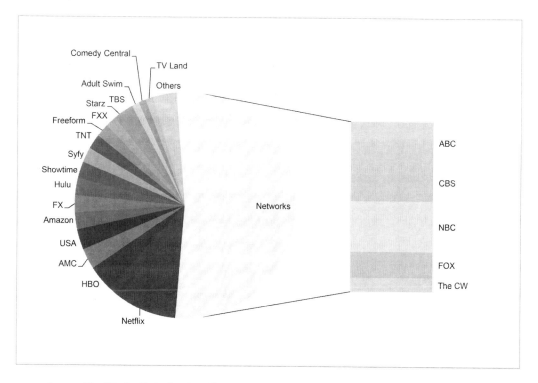

Source: Tim Westcott, technology.ihs.com MIP 2015 PowerPoint presentation. IHS Markit TV Programming Intelligence © 2016 IHS Markit; technology.ihs.com.

cable and online services in the US — that's double from just 2010. And this is just scripted. It does not include reality TV, live events, sports, news, etc.

This gives you just a hint of the grueling, ultra marathon churn. With uncertainty so endemic to the system, it's not surprising that viewing audiences are leery of investing their own precious time and emotional commitment in characters and worlds that capriciously disappear, resulting in a lot of seemingly ignored fan frustration. This might be part of the motivation driving many of the OTT platforms to commit outright — and very publicly — to an entire first season.

While film studios focus on blockbuster franchises, sequels and prequels, originals are what attract new subscribers and advertising dollars to television. Some of the very best independent filmmakers who have been unable to overcome the many financing, distribution and marketing obstacles in the film arena have instead joined the incredible diaspora of writing and acting talent migrating from the big screen to the small and mobile screens, fueling the current renaissance in television. The new hub of independent storytelling, digital storytelling truly is the Wild West frontier for independent content creators.

NOTES

1 "Spec" is short for "speculative," meaning unsolicited.
2 FX Networks research department.

The Players on the TV Market Stage 10

DISTRIBUTORS

What a TV distributor is, is changing perhaps more rapidly than any other element of our entire media landscape. In the world of television, distributors are usually broadcast or cable networks, though they can also be satellite or Internet TV providers (OTT),[1] syndicators or station groups. Just like "buyers" at film markets, TV distributors invest money and time to exhibit their inventory at the TV markets. While traditionally represented at the TV markets, these outlets are increasingly significant attendees at film markets, as well.

Broadcast Networks

Broadcast networks are entities that provide live or recorded content over the air via radio waves. This content ranges from scripted programming such as sitcoms and one-hour dramas, movies, limited-event series, to reality programming such as talk and game shows, local and international news to sports, event spectacles and local public affairs. Their competitive linchpin continues to be live events such as sports (especially championship series), talent or other reality competition finales and awards shows (such as the Oscars, Emmys and Golden Globes). Broadcast networks are looking to sell (i.e. license to distribute) their existing (original or licensed) product to other networks in other countries or to syndicate it to other domestic channels.

EXAMPLE BROADCASTERS

- ABC
- ARD
- BBC
- CBS
- FOX
- NBC
- Televisa
- The CW
- Univsion

Cable Networks

Cable networks deliver programming to paying subscribers via coaxial or fiber-optic cables. Cable has traditionally tried to offer more premium content that viewers are willing to pay extra for: events viewers might have bought a ticket to go see in the real world, such as concerts, seasonal or sporting events. As an example, in terms of original, exclusive programming, **W**orld **W**restling **E**ntertainment (WWE) accounts for 8 percent of the USA cable network's viewership.

Some cable channels are subscription-based while most are ad-supported. Still others offer both options. Many large conglomerates have invested in both broadcast and cable infrastructures to compete in both sectors. Some cable providers are integrated into some of Hollywood's biggest oligopolies (i.e. Comcast acquired NBC Universal) or were formerly affiliated (Time Warner Cable used to be a sibling division to Warner Bros. before being spun off) and many broadcast networks have multiple cable channel siblings. For example, NBC Universal produces and distributes its own broadcast content under various banners, most notably NBC Entertainment (mainstream content for the mass market); Universal Television and Telemundo (both competing for the Hispanic market with Televisa and Univision); while its cable offerings include: USA, Syfy, E!, Bravo, Oxygen, Chiller, Cloo, Sprout, The Esquire Network, NBC Universo (formerly Mun2, also targeting Latinos) and The Weather Channel — to name but a few.

MSOs

Most cable systems operate in more than one community and are thus referred to as "Multiple System Operators" (or MSOs). The studios, networks, cable outlets and larger independent distributors have consolidated over the past decade, so fewer buyers remain as outlets and partners for independent content creators.

🐜 HOT TIP!

Even though their hierarchical names may be confusingly similar, there is a vast difference between a cable *channel* or *network* versus a cable *operator* or *provider*. These latter pros may be very far removed from the creation of the content they carry — and thus may not even be prospects for you (while the former
might be).

Satellite TV

Satellite television relays broadcast signals from communication satellites via an outdoor dish to a set-top box or a built-in television tuner that receives and decodes the signals for the desired (or paid for) programming to be viewed on a television set.

CABLE EXAMPLES

Subscription-Based (Pay TV) Cable Networks:

- Canal+
- FOX Sports
- HBO
- HereTV
- OSN
- Showtime
- Starz

Subscription-Based (Pay TV) Cable Operators:

- Comcast
- DEN Networks
- Shandon Cable
- Time Warner Cable
- Virgin Media

Ad-Supported Cable Networks:

- A&E
- ABC Family
- Adult Swim
- AMC
- BBC America

- BET
- Cartoon Network
- CNN
- Discovery
- Disney Channel
- ESPN
- FOX News
- FX
- Hallmark Channel(s)
- History
- MSNBC
- Nickelodeon/Nick at Nite
- TBS
- Televisa
- TNT
- USA

EXAMPLES OF SATELLITE TV PROVIDERS

- DD Free Dish
- Direct TV
- Dish TV
- DStv
- Echo Star
- PrimeStar
- Sky Digital
- Sky TV
- Star Sat

Telcos and ISPs

The advent of high-speed Internet has revolutionized our media world, blurring the distinction between telecommunication companies (often called "Telcos"), **Internet Service Providers** ("ISPs") and broadcast and cable networks (often referred to as "the nets"). AT&T U-verse uses **Internet Protocol TV** (IPTV) to deliver their content to paying subscribers but in areas without their fiber-optic network, AT&T partners with satellite providers, offering the same service, still under the unifying U-verse brand. Verizon FiOS had a false start dipping their toe into the online VOD market with RedBox Instant. RedBox, with their 35,000 tiny footprint kiosks, is perhaps the last vestige of the physical disc rental market, dying a slow death on the heels of brick and mortar video stores, like Blockbuster Video, which have become endangered species in many parts of the world. Although net neutrality battles rage on with the FCC, telecos are trying to hold their ground as triple threats: bundling telephone, television and Internet services. It will be interesting to see if any of these deep-pocketed, technical, binary companies try their hand at the original content creation game, perhaps rekindling the 1948 debate[2] of whether a "studio" (a production entity) can control the means of distribution (theaters, televisions, computers, smartphones, etc.) of the content it manufactures — especially in light of the FCC's 1992 repeal of the financial-syndication rule.[3]

Over the Top Television (OTT)/Internet Networks

Internet networks are often referred to as "**O**ver the **T**op **T**elevision" (OTT). These platforms are relatively new but exponentially significant attendees at both marketplaces. As discussed earlier, these "**V**ideo **o**n **D**emand" providers can be either subscription-based (SVOD), **a**d-supported (AVOD) or simply transactional, which used to be called TVOD (for either **T**ransactional or **T**rue) or iVOD (for the **I**nternet), they are often lumped together as "VOD" as a master category.

The OTT powerhouse currently leading the pack is Netflix. Launched originally as a DVD-by-mail subscription service provider, Netflix has evolved into not only the world's most prominent online distributor — available in 190 countries — but also a formidable producer of original "film" and "television" content — which 70 percent of their customers binge watch.

Netflix has over 83 million subscribers worldwide.[4] Netflix's subscription base is broken down approximately as follows: 47 million in its native US, 13 million in Latin America, 8.8 million in the UK and Ireland, 3.5 million in Scandinavia with many of its newer markets nearing the 1 million mark: France, Germany, Japan, and the combined Southern European territories of Italy, Spain and Portugal. Their content exposure is

OTT AVOD Network Examples:

- CBS All Access
- Google Play
- Hulu Plus
- iTunes
- Roku
- Sony's Crackle
- YouTube

OTT VOD Examples:

- Cinema Now
- Google Play
- iTunes
- Sling TV/Epix (Dish)
- YouTube

OTT SVOD Network Examples:

- Amazon Prime Instant Video
- Blockbuster On Demand (SingTV; Roku)
- CBS All Access
- HBO Go/HBO Now (w/Apple)
- Hulu Plus
- iROKOtv
- Netflix
- Showtime

Set-top Boxes, Sticks, and Mobile Apps:

- Amazon Fire HD
- Apple TV
- Freeview
- Google Chromecast
- Microsoft Xbox Live
- Roku
- Sony PlayStation Vue

further extended by the fact that almost 30 percent of account holders share their credentials. China remains the largest holdout — and the world's largest potential market with almost 650 million Internet users.

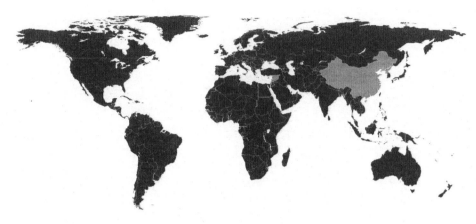

Source: © Netflix.

SYNDICATORS

Syndicators are sales people or companies who buy original content after it has premiered on its debut platform. When syndicating a show, the production company, distribution company, or syndicator attempts to sell the show to one station in each television market or geographic territory around the world. Syndication can be wildly lucrative and is a model used across virtually all forms of media.

> ## SYNDICATION EXAMPLES
>
> - **Newspaper columnists:** *Dear Abby, George Will, Salman Rushdie, Garrison Keillor*
> - **Cartoons:** *Peanuts, the Far Side, Garfield and Doonesbury*
> - **Rush hour radio talk shows:** *Howard Stern and Rush Limbaugh*

Most broadcast shows air across all of a network's affiliates on the same day and time (sometimes adjusted for time zones). But when network affiliates (local stations not owned and operated by the network), satellite and cable channels or station groups buy the syndication rights to popular, already-aired-elsewhere shows, they get to dictate the best time slots for their individual markets considering their individual schedules, local culture and psychographics.[5] They expect these shows will either be new — or at least of repeat interest — to their local viewers. More importantly, they are banking that these already proven popular shows will be much easier and far more profitable to sell commercial time for.

If the original outlet is a vertically integrated conglomerate, odds are, they have their own internal divisions or sales, legal and marketing departments to syndicate their own content, which creates inherent efficiencies.

But, if you're an independent content creator, syndication can be a bit like trying to sell your intellectual property door-to-door. Local station groups (see below) can accelerate this process exponentially by amalgamating markets but it's still very unlikely you'll hit a home run and sell out every possible international territory or ancillary window — but hey, *Oprah* did all right by it!

THE KING OF TELEVISION SYNDICATION

One of the original trailblazers in the syndicated television arena was the great salesman, Charles King, who founded King World Productions and was succeeded by his six children. King World Productions forged the path of joint venture programming between advertisers and station groups as well as international distributors. For a good couple of decades, they led the charge with some of the highest rated shows on the air including: *The Oprah Winfrey Show* and its spin-off, *Dr. Phil*; games shows like *Jeopardy!*, *Hollywood Squares* and *Wheel of Fortune* (one of the most popular shows in syndication history for over a quarter of a century); sitcoms like *Everybody Loves Raymond*; several iterations of the *CSI* drama franchise; *America's Next Top Model* and *Inside Edition*. Their legacy will forever impact television business models.

The skyrocketing potential of — and speed of access to — worldwide coverage has revolutionized the syndication landscape. The dramatic increase in the quality of local productions and other would-be imports have created unprecedented competition for the finite number of time slots for television and online outlets around the world — not to mention our own personal attention bandwidths! A fixed asset like real estate, every channel has only the exact same 24 hours of "time" to program; whereas magazines and newspapers (or even phone books back in the day) have a set amount of "space" to sell ads in; the Internet has truly rocked the world of the time–space continuum (at least in the world of entertainment ads), as all bets are off — and the possibilities are infinite! Yet syndication remains a robust (and evolving) business that makes the television world go round. You will see these pros on virtually every TV market floor, buying and selling programming year-round.

The Coveted 100th Episode

Q: Have you ever seen *The Hollywood Reporter* or *Variety* celebrating a show's 100th episode? Or the cast and crew popping champagne at the end of taping such a significant benchmark? What's that all about? Why is it such a big deal?

A: Historically (in the US, at least), the centesimal episode has long been the golden benchmark for most television series (especially for primetime sitcoms and scripted dramas) because once that threshold has been achieved, the show can then be packaged and sold into syndication (often making a few millionaires in the process). This is because the reruns can be "stripped" into 20 weeks of shows, five days a week, without repeating an episode.

LEADERS OF THE SYNDICATED TV PACK TODAY INCLUDE:

- 20th Television
- Anchor Bay
- CBS Television Distribution
- Debmar-Mercury[6]
- Disney–ABC Domestic Television
- MGM Television
- MyNetworkTV
- New Line Television
- Paramount Domestic Television
- Rysher Entertainment
- Sony Pictures Television
- TriStar Television
- Warner Bros. Television Distribution

Strip Shows[7]

Strip shows air at the same time every weekday, extending a stripe across the entire week in viewing guides. Strip programming is not synonymous with syndication. Original programming, such as telenovelas, talk shows or news, can also be referred to as strip shows, signifying that same calendar band.

The 100-episode landmark has been lowered in recent years to 88 (i.e. 22 episodes per season for a four season run rather than five) — or even lower. This is the primary

Table 10.1 A Hypothetical Sample Week of Strip Programming

	Monday	Tuesday	Wednesday	Thursday	Friday
3:00 PM	Soap Opera	Soap Opera	Soap Opera	Soap Opera	Soap Opera
3:30 PM	Talk Show	Talk Show	Talk Show	Talk Show	Talk Show
4:00 PM	Local Program	Local Program	Local Program	Local Program	Local Program
4:30 PM	Game Show	Game Show	Game Show	Game Show	Game Show
5:00 PM	*Modern Family*	*Modern Family*	*Modern Family*	*Modern Family*	*Modern Family*
5:30 PM	*Big Bang Theory*	*Big Bang Theory*	*Big Bang Theory*	*Big Bang Theory*	*Big Bang Theory*
6:00 PM	Local News	Local News	Local News	Local News	Local News

The grey shows sindicated "re-runs"

reason you see shows waning in popularity being moved to graveyard slots — just to eke out the tail end of their run to reach the lowest packageable pinnacle.

Game shows, reality programming, cartoons and other children's programming have varying syndication run numbers and profitability. The reasons for this are myriad but include:

- kids have a much higher tolerance for reruns;
- topical material gets dated quickly;
- surprise endings, suspenseful plot twists, and game show contest winners are often spoiled by media or Internet disclosure;
- reruns don't enjoy the social media buzz that buoyed the original run;
- licensing rights limitations.

Q: Have you ever seen the end credits on a rerun fly by at an accelerated speed? Or compressed to a split screen at the end of the show as the next program is teased? Or recognized that a beginning or end tag has been cut?

A: This is likely because the buying or licensing entity has trimmed up to two and a half minutes off the ends of a show to add up to five more 30-second slots to sell to advertisers.

Deficit Financing

A common practice for the first season of original scripted programming is for the networks (distributors) to pay a license fee (the right to air the show) that doesn't cover the entire production expense, thus forcing the television series producers (sometimes studios) to share in the financial risk of unproven content. They are both banking on the popularity of the show to drive profits in syndication. As an example, ABC *Studios* produces content that often airs on the ABC Television *Network* (which includes: ABC Daytime, ABC Entertainment, ABC News, an 80 percent controlling ownership in ESPN, Inc. and a 50 percent stake in A&E Television Networks).

A distributor might strike the same kind of deal with an independent producer, expecting them to assume a portion of the financial risk so they, too, will have what's called "skin in the game."[8] This limits the network's immediate financial exposure while positioning the "studio" (or independent production company) to retain ownership of the program, which enables them to profit much greater, later, off the other windows in syndication (first run, second run, cable, etc.), should the show be a breakout hit.

An analogy in the feature film arena could be made to an independent film's initial domestic theatrical run not fully recouping its equity investors' capital but that distribution being critical to drive awareness and momentum at the international markets so they can realize profits territory-by-territory and via other platforms.

Time Buy or Barter Syndication (Client Supplied Programming)

The old "infomercial" model involved buying a half-hour to an hour of airtime to directly sell product to consumers. Many hybrids divvy up this ad space including the content being outright given, traded or "bartered" (the usual industry term) in exchange for the airtime. This allows the syndicators to retain ownership of the programming and control and sell about half the ads themselves.

Major channels such as Discovery (TLC) and A + E Networks are proactively experimenting with these models, allowing individual content creators to get their shows on the air by buying time — even just a handful of approved, quality episodes. Proactive producers who are able to secure a product placement title sponsor and/or sell their share of the ad holes themselves (or even better: both) can cut out a whole daisy chain of middlemen. Of course, this approach takes a great deal of financial and labor commitment (read: sales, sales, sales!) because you have to completely underwrite the production in advance and deliver premiere-ready content in order to buy the time — but owning and controling the intellectual property (i.e. copyright) can be priceless and lucrative to a lot of independent content creators in this shifting media marketplace.

The embedded advertising for brands can prove incredibly effective if appropriately aligned and creatively developed. Conversely, it can also limit the appeal to competing brands to buy ad spots around competitors already organically embedded into the content. Producers must carefully weigh all their options and potential outcomes.

WHAT'S THE DIFFERENCE BETWEEN LICENSING AND SYNDICATION?

While the terms are often used interchangeably, technically: it all comes down to what restrictions and permissions are negotiated — on which assets. As an example: you license *rights* to *use* music, *adapt* characters or *distribute* (i.e. "syndicate") *content*. You could *syndicate* five seasons of a show that's in the can for another country to air in their territory or they might prefer to *license* just the format (scripted or reality) to reshoot a more culturally relevant version in their own language, with familiar ethnic faces, in their own local settings.

Station Groups

Station groups are exactly what they sound like: groups of local stations bound together for cooperative buying power and unified reach. Raycom is an excellent example of a station group. Created in 1996 with 15 initial stations, they now provide over-the-air syndication, regional cable and digital media services to 53 television stations in 37 markets and 18 states, covering 13.1 percent of US television households. Station groups are increasingly open to considering independent content. But there is increased — and potentially favored — competition from producers creating indigenous content specific to their own communities.

AGGREGATORS

Aggregators have direct relationships with digital platforms and, like other reps, do not take an ownership stake in the properties they represent but rather charge commission fees (usually about 30 percent). Aggregators usually assist one-off producers with the technical deliverables such as converting files to the various platforms' specifications, supplying metadata, key art images, trailers to platforms in their preferred formats as well as collecting revenue from the many outlets and dispersing revenues to the rights holder(s).

Many digital platforms will not work with producers with just one project directly, preferring their deal flow to come from distributors or aggregators with a larger, more consistently professional volume — but these barriers to entry are dropping, too. Since all the above elements must originate from the creator anyway, more self-serve options facilitate these submissions as the technical savvy of the average content creator rises. While most distributors have direct relationships with digital platforms, aggregators can provide a good tertiary conduit between independent producers and digital platforms.

AGGREGATOR EXAMPLES

- BitMAX
- Digi Distribution
- Distribber
- GoDigital
- Gravitas
- Inception Media Group
- Kinonation
- Premiere Digital

EXHIBITORS

As covered earlier in Chapter 3 "The Players on the Film Market Stage," "exhibitors" can be any market participant who chooses to market themselves via a physical footprint at any market.

MARKET MAKERS

Also covered earlier in the Film Market section (Part II), don't forget the event hosts, staff, and volunteers can be invaluable resources to you in navigating and making the most of your market experience.

That's a Wrap!

NOTES

1 Over-the-Top TV.
2 The Paramount Consent Decree, a landmark Hollywood anti-trust case.

3 Limited networks to owing or producing only 2.5 hours of entertainment programming.
4 As of July 2016.
5 The study of IAO variables (interests, attitudes and opinions), as well as personality, values and lifestyles.
6 A wholly owned subsidiary of mini major, Lions Gate Entertainment.
7 No, not a burlesque dance.
8 A term coined by renowned investor Warren Buffett mandating that C-level stakeholders own stock in the companies they run to ensure they are personally invested in its wins and losses.

The TV Markets

The MIP Markets

Source: © Reed MIDEM.

Just like the film markets, there are television markets all around the world. TV and digital content creators attend their industry segment events for much the same reasons as their feature film counterparts do: to finance projects, find co-production partners, launch and promote new programs, license formats internationally and network with their peers. On the buyers' side, they come to discover and acquire new properties and channels to add to their own line-ups.

While it's possible to find TV distributors at film markets and vice versa, if you're looking to sell your independently produced television program, feature or documentary to international television, VOD or OTT buyers, or to meet broadcasters to pre-sell the first season of your television show, you really need to hit a TV market. The concentration of television-specific expertise, knowledge, opportunities and leads at TV markets for television projects is, understandably, unparalleled. This is where the TV action is.

Just like at the film markets, sales agencies set up booths in the pavilions, on the market floors and in suites at the surrounding hotels to pitch and negotiate. But here, the deal flow ranges from reality and factual formats to scripted television series of every genre and subgenre to game shows, telenovelas, kids' programming, documentaries, webseries, new media (as well as feature films).

The TV markets provide access to distributors, ranging from the major networks, broadcasters and cable companies from all around the globe to OTT platforms and DVD experts, to major production houses, financiers and advertisers. And of course, the whole litany of ancillary affiliates follow the TV pack wherever it goes from production services companies and locations' commissions to entertainment attorneys, media reps and publicists to teleprompters, subtitlers, customized software and hardware vendors.

These venues offer glamorous opportunities to launch and publicize major series. The conferences, integral to all these events, feature key industry figures and professionals offering priceless, contemporary, educational insights. Nowhere, perhaps, is the shift from the big to the little screen more obvious than at the TV markets, where filmmakers, talent and distributors are better learning how to target the mass and niche audiences that TV and the Internet can reach. Hot topics at the booming intersection of all the media industries are multi-platform distribution, viewing habits, embedded product placement, advertising versus subscription funding models, rights management and piracy, and, of course, social media — but dead center (thankfully) remains original content.

The most significant television markets in the world are MIPCOM and MIPTV, sibling events in the autumn and spring at the same facilities in France where Le Marché du Film and the Cannes Film Festival are presented. Next comes NATPE, now in Miami (and in Europe), and Real Screen in Washington, DC. Bringing together virtually every sector of the digital content business, these "TV" markets have all broadened their foci to encompass all the "content" industries including film, documentaries and "digital content" but also, significantly, brands and advertising.

THE MIPs

The world's most established and biggest content markets for buying, selling, financing, co-producing and distributing TV, film, digital and audio-visual content are Le **M**arché **I**nternational **d**es **P**rogrammes. The MIP markets are a series of television events originally scheduled around the spring and fall TV schedules. MIPTV traditionally kicks off the year in April, launching early-stage projects followed by MIPCOM in October, which is usually the busier event, bustling with a much more mature and robust deal flow. As their business cycles hinge around these landmark events every six months, many of the almost 13,000 attendees either overlap between the events or returning firms rotate delegates.

BACK AT THE PALAIS

Source: MIPCOM © V. DESJARDINS: IMAGE & CO.

Hosted in the same 20,000 square meters of the Cannes' Palais des Festival's exhibition space, all the MIP events have been professionally coordinated for over 40 years by Reed MIDEM, a global event organizer that specializes in international professional markets (primarily for the entertainment and real estate industries). The weekend before MIPTV, Reed MIDEM concurrently and logistically (but with separate badge fees and access) hosts MIP Formats, for scripted and unscripted intellectual property, and the documentary/media showcase MIPDOC. Come autumn, MIPCOM is prefaced by MIPJr., a mini-market, two-day showcase of content for kids and teens.

ACCESS TO IT ALL VIA MYMIP AND MOBILE APPS

Technology is revolutionizing the market experience, helping attendees around the globe maximize their ROI[1] on these events by enabling them to research, interact, and market their projects before, during and after the actual events. The full suite of MIP events are organized via their MyMIP[2] website and show-specific mobile apps. Convenient portals to all MIP-related data, you can make the most of your travel and accommodations arrangements through their list of hotels and apartments available with descriptions and pricing as well as access a complete online database of all of each event's attendees.

Source: © Reed MIDEM.

With over 30 percent of the attendees "first timers," this can be a priceless platform for you to introduce yourself and your company and to launch projects to the marketplace. You can build an online profile, share your one sheets, press releases, articles and reviews, link to YouTube or Vimeo sizzle reels, trailers, episodes, and link to your other social media accounts — and showcase your screenings to the thousands of powerful connections in the database.

A network matching system suggests prospective mutually beneficial meetings. You can bookmark sessions or screenings you plan to attend, speakers you wish to track down and participants or companies you wish to connect with. You can easily share your customized schedule and contacts with assistants and colleagues, inviting them to join key conferences, screenings, educational or networking events with you or to do their own due diligence on proposed leads you share. You can also share your itinerary with prospects to facilitate mutually logistically convenient market meetings.

From your office desktop, to your laptop at home, tablet on the road, or smart-phone onsite, the MIP apps synchronize with your online database account daily. Seam-lessly integrated, you can use your GPS and interactive map to dynamically navigate the campus, take session notes or leave yourself reminders of adjacent meetings or screenings right in your personal agenda. Daily reports of market goings on and indus-try trends and insights make these robust and well-thought-out tools for veterans and rookies alike.

MIPTV

The first of the MIPs is an essential date on any annual tele-vision calendar. MIPTV in April is a quieter market than its larger sibling MIPCOM in October, but the whole breadth of scripted and factual content, formats, kids' programming, docs and films do a bustling trade with international broad-casters and platforms here. Obviously, don't come to the MIPS looking for theatrical distribution: these are interna-tional TV and video markets.

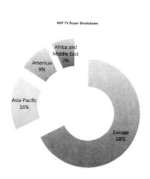

Source: © Reed MIDEM/MIPTV.

MIPTV offers a full conference curriculum, match-making services and networking forums to discover future trends and trade content rights on a global level. The market highlights the hot entertainment trends and TV companies, personalities, and emerging media players and their strate-gies that are driving the next wave of international content. MIPTV attracts top television execs and creative talent from 100 countries to forge content development partnerships and seal international distribution deals for the year ahead. While a microcosm of the entire digital and online ecosys-tem, MIPTV skews European.

Welcome to the Club(s)!

MIPTV has a variety of lounges to facilitate networking, preparation and relaxation by specialty, market intent and goals. **The Participants'** and **Producers' Clubs** are open to all badge holders attending MIPTV without a stand. These meeting areas provide free coffee service, mobile telephone charging stations and a message system. **The Match-making Lounge** is a great place for attendees to network over a cup of coffee around the Grand Auditorium conference sessions.

The Buyers' Club is reserved for program-purchasing executives. Their lounge area enjoys a complimentary bar and hostess support in addition to charging stations and an electronic message board. With entry by invitation only, the exclusive **VIP Club** allows high-profile delegates to relax and discuss business in more private surround-ings. A professional concierge service and dedicated staff attend to these players' needs while they enjoy refreshments and the daily press. The **Gold Members** of **MIP's Cus-tomer Recognition Program** enjoy complimentary and personalized business services including PCs and Internet access and refreshments.

Of course, journalists are accommodated as well with a sea-view terrace room fully equipped with computers and a complimentary bar and the press section at MIPTV.com empowers reporters and bloggers with access to official MIP and client press kits, press releases, the latest news and background information on projects as well as facilitating interviews.

MIPDigital Fronts

Just launched in 2014 and now an integral part of MIPTV, MIPDigital Fronts is the only international screenings showcase for multi-channel networks (MCNs), digital studios and online publishers. Original online content is curated and showcased followed by Q&As with the creative talent. Game-changers discuss innovative new technologies, the state and future of production, distribution and acquisitions of original digital content primarily targeting online audiences and the future of the ever-closing gap between the traditional entertainment ecosystem and the burgeoning online video marketplace.

This new breed of international digital content creators, buyers and distributors are impacting the traditional landscape the world over. Reed Midem revealed that 800 of the 4,000 program acquisition executives who attended MIPTV in 2015 were digital buyers — that's a 30 percent increase over the year prior. The European Audiovisual Observatory reported that 45 percent of the 920 VOD services available within the EU were run by US companies.

MIPFormats

Just launched in 2010 and offered the weekend before MIPTV, MIPFormats gathers aspiring creators, producers, commissioners, buyers, distributors and licensing agents to incubate, discover and develop the next wave of big ideas and must-see formats trying to break through the noise. The latest scripted and non-scripted entertainment formats are pitched and screened to get a jump-start on closing deals in the subsequent days at MIPTV.

Source: © MIPTV/MIPFormats/Reed MIDEM.

MIPDoc

The weekend before MIPTV, the factual community heads to **MIPDoc,** the leading factual co-production, screenings and conference event, to browse, screen, buy, negotiate co-productions, and finance the newest documentary and factual programs from around the world. The world's larg- est screenings library, integrated with a rich conference

Source: © Reed MIDEM/MIPDoc.

curriculum and matchmaking services, helps international buyers, sellers, producers and commissioners of documentary and factual programs facilitate connections to bring quality non-fiction content to the broadest audiences possible.

MIPCOM

The grand daddy of them all, known colloquially in the industry as MIPCOM, Le **M**arché Interna- tionale des **P**rogrammes **C**ommunications is per- haps the year's most anticipated global market for televised or digital content. Attracting 13,500 buyers and decision makers — all looking for the next big idea in multi-platform entertainment, MIPCOM is eagerly covered by more than 400 media (including journalists, bloggers, photogra-

Source: © Reed MIDEM/MIPCOM.

phers, and film crews) from 180 different international publications and outlets.

Source: © S.d'HALLOY/IMAGE & CO.

MIPJunior

Two days prior to MIPCOM, the spin-off, add-on event devoted exclusively to the chil- dren's television landscape is known as MIPJunior. With over 46 regional and national

mipjunior® pavilions including Russia, South Korea, France, UK, China, India, Italy, Mexico, Spain, Nigeria, Malaysia and Singapore, MIPJunior is the leading showcase for children's programming and animation around the world. Influential buyers, distributors, commissioning editors, digital players, publishers and licensing executives present, discover and screen the very latest content, giving them the edge to close their deals at MIPCOM.

With the biggest international digital library of kids' programs, it's a great forum to get real-time feedback on your show, track new buyers, find co-production partners and finance projects. Of course, there is an entire line-up of specialized conferences.

Source: MIPJunior © S.d'HALLOY/IMAGE & CO.

Source: MIPJunior © S.d'HALLOY/IMAGE & CO.

HOT TIP!

If you need to economize: the two days of MIPJunior cost almost as much as the four days of MIPCOM — and almost everyone you'd want to meet at MIPJunior will likely also be at MIPCOM, so you can save money by hitting just MIPCOM. However, if you're selling exclusively kids/teens content, it might behoove you to attend this more intimate, niche event to capitalize on the targeted pitch and networking opportunities afforded to one-tenth the crowd.

MIPCANCUN (THE LATAM TV BUYERS SUMMIT)

Going into just its third year, **MIP Cancun**, the Latin American TV Buyers Summit, is growing at a rate reflective of the growth of the **Lat**in **Am**erican TV market. Mid-November in Mexico, more than 100 buyers and 33 international sales agents from 23 Latin American countries will come to view the 70 exhibiting distributors' content. Channels that came to network on the beautiful Yucatan Peninsula included: Fox Networks Group Latin America, Disney Latin America, Telefonica, Telefe, Turner, Grupo Bandeirantes, Blim, Televisa, Canal 22, TV Unam, A&E Networks Latin America, AMC Networks International, BBC Latam, Google/YouTube, HBO, NBC Universal and Nickelodeon Latin America. The event includes one-on-one matchmaking and summits of digital and creative minds.

ASIA TV FORUM & MARKET (ATF)

Another growing event produced by Reed Exhibitions in association with MIPTV and MIPCOM is the Asia **TV** Forum & Market (ATF). Over four days in early December in Singapore, 905 international buyers and 723 exhibitors in 16 pavilions from 60 countries focus on Asian content. Held in conjunction with the **S**ingapore International **F**ilm Festival (SGIFF) and the Asian Television Awards, the ATF is attended by close to 5,000. The first day is a pre-market conference and in keeping with its sibling events, there is a day focused on formats and one on children's programming, as well as animation, digital and cross-border futures.

NOTES

1 **Return on I**nvestment.
2 www.my-mip.com.

National Association of Television Program Executives (NATPE)

12

The **N**ational **A**ssociation of **T**elevision **P**rogram Executives (NATPE) is the biggest television market in North America. Organized by the entity of the same name, NATPE is similar to the AFM in that their markets are both hosted by global, non-profit trade associations. Almost like industry-specific Chambers of Commerce,

the paid staffs, board members and committee volunteers coordinate these educational and networking opportunities for the benefit of their members and industry at large.

Source: Courtesy SWPix and NATPE.

NATPE has long been dedicated to the creation, development and distribution of televised programming in all forms, across all media. NATPE's charter members were originally syndicated programming salesmen who pulled together the first conference by enticing 71 registrants, primarily program directors, to join them at the New York Hilton in 1964. Now, more than 50 years later, NATPE's Annual Market & Conference brings together more than 5,000 global industry leaders and innovators in content creation, cross-platform production and distribution, advertising, marketing and business development. Speakers such as senior executives from A&E Television Networks, Bravo, Creative Artists Agency (CAA), CBS Entertainment, Disney Channel, Endemol USA, Fox Television Studios, Twitter, Microsoft Xbox and YouTube — to name just a few — share their experiences and insights, discuss creative and technological challenges and collaborations as well as their visions for the future.

NATPE had to redefine itself from its 1980s heyday when its peak events alternated between Las Vegas and New Orleans. The rolling economic downturns that impacted our entire world caused an unprecedented consolidation in the Western television industry. Large US and European media conglomerates (i.e. Discovery, ITV and FremantleMedia) acquired many promising boutique independent producer shingles.

2015 was a watershed year for NATPE. The half-century event and organization leapt prominently back on the industry's stage as an increasingly relevant, constructive and driving force in the industry. To this end, NATPE strives to offer something to all the players in the television and digital space. NATPE's most recent initiative, "Content First," sees the morphing organization now actively pursuing new media and technology and breaking down barriers between the linear and digital communities and brands and advertisers. Over 40 percent of their speakers in 2015 were from the digital space offering insights into trends in content creation, delivery, and monetization.

NATPE's President and CEO, Rod Perth, explains:

At no time in our industry has there been as much change as we are experiencing today. All of us are recalibrating how we monetize content because technology continues to improve access to new platforms. Advertising will continue to drive monetization because audiences are being measured no matter how or where they watch. Our business is increasingly interdependent and past silos between new and old media are disappearing.

Source: Courtesy SWPix and NATPE.

Today, getting off your feet to charge your phone in a lounge on NATPE's market floor, you could find yourself sitting next to program development and acquisition executives from TV station groups or broadcast, cable, satellite or Internet networks; home entertainment (DVD/VOD) distributors; advertising brand managers; bankers; new media producers; and YouTube or television stars. Whether legends or the next generation of big stars, anyone you meet could be a valuable resource — or your next partner.

> ### 🔥 HOT TIP!
>
> A searchable list of all the buyers, attendees and press since 2012 is available at:
>
> www.natpe.com/market/lists
>
> Only exhibitors and sponsors can download all the lists' contact information for the current year in excel or .pdf.

PROFESSIONAL PITCH OPPORTUNITIES

It's one thing to cold call Bravo. Or e-query ITV. But how easy is it to actually get in to pitch to The CW? Even with representation? Even if you manage to get past all the gatekeepers to get in that seat opposite a legit buyer, how often are you armed in advance with the inside scoop of what they're really looking for? Or if they are even buying right now? Much less, get their undivided, one-on-one attention? It's rare. But NATPE has experimented with a wide array of iterations over the years. From huge speed-dating-like events filling an entire ballroom to live contests in front of an audience and a panel of judges to intimate behind-the-scenes coaching and mentoring on leave behinds, sizzle reels, hit list creation, approach strategies, and pitch practice. Most importantly, NATPE ensures that their membership (and event attendees) actually pitch to someone on the decision-making ladder at active, fully funded entities with distribution resources (if not household names).

In 2015, Jenean Atwood Baynes, the Director of Buyer Initiatives at the time, recruited almost 30 "catchers" (buyers) from major reality-based networks and emerging media platforms who agreed to share their internal brand mandates. To ensure that the buyers weren't wasting their time either, NATPE vetted professionals from their membership, established guilds and academies or production companies with a qualifying threshold of at least one nationally broadcast show on the air in the past three years. Pitchers who met the eligibility criteria were offered the unprecedented opportunity to pitch their ideas directly to reality and format executives from domestic and international distributors and broadcast, cable and syndicated outlets in 160 curated pitches.

Source: Courtesy SWPix and NATPE.

First Show of the Year

In 2014, NATPE and the Washington DC reality TV market, Realscreen (see below), directly overlapped, which significantly impacted both their attendances and ability to attract the same heavyweights. NATPE adjusted its calendar to be earlier in January, positioning it as the first market of the year for the television and digital content communities. This may be partly what inspired its 2015 theme: "Content First."

⚡ HOT TIP!

NATPE offers Discount Codes Galore. The Screen Actors Guild, Women in Film, National Association of Latino Independent Producers (NALIP), Hollywood Radio and Television Society (HRTS), to name just a few — but Jeffrey R. Gund's InfoList.com usually offers the lowest price possible.

NATPE Hotels

In addition to the Fontainebleau home base, the Eden Roc next door hosts a great many NATPE suites and events. The Grand Beach and even the Holiday Inn are good options if the main hotels are booked solid or too expensive.

LIVE STREAM VIRTUAL NATPE

Just as filmmakers are looking to digital outlets to expand their audience reach, so, too, are the conference providers. Realizing that they can only reach a certain percentage of their would-be audience through geographically specific bricks-and-mortar events, live streaming opens up the whole world and builds cyber-bridges to underserved populations of the globe. Thus, if cost or travel are obstacles for you, NATPE offers live streaming access to all the sessions and enables you to customize your virtual show experience at a very reasonable price point.

CONTENT WITHOUT BORDERS: NATPE BUDAPEST

In recognition of our increasingly international marketplace, in 2011, NATPE Miami, the "Market of the Americas," acquired DISCOP East to better serve the Central and Eastern European television communities.

Much as the European MIP suites anchor their events on bi-annual calendars, NATPE now offers its members January and June forums to conduct deals from both sides of the Atlantic. Vital for those who aren't able to attend the LA Screenings in May, international acquisitions execs, brands and advertisers can get a "first (European) look" at US studio programming.

Source: Courtesy SWPix and NATPE.

A much more intimate event, the market, screenings, special events, networking and social events all take place under one roof.

AWARDS

For information on NATPE's Brandon Tartikoff Legacy Awards and/or NATPE's Reality Breakthrough Awards, please see Chapter 32 Awards Shows — Key Television Awards, p. 270.

Realscreen

The Realscreen branded series of events (and the BCON Expo) are all coordinated by Toronto-based Bruinco Communications, Ltd. and its California subsidiary, Bruinco Marketing, Inc., which also publishes *Realscreen Magazine*. Historically providing a forum to explore issues, uncover trends, identify the best new ideas and recognize top industry talent, they are increasing their efforts towards facilitating sales. If you are a content creator, buyer or commissioner, agent, distributor or multi-platform broadcaster of unscripted entertainment — or if you are an affiliate vendor or have products or services that cater to this business arena — these events provide fertile ground to initiate and nurture meaningful industry connections.

Practical business and creative intelligence is shared and debated through a variety of high-level keynotes, panel discussions and both structured and informal networking opportunities with the shared goal of fostering business collaborations. Realscreen topics range from: case studies analyzing the best sizzle reels; how to hire the right show runner or contend with the demands of reality talent; the pros and cons of hiring an agent; how to fight for your rights; and the future of formats.

Commissioning editors tell you precisely what they're looking to commission while some of the busiest agents in the unscripted game share who's buying what — and why, what's on the way out and where the next hit might come from — and they're not always unanimous on what they think producers need to know — and do — to get that green light.

REALSCREEN SUMMIT

The Realscreen Summit in Washington DC is an exclusively non-fiction and unscripted content conference and market. With steady growth over its 18 years, Realscreen Summit now attracts over 2,600 reality and factual entertainment global commissioning editors, distributors, broadcasters and content creators from all around the globe.

🔥 HOT TIP!

The entire Washington Hilton hotel is closed to anyone without a Realscreen badge.

First come, first served (not guaranteed) are: Luncheon Roundtables, Meet a Mentor and Meet an Expert sessions. Also not guaranteed but available to all delegates via a lottery (based on ranked preferences) are up to two Speed Pitching opportunities. For an additional fee, you can also sign up for a couple of Masters Classes.

Luncheon Roundtables

While choices can't be guaranteed, each delegate is afforded the opportunity to break bread with one of a couple dozen green-light empowered commissioning executives while conversing with a small group of your peers over lunch.

Meet a Mentor

Designed to give delegates rare access to some of the top producers in factual programming, Realscreen's "Meet a Mentor" series provides opportunities to glean valuable information in an intimate, "off the record" setting with A-list producers (like Thom Beers[1]) through a Q&A about how they charted their paths, faced and overcame challenges, and learned invaluable lessons along the way.

Meet an Expert

Top agents and distributors in factual entertainment share what they can offer you and your production.

Speed Pitching: Now You're Talking — FAST!

Realscreen's speed pitching offers lottery winners coveted, three-minute, one-on-one, face-to-face pitches with top executives who have the power to green-light your project.

30 Minutes With . . .

With seating limited to 40 delegates, Realscreen's signature "30 Minutes With . . ." sessions provide unprecedented, intimate access to the most in-demand, unscripted buyers (such as Executives from A&E, Travel Channel and OWN) and commissioners who candidly share their programming strategies, future plans and priorities. This up-close-and-personal vibe is often followed by hosted cocktails for further networking opportunities.

Master Classes

As optional, add-on to the general conference agenda, Realscreen assembles a slate of high-value, classroom-style, practical presentations. Delegates can sign up for a pair of these Master Classes.

A searchable delegates list is available to the public:

By title at: http://summit.realscreen.com/2016/delegates/bytitle/.

By company at: http://summit.realscreen.com/2016/delegates/bycompany/.

Summit Showdown Pitching Contest

Pitching hopefuls who make it through the advance gauntlet enter the interactive, international pitch competition where they are judged not only on the all-important quality and execution of their pitch but also (even more importantly) on the creativity and marketability of their unscripted/non-fiction series concept or non-fiction documentary/one-off idea.

Awards

🎬 HOT TIP!

Book your Realscreen Summit meetings the first two weeks in January. Before the holidays is too soon because most professionals are ready to take a break from the business (and you'll get buried in their inbox) but if you wait until you get too close to the event, you'll be too late, as their agendas will cram full shockingly fast. Most come back after New Year ready to start booking appointments, so that's the perfect, proactive sweet spot to start booking meetings.

If you're coming from abroad, one way to make the most of your trip to the states might be coordinate a layover in NYC. This might not make any difference in your airfare and might enable you to connect with New York-based firms. If you're traveling East, an extra night or two might also ensure that jet lag doesn't diminish your charm during the intense market days (and you could hit a few Broadway shows while you adjust to the time zone!).

If National Geographic, Discovery and/or Smithsonian are on your hit list to meet and greet (or pitch to) and they are booked solid during the market, they are all headquartered in Washington, DC, so you might be able to schedule quieter, longer meetings with them on the days bookending the Realscreen Summit market craze.

A few weeks after the summit, all registered delegates will receive an email with instructions on how to access audio recordings of all the sessions.

REALSCREEN WEST

Essentially "Realscreen Light," all the same offerings are brought to the West Coast for a conference that is currently half its sibling's age, length and size. About 1,000 delegates, including about

200 unscripted programming buyers, come to the sunshine of Santa Monica (specifically the Fairmont Miramar Hotel where the AFM Conferences are held) for two days worth of panels, pitching, networking and deal making.

REALSCREEN LONDON

In just its second year, Realscreen London hosted its two-day, 2016 program at the London Marriott Hotel Grosvenor Square to over 400 UK and international producers and global buyers.

REALSCREEN MAGAZINE

Realscreen Magazine keeps its readers informed about emerging audience and production trends, best business practices, and industry opinion in the non-fiction film and television industries. It is published six times annually, mailed globally to over 6,600, producers, distributors, broadcasters and suppliers, and is distributed at major international markets and festivals dedicated to non-fiction.

REALXCHANGE

RealXchange is Realscreen's online community. This messaging platform offers year-round networking opportunities for you to post your bio and showcase projects you're working on. Once registered for the event, you'll be able to easily connect with others attending the event to book pitch or networking meetings in advance or discover potential new partners before or after the event — all from the convenience of your laptop, tablet or smartphone.

KIDSCREEN SUMMIT

Another in the Bruinco suite of events (the producers and publishers of Realscreen), their Kidscreen Summit follows their proven format. In 2016 it was held in February at the InterContinental Hotel in Miami and attracted 1,700 delegates made up of 450 kids, programming buyers and over 900 producers and distributors from 54 countries.

To support this niche community, *Kidscreen Magazine* is published seven times a year and delivered to 10,000 executives and industry decision makers in kids' entertainment around the world. The Kidscreen Daily email newsletter highlights breaking news and trends. Kidscreen.com is an online affinity group forum while Kidscreen-Xchange connects you to buyers and investors by providing a showcase platform for kids' entertainment.

BCON EXPO

Programmed by Realscreen's Branded Entertainment Forum advisory board, the BCON Expo focuses on unscripted/factual brand integrations and brand-created content. Dates and locations of the one-day event have varied from March in Toronto to late October in Manhattan.

BCON Xchange is its online marketplace that connects creative and media buying agencies, marketers, content producers and execs from television networks and digital platforms.

STREAM MARKET

Also hosted by Bruinco, stream market is the leading marketplace and conference for online originals attended by content creators, leading development executives, multi-channel networks, media agencies and brands. Held in June at the Fairmont Miramar Hotel & Bungalows (where the AFM Conferences are  held), the event includes their regular line-up: 1:1 Speed Pitching; "Lunching With . . ." (green-light capable commission execs); "30 Minutes With . . ." (the online video industry's major content investors); the Business Exchange Breakfast (to get expert advice on pitching and packaging original online content deals from top digital agents); and finally the Tech Showcase, where innovative and potentially disruptive technology companies showcase their product concepts.

NOTE

1 Credits include: *Deadliest Catch*, *Ice Road Truckers*, *Storage Wars* (among many others).

Regional TV and Serialized Video Content Markets

14

There are so many television (and now digital video) events around the globe, with new ones popping up, old ones merging and all of them overlapping all the time (in addition to the major international events of the three industry leaders detailed in earlier chapters) that what follows are just a few of the more influential regional markets where television and serialized video content is bought and sold.

BOGOTA AUDIOVISUAL MARKET (BAM)

Bogota Audiovisual Market (BAM) is organized by the Bogota Chamber of Commerce and Proimágenes Colombia with the support of the **Film Development Fund** (FDC) to publicize Colombia's finished films, projects in development, audio-visual production services and locations. The market occurs in July but BAM has a permanent exhibition site of finished movies available to attendees as well as an online video library and a screenings program of the latest Colombian projects in the final stages of post-production that are looking for sales agents or distribution. BAM also hosts academic talks and brunches that are open to interested individuals who might not qualify for market credentials.

DISCOPs

Launched in 1991, the DISCOP markets are regionally focused trade shows centered on pre-organized meetings between buyers and sellers of film, finished programs, formats, live events and packaged TV channels. This series is organized by Basic Lead, a business event organizer headquartered in Los Angeles with offices also in Johannesburg. Specializing in large-scale, international, B2B and B2C[1] events that engage entertainment content producers, distributors and consumers, they have planned events in more than 30 countries including Budapest (since purchased by NATPE). They increasingly focus on world regions with a fast growing percentage of young, urban, literate, media-savvy and wired demographics, such as: sub-Saharan and North Africa, Central and Eastern Europe, the Commonwealth of Independent States and the Middle East. While their events evolve to meet market demand, their offerings at the time of our publishing are as follows:

DISCOP Africa

Africa's #1 film, TV content, adaptation rights and packaged channels market, DISCOP Africa was launched in 2008. The most important pan-African media market, it is a bi-annual, three-day event, currently rotating between Johannesburg, South Africa in November and Abidjan, Cote D'Ivoire in May/June with an estimated 2,500 delegates representing 1,250 companies from 100 countries and more than 250 exhibitors.

DISCOP Abidjan

DISCOP Johannesburg

Key broadcasters, pay TV and online platforms, mobile networks, producers, advertisers, influencers and investors driving multi-platform, multiscreen content business across sub-Saharan Africa meet to pursue commerce and co-production as well as screenings, workshops and a pitching competition.

In an effort to support regional television content production and distribution, three months prior to each event, the multilingual organization prepares locals to promote everything home-grown from film, drama and thriller series, to reality and competition shows, sports and children's content to documentaries, transmedia and webseries. Visitors are not eligible for any of these services, nor the matchmaking, pitching opportunities or personalized online tools, all of which are reserved for African nationals.

🎯 HOT TIP!

With offices in Los Angeles, Johannesburg and Istanbul, and field stations in France, Russia and China, DISCOP's multilingual staff is ready to assist in 22 different languages (in alphabetical order: Afrikaans, Arabic, Bemba, Chinese, English, French, Lingala, Ndebele, Portuguese, Romanian, Russian, Sepedi, Sesotho, Setswana, Shona, Spanish, Swahili, Tagalog, Turkish, Ukrainian, Xhosa and Zulu).

See Chapter 17 Other Major Co-Production Markets, for information on DISCOPRO.

DISCOP Istanbul

DISCOP Istanbul was launched in 2010, targeting Turkey, CEE,[2] MENA[3] and CIS[4] countries. In a business region with a history as long and as rich as the Silk Road, and a marketplace of 850 million people from more than 45 countries, this area saw a 50 percent increase in its market share in the past five years alone and now accounts for 20 percent of the global entertainment content business revenue.

DISCOP Istanbul pride themselves on their high percentage of decision-making participants, their advance, online matchmaking and face-to-face meeting scheduling, as well as their experienced, multilingual staff. Delegates include entertainment brand licensors, agents, consumer goods manufacturers, major retail chains and trade associations looking to buy and sell licensing and merchandising rights for Turkey and neighboring countries from international licensors representing popular film, television, online and video game brands.

The fifth anniversary edition of the DISCOP Istanbul TV content and adaptation rights market dedicated a whole day to the staying power of scripted and unscripted formats and to the challenges in adapting these story lines and concepts so that they remain relevant across diverse markets and cultures. This new "format day" features a presentation on adaptable dramas, a discussion and analysis of innovative unscripted TV format concepts, a format pitching competition for independent producers and an award ceremony.

Geopolitical unrest in Turkey caused the event programmers to put this event on hiatus for 2017.

DISCOP Dubai

The inaugural DISCOP Dubai will run during the last three days in January 2017 at the Madinat Jumeirah resort, the same venue where the Dubai Film Festival is held. Targeting countries from the Middle East, North Africa, the Gulf and the Asian subcontinent, including India, Basic Lead expects more than 1,500 attendees.

HONG KONG FILMART

Covered extensively in Chapter 7 Regional Film Markets. Hong Kong FILMART is jointly organized by the HKTDC (**H**ong **K**ong **T**rade **D**evelopment **C**ouncil) and the **H**ong **K**ong **T**elevisioners **A**ssociation (HKTA). Launched in 2007, 2016 saw over 801 TV-related companies specializing in animation, digital post-production, video games, and edutainment software exhibit to 7,362 visitors from 60 countries. Highlights of this trading platform include: the Digital Entertainment Summit, the Hong Kong Animation and Digital Entertainment Pavilion, and the Hong Kong International Mobile Film Festival Mobile Film Awards Ceremony.

Hong Kong Televisioners Association
香 港 電 視 專 業 人 員 協 會

MYCONTENT

MYCONTENT is the leading international entertainment content and media marketplace in the MENA[5] region, held in conjunction with the Dubai International Brand Licensing Fair and the Dubai World Game Expo, under the umbrella event: "The Big Entertainment Show," in early November at the Dubai International Convention and Exhibition Centre. Like other markets, MYCONTENT is a business-to-business marketplace for networking, showcasing, producing,

co-producing, selling, buying, financing and distributing entertainment content including: TV, film, animation, kids' programs, Internet content, mobile content, social media, creative art, interactive entertainment, comics, apps and digital media content.

Over 85 percent of the buyers are from the MENA region, 65 percent of whom are the direct, final decision makers with 32 percent being purchase influencers. Almost a third represent television channels, fairly well balanced between formats/unscripted, drama/scripted, kids, docs/factual and Interactive/Apps.

Source: © 2016 INDEX® Conferences and Exhibitions Organisation Est.

TIFFCOM

Please see Chapter 7 Regional Film Markets.

WORLD CONTENT MARKET

Founded in 2008, the World Content Market attracts almost 1,200 international television and digital buyers and sellers from over 480 companies and 40 countries, three times a year (in Autumn, Spring and Summer) to the heart of Moscow, steps from the Kremlin and Red Square. In addition to workshops, screenings and networking events, they offer an online matchmaking tool to connect buyers and sellers with appropriate content and facilitate scheduling the appointments. Russia and CIS countries are typically well represented in addition to firms from America, Europe and Asia.

NOTES

1 Business to Business; Business to Consumer.
2 Central and Eastern Europe.
3 Middle East and North Africa.
4 Commonwealth of Independent States.
5 Middle East and North Africa.

Part IV
Co-Production Markets

Securing financing can often be the greatest hurdle for independents to overcome. The second-most enduring challenge that many creatives on the autonomous path experience is a feeling of isolation or lack of support — especially when they're not in the community phases of production. The bookends of getting from concept, development and soft prep to funded pre-production — and then what do once the project is polished and out of post — can be grueling, lonesome journeys for the self-determined entrepreneur. A vast chasm has opened between studio franchise blockbusters and cookie-cutter, derivative genre pabulum at one end of the spectrum and self-indulgent clutter or tiny, indigenous, multi-media storytelling on the other. A nurturing community of mentors and resources has arisen to fill the void to support low- to mid-budget independent original content creators between these two extremes.

Often embedded in festivals or traditional markets, co-production markets or "media development labs are like the studio system but for early-stage indies," explains Gabrielle Kelly, author of the soon-to-be-published book, *Global Media Labs: The New Development Deal* (and also *Celluloid Ceiling: Women Directors Breaking Through*). "Springing up all over the world, especially in Asia, they have come to almost replace the indie development scene, mostly generating feature scripts which are often co-productions."

Sadly for US content creators: "Americans are not eligible for many of the labs because they are funded by European and Asian governments." "In the US," she explains, "they are largely funded by corporate sponsors like Sundance or Tribeca." Gabrielle's book offers worksheets to determine the most appropriate lab for a given project at various stages and most importantly: what each lab really offers and how to actually get into them. Since her book will do such deep dives into this rich terrain, I will simply highlight the highest profile ones herein, starting with the original innovator, CineMart, and Berlinale, which so beautifully illustrates the integration between a market, a co-production market and festival. These two are followed by top notes (in alphabetical order) for similar events affiliated with the markets and festivals covered herein, listed in a mini calendar for context. These are all also listed on the Annual Calendar of Key Industry Events in the Introduction and on this book's website at: www.HeatherHale.com/HowtoWorktheFilmandTVMarkets. A more exhaustive list of global co-production markets and media labs is at the end of Chapter 17.

🔥 HOT TIP!

Be sure to check out Gabrielle Kelly's brand new website, www. thelabs project.com, maintains updated information on the hundreds of Co-Production labs around the world.

MINI CALENDAR OF KEY CO-PRODUCTION MARKETS

January	CineMart and the IFF Rotterdam Lab
February	Berlinale Co-Production Market
March	Sofia Meetings and Balkan Screenings
April	Frontières International Co-Production Market (Brussels)
	Beijing Film Market
June	Moscow Business Square
July	Frontières International Co-Production Market (Montreal)
August	CineLink Co-Production Market
September	Europe-Latin America Co-Production Forum
	Holland Film Meeting
	IFP No Borders International Co-Production
October	Asian Film Project
	Boat Meeting
November	CPH:FORUM
	TorinoFilmLab
December	Paris Co-Production Village

CineMart (IFF Rotterdam Co-Production Market) | 15

The original and possibly still the best, CineMart was launched in 1983 as a regular film market but it soon became clear that there was a great, underserved need for projects seeking access to the gears that drive the industry and a whole new kind of platform was born. CineMart deserves recognition and praise for originating the co-production market concept and inspiring and nurturing this evolving, innovative scene. Concurrent and co-located with the Independent Film Festival Rotterdam,[1] CineMart heralds the start of each new film year.

By invitation only, CineMart offers filmmakers the opportunity to introduce their ideas to the international film scene and find the right connections to get their projects financed, made and out there. The invitation process is quite selective, seemingly ranging between 25 and 35 projects. After the project selection is completed, the CineMart staff meets with filmmakers prior to the market and creates an elaborate dossier highlighting all the selected projects and invited professionals. Directors and producers present their film projects to prospective co-producers, film funds, sales agents, distributors, TV stations and other potential business partners. The industry delegates attending CineMart are carefully reviewed each year to ensure that they can truly contribute to that year's projects.

The four-day informal yet highly productive event takes place at the festival center, De Doelen, in the heart of Rotterdam. CineMart-accredited guests are provided access to all festival and CineMart activities, access to press and industry screenings, the Video Library and free admissions to public screenings. CineMart's rich history of presenting daring, innovative and independent film projects has resulted in unprecedented success. More than 454 CineMart-selected films have been completed and distributed. Each year, about 20 CineMart titles premiere at major international festivals including Cannes, Venice, Locarno, Toronto, Berlin and, of course, Rotterdam.

CineMart's design and execution of facilitating these one-on-one meetings has proven to be so effective that many festivals have used the same blueprint to create their own co-production markets. CineMart is pleased to be working together with many of them, including Cannes, Berlin, Hong Kong, the Independent Filmmaker Project (IFP), Paris Cinema and Sarajevo.

ROTTERDAM LAB

In 2001, to further support emerging filmmakers, the CineMart staff organized the Rotterdam Lab, a five-day training workshop designed to give them first-hand experience at an international festival and market and to enhance their international networking. Participation in the Rotterdam Lab provides producers with the confidence and skills to navigate the festival circuit and meet professionals who can help finance their projects. The participants of the Rotterdam Lab are nominated through the partnering organizations of CineMart.

NOTE

1 More on the IFFR in Chapter 28 Top Ten Market-Like Film Festivals.

Berlinale Co-Production Market

16

It is nearly impossible to extract the EFM from Berlinale (the Berlin International Film Festival), their events are so seamlessly intertwined, but straddling both events is the Berlinale Co-Production Market, a three-day event, embedded in the middle of the EFM week (Sunday through Tuesday), just steps across the street at the Berlin House of Representatives.

By Christmas, the Berlinale Co-Production Market has selected approximately 35 projects submitted by production companies seeking partners. In 2016, 35 new feature film projects from 28 countries were selected, as well as 6 drama series projects, 10 books for adaptations and 5 high-profile companies without projects, to be promoted to 500 international producers, sales agents, distributors, broadcasting and funding representatives active in the field of co-production.

Source: Richard Hubner © Berlinale 2012.

Each Berlinale Co-Pro project must have a minimum of 30 percent of its budget secured in advance in order to be eligible to participate.

"It's a matchmaking service," Matthijs (the EFM Director) explains. "If you are selected as a producer, we will look with you and for you to set up a wide range of one-on-one meetings with co-producers with funds — and we'll help you prepare for those meetings." Over 1,200 pre-scheduled, 30-minute meetings took place in 2016. These meetings often diverge from the submitted project to other business ideas, company strategies and potential common grounds for future collaboration and international alliances to even slate discussions.

Hugely significant: over 190 of the projects that have passed the Co-Pro team's "market viability check" (in form and content) that were matched with co-producers, sales agents, TV representatives, distributors, fund representatives and financiers — have been produced. The main partners of the Berlinale Co-Production Market are the MDM (Mitteldeutsche Medienförderung) and Creative Europe MEDIA. Like bragging rights for your Fantasy Dream Team, as talent is recognized, nurtured and promoted, it reflects admirably upon the program.

Source: Oliver Most © Berlinale 2013.

Source: Juliane Eirich © Berlinale 2014.

BERLINALE CO-PRODUCTION MARKET PRODUCERS HUB

The Berlinale Co-Production Market's Producers Hub at the Berlin House of Representatives provides a forum for informal meetings between potential co-production partners, funds and broadcasters attending the EFM conveniently across the street.

BERLINALE DIRECTORS

Keeping it in the family, three highly promising projects are selected among directors whose previous films were past Berlinale program selections. Their newest projects are presented in the Berlinale Directors tract. Although most of these projects do not fulfill the 30 percent financed criteria, they have clearly recognizable potential with helmers with established track records and are thus supported in their efforts to solicit funding and production partners early in the process.

ROTTERDAM-BERLINALE EXPRESS

A few projects are selected each year to participate in both Rotterdam's CineMart and Berlinale's Co-Production Market.

COPRO SERIES (DRAMA DAYS)

As further evidence of the ever-merging industries, CoPro Series is an exclusive event embedded in the Drama Series Days, the official new platform for serial content at both the European Film Market and Berlinale Co-Production Market. The CoPro Series aims to encourage film producers from the Berlinale Co-Production Market to take a look at (and possibly embark upon) serial production and financing ventures. The goal is to create a space for networking and the exchange of information between the film and drama series industries. A central meeting point for the series industry at the Berlinale, the CoPro Series invites producers and financiers to screen and hear pitches on new, high-quality international drama series looking for partners. In its first two years, projects have come from Canada, Denmark, Germany, Israel, the Netherlands, Norway, Spain and the US.

BOOKS AT BERLINALE

Literary material, whether best sellers, timeless classics, cinematic genre books or even promising, unpublished manuscripts, has always proven ripe fodder for adaptations and a steady source for all sizes of screens. First launched in 2006, Books at Berlinale was the world's first market for literary adaptations. Together with the Frankfurt Book Fair, the Berlinale Co-Production market's "Books at Berlinale" provides an innovative new forum where interested film producers can meet with authors, publishers and literary agents — the copyright holders — and negotiate filming rights right there on the spot! Talk about accelerating and streamlining networking between the film and publishing worlds!

Approximately 130 books from more than 25 countries are submitted. In 2016 and 2015, 11 titles were selected that were deemed to have a great film adaptation potential.

Source: Juliane Eirich © Berlinale 2014.

International publishing houses and literary agents from Austria, Denmark, Finland, France, Germany, Italy, the Netherlands, Spain, Sweden, Switzerland, Turkey and the UK have recently presented their material, which ranged from new publications, best-sellers and/or award-winners with genres spanning the full spectrum.

WORLD CINEMA FUND

A collaboration between the Federal Foundation for Culture, the Goethe Institute, the Foreign Ministry and German producers, the World Cinema Fund works to develop and support cinema in regions with a weak film infrastructure, such as Latin America, Central America, the Caribbean, Africa, the Middle East, Central Asia, Southeast Asia and the Caucasus, while fostering cultural diversity in German cinemas. With an annual budget of approximately €350,000, the World Cinema Fund supports the production and distribution of feature films and feature-length documentaries that could not be made without additional funding: films that stand out with an unconventional aesthetic approach, that tell powerful stories and transmit an authentic image of their cultural roots.

COUNTRIES IN FOCUS

Public funders and representatives from various countries give short, ten-minute over-views on producing and accessing financing in their respective countries. After each panel (usually two panels of six countries each), they field audience questions and offer concrete answers specific to their regions and territories. 2015 saw: Brazil, Brussels (Belgium), Canada, Colombia, Germany, Lithuania, Mexico, Norway, the Netherlands, Poland, Screen Flanders (the central film commission for the Dutch-speaking region of North Belgium) and Wallonia.

Other Major Co-Production Markets

17

ASIAN PROJECT MARKET

Launched in 1998 at the Busan[1] International Film Festival, the Asian Project Market (APM, formerly known as the Pusan Promotion Plan (PPP)) was originally designed to connect talented Asian directors with new projects to global film investors, producers and distributors. In 2007, they broadened their field to projects outside of Asia, though the predominant synergy seems to be between Korean innovation and Chinese financial power and massive media consumer market.

Their Entertainment-Intellectual Property (E-IP) Market highlights ten original works ranging from unproduced scripts to in-the-can dramas to on-the-web cartoons. Focusing on the myriad ways original source material can be repurposed, other strands include book-to-film adaptations, legal workshops and co-production matchmaking meetings.

BEIJING FILM MARKET

The Beijing Film Market is the key industry event of the Beijing International Film Festival, the largest film market on mainland China, which celebrated its fifth year in 2015. Held for three days in April at the China Millennium Monument, it attracts over 7,000 participants, predominantly from Hong Kong, Macao and Taiwan. About 250 exhibitors attend, about half of which are international, from all five continents, including: Australia, Britain, Bulgaria, Canada, the Czech Republic, Estonia, France, Germany, Hungary, India, Italy, Namibia, New Zealand, Norway, Romania, Russia, Singapore, South Korea, Thailand, the Ukraine and the United States.

As part of the Chinese film industry's drive to raise the professionalism of, pitch and promote mainland Chinese projects, they offer two professional platforms: the Film Project Market, which serves as an incubator for Chinese films and mainland movie talent, and the Film Factor Market, which is more of a transactional and collaborative platform. Over 250 pitches or co-production projects are typically submitted to the Film Project Market with less than 20 percent being selected for the four days of pitching, training, project assessment and negotiations and a final judging by a jury panel that awards grants of international training, promotion and financial support.

The Film Factor Market runs concurrently, offering workshops and panels on script development, principal photography, post-production, distribution, copyright transaction, derivative and licensing.

BOAT MEETING

Hosted in a hotel built in a boat, the Boat Meeting is part of the Kyiv Molodist International Film Festival, an almost 50-year-old festival and the only film festival in the Ukraine ranked by FIAPF.[2] The late October/early November festival strives to recognize debutants, thus awarding student films, first shorts and features in its competition but also presents more than 250 films from all over the world — especially acknowledging young cinema. Its international co-production market honors less than ten first or second feature film projects, inviting the directors or producers with selected scripts with at least 20 percent funding, to constructive meetings with influential industry players.

CPH:FORUM

CPH:FORUM is the financing and co-production event of CPH:DOX, the Copenhagen International Documentary Film Festival, which, with a selection of more than 200 films from around the world, is the largest documentary film festival in Scandinavia. Provided 20 percent of the production budget has been raised, documentaries and experimental hybrids in all stages of development with an eye towards a cinematic release (even if just within the art world) are welcome to submit. In addition to participation in the festival and eligibility for the Eurimages Co-Production Development Award, accepted participants enjoy pre-arranged, one-on-one matchmaking meetings with professionals who could really make a difference with their projects and careers as well as engage in a suite of activities (master classes, case studies, seminars, etc.).

CPH:FORUM 4 FOCI

- **FICTIONONFICTION:** Challenging works in the hybrid landscape between fiction and non-fiction.
- **CINEMA:** High-end theatrical feature-length documentaries with international distribution potential.
- **F:ACT:** Projects bridging the fields of filmmaking, investigative journalism and activism.
- **ART:** Film projects positioned in the borderland between art and film and screened both within the institution of cinema and that of visual arts.

CINELINK CO-PRODUCTION MARKET

As part of the Sarajevo Film Festival in August, the most promising Southeast European and Caucasus[3] projects are presented for production and distribution funds, support and services. The Doha Film Institute, IMCINE and the Arab Fund each present one project for Arts and Culture. Their Works in Progress showcase is also open to North African and Middle Eastern countries bordering the Mediterranean Sea.

DISCOPRO

As part of the multiple-destination DISCOP Africa TV markets, the flagship **DISCOPRO** celebrated its fifth anniversary in 2016 in Johannesburg with 426 independent producers from 31 countries and 451 television executives representing broadcasters operating across the continent. Thirty competing projects in a variety of formats (TV and web series, comedy, animation and documentaries) were pitched in front of a panel of experts and developed through the educational component, which included 32 hands-on workshops over the three days. The exhibition showcased production services and providers of broadcasting technologies under national umbrellas representing South Africa, Cote D'Ivoire, Nigeria, Kenya, Cameroon, the Caribbean region, Ghana and Botswana.

Designed to stimulate co-production and distribution opportunities between **Western, Eastern and Southern Africa**, this initiative promotes intra-African trade and strives to develop and enhance sustainable content production and distribution opportunities across the continent. Recently expanded to Abidjan, a new satellite event is being launched in Nairobi, co-located with the new Kalasha Festival, organized by the Kenya Film Commission and the French Embassy in Kenya.

EUROPE–LATIN AMERICA CO-PRODUCTION FORUM

In 2012, the San Sebastian Festival launched the Europe–Latin America Co-Production Forum with a mission to foster the development of audio-visual projects, encourage collaboration between professionals and outwardly promote new international markets. Ideal for works-in-progress, this Co-Production Forum is open to film projects from Europe and Latin America.

The Industry Club is the Festival's Industry Department, an open space where accredited professionals can relax and network, take meetings and view films. Display stands promote completed films and those in production. There are private meeting rooms available for reservation, computers with Internet connections and access to the entire Online Film Library. A personal agenda of pitching appointments with prospective matched professionals is scheduled for each participant. Egeda, the Audiovisual Producer's Rights Management Association and program sponsor, presents a 10,000 EUR award to the producer of the best project. The Producers Network of the Marché du Film (Cannes Film Market) and Argentina's **I**nstituto **N**acional de **C**ine y **A**rtes **A**udiovisuales (INCAA) signed a collaboration agreement, which would help support these projects and magnify their international promotion as they continue their journey beyond the San Sebastian Forum to participate in the Cannes Producers Network and the Ventana Sur market.

FRONTIÈRES INTERNATIONAL CO-PRODUCTION MARKET

The only co-production market in the world dedicated exclusively to genre films, the Frontières International Co-Production Market recognizes both emerging and established horror, science fiction and fantasy filmmakers for innovation within their genres. Their two bi-annual footprints: at the Fantasia International Film Festival in Montreal in July, and in April at the Brussels International Fantastic Film Festival, are underwritten by Creative Europe, Telefilm Canada, SODEC, la Région de Bruxelles Capitale, Visit Brussels, Wallimage, the Netherlands Film Fund and the Fédération Wallonie-Bruxelles. Seasoned North American and European industry professionals join the selected participants for one-on-one meeting sessions, consulting services, workshops, panels and networking cocktails.

HOLLAND FILM MEETING CO-PRODUCTION PLATFORM

Hosted by the Netherlands Film Festival, every year, about 20 Dutch and European Union film projects, 70 minutes or longer with partial local financing raised, are selected to be presented to influential financiers, distributors, sales agents and co-producers via the Holland Film Meeting Co-Production Platform. Sponsored by the Ministry Dutch Film Fund, there are 5–10 minute pitches, moderated sessions with visuals, roundtable discussions covering all areas of the film industry, one-on-one meetings and works in progress sessions and awards.

IFP NO BORDERS INTERNATIONAL CO-PRODUCTION MARKET

No Borders offers 35 projects with 20 percent or more of their budget raised and some cast and/or key attachments in place (but little to no previous marketplace exposure) the opportunity to take part in a variety of business and artistic activities. Over 800 one-on-one meetings are scheduled with buyers, financiers, sales agents, pitch training, expert consultants and established US and international producers who have strong track records for producing films in the international marketplace. Workshops and master classes with business and artistic leaders and high-level social events broaden their knowledge and networks.

IDFA FORUM (DOCS FOR SALE/IDF AMSTERDAM)

Europe's biggest co-production and co-financing market for new documentaries is the International Documentary Filmfestival Amsterdam (IDFA)'s Forum. Held in conjunction with the world's biggest documentary festival, which welcomes 3,000 international documentary professionals for 11 days and its popular international doc market, "Docs for Sale," launched in 1996, which attracts more than 300 TV buyers, sales agents, distributors and festival programmers.

The Co-pro Forum selects approximately 50 writer/producer/director teams to pitch via roundtable as well as central pitches in the larger hall in front of 25 commissioning editors and 300 observers (mostly made up of other independent documentary producers and filmmakers, financiers and other stakeholders). Some 800 one-on-one meetings and rough-cut screenings are also facilitated. With a keen focus on creative storytelling, their IDFA Crossmedia Forum focuses on creative non-linear new media projects that tell a documentary story or explores unknown realities with an emphasis on interactivity (including webdocs, virtual reality and artificial intelligence projects, physical installations, multimedia journalism and live performances).

MOSCOW BUSINESS SQUARE

Supported by the Russian State Ministry of Culture, the main industry event of the Moscow International Film Festival is the Moscow Co-Production Market known as "Moscow Business Square," at which 200 professionals from several countries participate in film pitches, co-production meetings, roundtables, master classes, seminars and conferences on financing and theatrical distribution.

PARIS CO-PRODUCTION VILLAGE

Organized by Les Arcs European Film Festival[4] and hosted by the Champs-Élysées Film Festival in June, the Paris Co-Production Village is a development and financing forum for Europeans. Over a dozen selected projects are pitched in about 550 meetings to more than 150 producers, sales agents, distributors and financiers from the European Cinema Industry. Prizes include cash and post-production services. Since 2009, nearly 120 feature film projects have solicited financing, development and promotional support and were made into successful films, launching careers on the distribution and festival circuits. The Champs-Élysées Film Festival also hosts half a dozen American films in late post-production stage in their "US in Progress" series. Over at Les Arcs European Film Festival, the European Film Agency Directors group (EFAD) hosts a workgroup designed to engage European distributors with EFAD members on topics such as digital single market, piracy and copyright. The Film School Village, works in progress and market screenings, Low Budget Film Forum (organized in collaboration with the London Film School) round out their coherent platform.

ARC 1950 COPRODUCTION VILLAGE

Hosted at the actual Les Arcs European Film Festival in December, Arc 1950 is their three-day event that selects 22 European feature films to be presented to the marketplace for financial and production support. One-on-one morning meetings with national and regional funds, producers, sales agents, and distributors are capped off by conferences then cocktail parties and complemented by plenty of skiing and other leisure opportunities.

SOFIA MEETINGS AND BALKAN SCREENINGS

In Bulgaria in March, the Sofia Meetings are a co-production market embedded in the Sofia International Film Festival. First-, second- or third-time European filmmakers are encouraged to share their work via the Balkan Screenings with more than 100 key decision makers including film funds, distributors, TV buyers, sales companies, film market representatives and producers from the region. Of course, there are workshops, panels, case studies, lectures, keynotes and networking opportunities as well. Supported by CREATIVE EUROPE Programme of the European Union and Bulgarian National Film Center, the Sofia Meetings also partner with EAVE, Producers Network, Europa Distribution, Crossroads, Mediterranean Co-production Forum, Mediterranean Film Institute and the Moscow Business Square.

Table 17.1 World Wide Annual Calendar of Co-Production Markets

Worldwide Co-Production Markets	
JANUARY	
NISI MASA European Short Pitch — The Scriptwriting Workshop in Residency, Poznan (Poland)	nisimasa.com; www.facebook.com/nisimasa
EAVE + fourth edition, Luxembourg	www.eave.org
First Cut Lab — Trieste Film Festival (Italy)	www.triestefilmfestival.it
CineMart within Rotterdam Film Festival (Netherlands)	www.filmfestivalrotterdam.com/en/cinemart/
FEBRUARY	
Clermont-Ferrand Short Film Market within Clermont-Ferrand Short Film Festival (France)	www.clermont-filmfest.com
The Berlinale Co-Production Market (@ the EFM/Berlin IFF) (Germany)	www.efm-berlinale.de
Raccontare l'avventura (workshop/pitching forum for Documentary in Europe) — Trento (Italy)	www.docineurope.org
B2B Belgrade Industry Meetings — Belgrade International Film Festival (Republic of Serbia)	www.fest.rs
MARCH	
East European Forum (Pitching Workshop/Forum), Dok Tank/Project Market/East Doc Platform	www.dokweb.net
One World International Human Rights Documentary Film Festival, Prague (Czech Republic)	www.oneworld.cz
NISI MASA European Short Pitch/Co-Production Forum	http://nisimasa.com/wp/esp-luxembourg-events/
EAVE European Producers' Workshop (Luxembourg)	www.eave.org
Sofia Meetings within Sofia International Film Festival (Bulgaria)	www.siff.bg/sofiameetings/

Doc Market/Docs in Progress — Thessaloniki Documentary Festival (Greece)	www.tdf.filmfestival.gr
Script and Pitch, First Workshop, Ghent, (Belgium)	www.torinofilmlab.it

APRIL

MIPTV, Cannes (France)	www.miptv.com
Film Market/Beijing IFF (China)	www.bjiff.com
Docs in Progress/Pitching du Reel/Rough Cut Lab/Visions du Reel IFF, Nyon (Switzerland)	www.visionsdureel.ch
East–West Talent Lab, goEast — Festival of Central and Eastern European Film in Wiesbaden (Germany)	www.filmfestival-goeast.de
Ties That Bind — EAVE Asia–Europe Producers' Workshop within Udine Far East Film Festival (Italy)	www.eave.org
Hot Docs Industry Conference and Market /International Documentary Festival, Toronto (Canada)	www.hotdocs.ca/conference

MAY

Animation Production Day (May 7–8) — Stuttgart International Festival of Animated Film (Germany)	www.itfs.de
Visegrad Animation Forum, Anifilm, International Festival of Animation Films, Třeboň (Czech Republic)	www.asaf.cz/en/; www.anifilm.cz
Marché du Film, Cannes Film Festival (France)	www.marchedufilm.com
Producers on the Move in Cannes (France)	www.efp-online.com
Pitching Forum — Docs Barcelona, International Documentary Film Festival (Spain)	www.docsbarcelona.com
Transilvania Pitch Stop and Transilvania Film Festival Fund (Romania)	www.tiff.ro

(Continued)

Table 17.1 Continued

Worldwide Co-Production Markets

JUNE

International Animation Film Market (MIFA)/Annecy Animated FF (France)	www.annecy.org
Script and Pitch, Second Workshop, Brignogan (France)	www.torinofilmlab.it
B'EST — Producers' Workshop Baltic Bridge East by West	www.eave.org
Sunny Side of the Doc, La Rochelle (France)	www.sunnysideofthedoc.com
EAVE European Producers' Workshop 2 in Skopje (Macedonia)	http://eave.org/programmes/
Moscow Business Square with the Moscow Co-Production Forum within Moscow IFF (Russia)	www.moscowfilmfestival.ru www.miffbs.ru/en/

JULY

Works in Progress, Docu Talents from the East, Pitch and Feedback — Karlovy Vary IFF (Czech Republic)	www.kviff.com
NISI MASA Script FilmLab at Lago IFF (Italy)	http://nisimasa.com/wp/call-for-participants-acting-out/
New Horizons Studio, T-Mobile New Horizons Film Festival, Wroclaw (Poland)	www.nowehoryzonty.pl
Ex Oriente Film Workshop, the first session	www.dokweb.net

AUGUST

CineLink — Sarajevo International Film Festival (Bosnia and Herzegovina)	www.sff.ba
Nordic Co-Production and Finance Market, Norwegian International Film Festival, Haugesund (Norway)	www.filmweb.no/filmfestivalen/

SEPTEMBER

Producers Lab Toronto (Canada)	www.efp-online.com
Baltic Sea Forum for Documentaries, Riga (Latvia)	www.mediadesklatvia.eu/baltic-sea-docs-2014/
Baltic Bridge East by West (B'EST) Producers' Workshop in St. Petersburg (Russia)	http://eave.org/programmes/best-2014/
Cartoon Forum: European Co-Production Forum — Animated TV series, Toulouse (France)	www.cartoon-media.eu
Films in Progress and Europe-Latin America Co-Production Forum within San Sebastian IFF (Spain)	www.sansebastianfestival.com
Holland Film Meeting — Netherlands Film Festival, Utrecht (Netherlands)	www.filmfestival.nl

OCTOBER

EAVE The Ties that Bind 2014 Workshop within Busan IFF (South Korea)	www.eave.org
Busan Asian Project Market — Busan IFF, Seoul, South Korea	www.asianfilmmarket.org
Euro Mediterraneo Co-Production Forum, Taranto (Italy)	www.en.apuliafilmcommission.it
CentEast — Warsaw International Film Festival (Poland)	www.wff.pl/en/targi-filmowe-centeast/; www.centeast.org
MIPCOM, Cannes (France)	www.mipcom.com
Lisbon Docs, Docslisboa — Lisbon International Documentary Film Festival (Portugal)	www.doclisboa.org/lisbondocs/pt_home.php
Film London Production Finance Market within BFI London Film Festival (Great Britain)	http://filmlondon.org.uk/PFM; www.bfi.org.uk
Emerging Producers within Jihlava International Documentary Film Festival (Czech Republic)	www.dokument-festival.com
Ex Oriente Film Workshop (Production and Story Development) — Jihlava (Czech Republic)	www.dokweb.net

(Continued)

Table 17.1 Continued

Worldwide Co-Production Markets

OCTOBER

Boat Meeting Coproduction Market — Kyiv International Film Festival Molodist (Ukraine)	www.molodist.com
Leipzig Networking Days and DOK Leipzig (Germany)	www.dok-leipzig.de
EAVE European Producers' Workshop 3 in Strassbourg (France)	http://eave.org/programmes/

NOVEMBER

Crossroads Co-Production Forum (and Agora Works in Progress — Thessaloniki IFF (Greece)	www.filmfestival.gr
Connecting Cottbus — Cottbus International Film Festival (Germany)	www.connecting-cottbus.de
Mannheim Meeting Place — Mannheim International Film Festival (Germany)	www.iffmh.de
International Documentary Film Festival Amsterdam Docs for Sale/The Forum — (Netherlands)	www.idfa.nl
Script and Pitch Third Workshop — Turin (Italy)	www.torinofilmlab.it
Baltic Bridge East by West (B'EST) Producers' Workshop within Baltic Event in Tallin (Estonia)	http://eave.org/programmes/best-2014/
Baltic Event — Tallinn Black Nights Film Festival (Estonia)	http://be.poff.ee/

DECEMBER

3D Financing Market, Liège (Belgium)	www.3dstereomedia.eu/market

TORINOFILMLAB

Focusing on first- and second-time directors, the TorinoFilmLab is a global co-production market for early-stage independent feature films, adaptations and cross-platform projects from all over the world. Developed throughout the year with training, development and funding grants, awards and educational support, the jury makes its award selections based on reading everything from the scripts to financing plans and all marketing materials prepared in advance prior to witnessing the moderated 20-minute multi-media pitches, the culmination of all the work, shown off at the Torino Film Festival in November. The winners go into immediate development.

NOTES

1 South Korea's second largest city behind Seoul, formerly Romanized as "Pusan."
2 Fédération Internationale des Associations de Producteurs de Films (International Federation of Film Producers Associations).
3 The Caucasus Mountain range at the Europe/Asia border (i.e. Armenia, Azerbaijan, Georgia, Iran, Russia and Turkey).
4 See Part VIII Important Ancillary Events for more information on working the film festival circuit.

Part V
Before
Preparation

Every minute you spend planning saves ten minutes in execution.

~Brian Tracy

Now that we've surveyed the landscape, let's talk about how to work these events. Just like production, the better your development and prep, the greater your odds for a more seamless and fruitful execution "on the day." "The real work happens before the market," explains Kevin Iwashina, Founder and Managing Partner of Preferred Content. "Sales agents and distributors start their work eight months in advance. Your projects will get the most attention four to eight weeks ahead of the market." If you have short notice to attend a market (*which shouldn't happen after reading this book! But, surprise opportunities do arise*), it's still likely worth attending for the chance networking and educational opportunities. What follows, however, are prudent strategies to effectively prepare to intentionally work a market with one to four months' advance planning.

Start with the End in Mind

18

If you don't know where you're going, you'll end up somewhere else.

~Yogi Berra

Rare is the producer who would begin principal photography without first fine-tuning the script, schedule and budget, yet every year thousands of "pros" around the world run off half-cocked to these markets without even slowing down to consider their objectives or to prioritize realistic goals, much less plan an effective strategy and schedule in alignment with them. Brainstorm the opportunities that lead to your end game in advance and you'll not only enhance your market coordination but you'll achieve better economies of scale, maximize your return on investment (ROI) and increase your odds of success. You're also bound to enjoy the entire experience more.

While all our expendable resources are limited, money is truly the most replaceable of all our assets. It's funny what a death grip so many of us have on our cold hard cash yet we will let our far more precious creative energy, professional relationships and universally limited time slip through our fingertips! Honor and respect your finite, less tangible commodities just as judiciously as you budget and dole out your currency.

Perhaps the most important question you can ask yourself in this entire process is . . .

WHY ARE YOU GOING?

Do you ever ask yourself: *"Why am I doing this?"* regarding a specific project or long-term career choice? Or even in terms of a personal relationship? Do you ever ask yourself: *"Why are you even in this business?"* (My parents ask me this all the time!). Just as you consider such important personal life questions (and professional development and production questions), so, too, should you give serious contemplation to: *"Why are **you** going to **this** specific market?"*

QUESTIONS TO ASK YOURSELF

- What do you hope to accomplish at this market?
- Where are you at in your career?
- Where are you at with this project?

What Are You Going With . . .?

Film Markets

- A finished film in the can?
- A rip-o-matic[1]?
- A look book?
- A script?
- A sizzle reel?
- A trailer?
- Completed scenes?
- A few elements of a package?
  - Partial funding?
  - Key attachments?
  - Deferred expenses or in-kind equity (in locations, equipment, services)?
  - Tax credits?

TV Markets

- A completed series or pilot?
- A pilot presentation?
- A series bible?
- A pilot script?
- A sample episode script?
- A treatment?
- Hypothetical reality scenarios?
- Hours of re-purposable footage to license?
- Attached talent?
- Talent reel, bio, headshot, book? (for aspiring on-air talent, hosts, subject matter guestperts)
- Tax credits?

- What are you looking to secure?
  - Distribution commitment?
  - An international sales agent?
  - Pre-sales?
  - Production funds?
  - Vetted cast lists?
  - Co-production partners?
  - Potential partner research?
  - Pitch practice to assess industry interest?
  - International or domestic locations?
  - Production incentives and resources?
  - Syndication?
  - Education?
  - A new job?
  - Expand your networking sphere?
- What are the realistic milestones and deliverables you could actually accomplish between now and when this market opens?
- Are there other projects you could present at this market?

People attend markets for all sorts of reasons. Make sure you know what yours are. Just as you must with each creative, production and financial decision, you should check in with yourself periodically to honestly reassess your underlying professional motivations and aspirations.

Are you in this business for the money? For the fame? For the power? For the (per-ceived) glamorous lifestyle? For the fun and travel? To work in a community of eclectic, artistic, go-getter dreamers? To change the world on an issue or topic? To be heard? To be empathized with? To have your story told? Are you making a go of show business because you're fundamentally unemployable in any other industry? Is this the highest and best appli-cation of your unique (and maybe odd) combination of skills? Or is it because you can't imag-ine a life without the art of storytelling?

Whatever your reasons, you should ask yourself before every event . . .

WHAT CAN YOU REALISTICALLY ACCOMPLISH AT *THIS* MARKET?

What are the concrete objectives you could realistically accomplish? Here? Now? Let's focus on that. This "Market Goals" chart is admittedly an oversimplification but details some of the possible points of entry for market attendees, in order of sales-readiness, based on a typical project lifecycle. Each stage inevitably overlaps and encompasses the one prior. These markets are but checkpoints along the annual market expedition. These relationships develop over time. Everyone benefits from networking and educa-tion at all stages of their career.

But What If I'm Not Really Ready Yet?

If you don't actually have an asset to sell or license (which is the primary purpose of these business-to-business *markets* — to *transact* business), only you can determine if this event — or a future one — are good investments of your time and energy.

If your film is not yet produced — or even funded: odds are fantastic that you're not *selling* it at this market (because your product doesn't really "exist" yet in a buy-able format). *That doesn't mean you shouldn't go.* You could raise money, find production resources or even tease interest for the next market with your work-in-progress.

If you just have an idea (*i.e. your script isn't even written yet and you don't have any elements in place*): odds are terrific that you're not going to get it *funded* during this period either. *That doesn't mean you shouldn't go.* Maybe you'll get development interest on the idea. Or meet new synchronistic partners. Or discover that the market is satu-rated with similar projects. Or by the collision of input, you'll get a great new twist for your idea.

If your concept or format isn't ready to be pitched yet (*i.e. it isn't executed well enough (yet) for you to pitch — much less protect*), you're probably best served keeping it closer to your chest and staying in "input and market assessment" mode. Catherine Clinch of Nuclear Family Films encourages (rookies especially): "Don't go in selling mode. Go in '*What can I learn?*' mode."

Even if you're not quite "ready," you can still have fun, learn a lot and network for your future. It might actually be years before you process all that you actually learn on the floor — or be in a position to apply any of it — but all the more reason to go — and the sooner the better.

Perhaps a reasonable neophyte or premature-for-the-project market-attendance goal might be to simply meet all your potential distributors and other prospective partners of interest face-to-face. Assess which first impressions most resonate with you. Maybe several of the speakers are on your hit list and you just want to sit back and listen to their panels or presentations to see if you jive with their personali-ties, values, sensibilities and work ethics. Sometimes what's revealed during public

Set Market Goals		
You're Ready With A (n). . .	@ The Film Markets	@ The TV Markets
Idea	Network; enhance industry education; and do due diligence research on concept, genre, format and comps.	
Project in development	Solicit financing, distribution, co-production or packaging interest and pre-sale potential; vet cast lists; secure more accurate comp numbers; pitch to prospects; research locations, and incentives	
Project in pre-production *(or soft prep)*	Secure a distributor or an International Sales Agent; solicit pre-sales, co-production partners, research tax and production incentives as well as production-support joint ventures — or just get on your hit list's (and others') radars so they will track your project's progress with interest and intent	Sell, license or syndicate your project; solicit co-production partners, research tax and production incentives as well as production-support joint ventures — or get on their radars so they will track your project's progress with interest and intent
Project in production *(in principal photography or post-production)*	Secure a distributor or an International Sales Agent; show trailer or scenes to solicit pre-sales, finishing funds — or just get on your hit list's (and others') radars so they will track your project's progress with interest and intent	Sell, license or syndicate your project; show trailer or scenes to solicit pre-sales, finishing funds or get on their radars so they will track your project's progress with interest and intent
Completed project *("in the can")*	Secure a distributor and/or an ISA	Sell, license or syndicate to domestic and foreign distributors, broadcast, cable, and OTT platforms
Active project in the marketplace *(with distribution and/or representation)*	Use the event and social media to: • support the marketing and promotion of your current project; • raise your career pedigree and network for your next project	

speaking can be just as off-putting as a blind date belittling waiting staff. Or the converse might occur as well: some heavy hitter you might have written off as out of your league or as too intimidating might surprise and delight you with shared affinity into sufficient confidence to approach them with something that might really be squarely in their wheelhouse. Trust your instincts. A cursory connection might translate what would have been an ice-cold-call into a far more effective, lukewarm query or pitch. Maybe your goal is to rekindle some old relationships and see who's new at your prospect companies, to get back on their radars before you're actually ready to unveil a project. Turn up the heat on those back burners and keep them simmering for when you're ready.

Always network two years ahead of your needs.
Build your net before you need to jump.

NOTE

1 A teaser video using clips from existing movies to portray a visual style or story potential, see www.HeatherHale.com/Samples/Ripomatics for examples.

Know Your Product 19

The entertainment industry is unique. In the early days until just a few decades ago, studios used to defer determining their promotional and distribution strategies until after each movie was in the can, leaving this critical last leg of the journey to be handed off to a whole new fleet of strangers — from totally different studio departments — brand new to the project. That may have worked fine in an era with very little competition for the big six Hollywood studios or just the big three networks, but with global competition at a fever pitch, flopping **R**esearch and **D**evelopment (R&D) and marketing until after manufacturing makes very little sense in our modern media-savvy world. That legacy method of operation, like so many other strategies, has not only shifted — but been turned inside out. Like it or not, modern producers must consistently fire on all cylinders. We must simultaneously coordinate development, financing, packaging, production, distribution, marketing, advertising and social media promotion right from conception.

Always keep in mind:

- Who is your target audience?
- Can you attach talent that will attract financing, distribution or paying audiences?
- Are your revenue projections realistic? For . . .
  - today's market?
  - this genre?
  - this level of talent?
  - these platforms?
  - this distribution strategy?
- Do you have a sound business plan to achieve these goals?
- Do you have a solid social media campaign strategy?

> There is one answer to everything in Hollywood: "It depends."

Every scenario "depends" on a whole host of symbiotic, interlocking variables such as:

- budget
- genre

- talent
  - the fame, power, connections, or resources of your team and attachments (and *their willingness or ability to actually catalyze them on your project's behalf*)
  - your own career pedigree (and that of this particular project)
- audience demographics
  - transient and unpredictable market tastes and psychographics
- intent
- the all-important "Mo" (momentum)
- a whole host of other factors

It's as if you're trying to decode the magic combination on a *Da Vinci Code* cryptex. Even if you could lay out all your options on an intricate choice flowchart, the nuances of this fickle business can never account for art, timing or pure luck — somehow all adding to the allure of show business an addictive gamble. You're just sure you can apply everything you've learned to catch lightning in a bottle "on the next one."

> **Preparation + Opportunity =** *(Create Your Own)* **Luck**

None of us have a crystal ball. The best strategy for achieving success anywhere in the world of mass or niche media is the same across the board:
Do Your Homework:

- Research your marketplace
- Do due diligence on your prospective or potential partners
- Know . . .
  - your competition (comps)
  - where your project fits in
  - what kind of performance might realistically be forecast
- Proactively develop worthy, marketable projects with professional but innovative execution
- Be responsible for your own preparation
- Be resourceful
- Create your own opportunities
- Perhaps the most important of all: *Keep Your Expectations Realistic*

Most disputes and failures can be sourced back to thwarted expectations. Like a good prepper, have a bug-out bag — a worst outcome preparedness kit at the ready — a break-even escape plan. But all the while, continually strive for the most creative, profitable best.

And Don't Be Delusional.

HIGH CONCEPT

High concept is a strikingly easy to communicate idea. Something that can be pitched in a few words. Or a sentence. A succinctly stated, emotionally intriguing, premise. Deceptively simple. WAY easier said than done. Its intent as an easily discernible "top note" premise is often confused with a lowbrow notion catering to the lowest common denominator — but it's much more elegant than that. High concept neither prohibits nor guarantees quality or profitability but it does promise the nugget of an idea that can be pitched up the ladder effectively then translated to audiences via sound bytes or images in posters, trailers and commercials. All genres and formats benefit from marketable high concepts and its importance cannot be overly emphasized — at least in terms of marketability: getting people to read your scripts, hear your pitches or ultimately pay to watch your programs.

 The best "high-concept" pitch I ever heard was just two words. It was for a great horror novel, the perhaps poorly titled *Meg*, by excellent *New York Times* best-selling author, Steve Alten, about an extinct dinosaur shark (a *Mega*lodon). It was pitched as "*Jurassic Jaws*." I don't know about you, but just off those two words alone: I can picture the poster, hear the theme song in my head, imagine how the film might start, who might star, as what kind of characters, what the likely catalyst and inciting incident might be, what the Act II escapades might be like, how it might climax, who their demographics are, how they might market to them — titles to credits to advertising — all off two words. And you know what? Knowing all that? It wouldn't stop me for a second from paying to go and enjoy every beat promised in the premise. That, my friends, is high concept.

FORMAT, GENRE AND SUBGENRE

One of the most annoying things a pitch-*recipient* must endure is when a project's creator beats around the bush, talking in circles about what their show is *like*, what it's better than or different from — but never actually gets around to spilling the beans on what their show actually *is*. Do us all a favor: *start* your pitch with its *format*, *genre* and *subgenre*.

Format is the way something is designed or arranged. A screenplay has a different format than a stage play. A bio has a different format than a resume. An epic poem has a different format than a haiku. Jingle versus symphony, trifold print brochure versus an interactive video website — you get the idea. One is not the other. They are different ways of expressing similar content. Format typically refers to what **<u>kind</u>** of show you are pitching (full feature film, one-hour procedural, sitcom, limited event series, talk show, etc.). Format can, of course, also refer to technical specifications (6K, 3D, etc.).

A **genre** is an artistic category characterized by subject matter or stylistic similarities (Comedy, Horror, Sci Fi, Thriller, Action, Adventure), often broken down into or combined with **subgenre** (Crime, War, Mystery, Police, Noir, Romance, Magical Realism, Paranormal, Psychological, Supernatural, Historical, Biopic, Slasher, Superhero, Western, Musical). For example: "comedy" is an umbrella *genre* that encompasses a full spectrum of *sub*-genres. Just a few are listed below.

COMEDY SUBGENRES

- Animated
- Black[1]
- Blue[2]

- Broad
- Buddy
- Dark[3]
- Family
- Gross-Out
- Horror
- Musical
- Physical
- Raunch[4]
- Romantic
- Slapstick
- Sports
- Stand-up

Any genre or subgenre can be expressed in virtually any *format*. Comedy could be in the format of a feature film, a sitcom, an animated short, a mockumentary,[5] a one-hour television show, a late night topical talk show monologue, a sketch comedy, stand-up or live variety musical ensemble series. Comedies, by their nature, tend to run shorter because the longer you have to sustain the lie or ruse, the more it challenges credibility. The more compressed the timeframe, the richer and more plausible the comedic conflict. Thus, most comedy feature films are closer to the 90-minute mark than 2 hours.

Sitcoms, One-Hour Dramas and Dramedies

Scripted television formats are often linked to length. Sitcoms are typically a half-hour and are frequently shot on a studio sound stage, often in front of a live audience to enrich the actors' comedic energy, with three cameras simultaneously capturing their physical comedy and expressions from triangulated angles as spontaneity can be hard to authentically replicate. Some half-hour comedy shows, like *Brooklyn Nine-Nine* and *Sex and the City*, are shot more like films, on various locations, with one camera. Most one-hour shows typically imply drama, however many "dramedies," like *Gilmore Girls*, straddle the comedy-drama line.

EMMY DEFINITIONS

For the purposes of Emmy competition, the Television Academy recently ruled that half-hour shows would be considered comedies and dramas would be defined as hour-long shows — unless a show petitions to switch categories and earns a waiver via a two-thirds vote. In March of 2015, *Jane the Virgin* (a 60-minute show that anyone who's watched it for one second knows it's intended as a comedy), *Glee* and *Shameless* were officially re-classified as comedies.

"Sitcoms" (*Situation Comedies*) is a bit of a misnomer. While undeniably exacerbated by the fabricated situation their creators thrust them into, they are really "character comedies." The comedy is born out of and *driven* — week after week, year after year (if you're lucky) — by the unique characters' distinct worldviews and *reactions* to their situations — especially as seen through the prism of the collision of their divergent worldviews.

Scripted Serial Renaissance

Analogous to movie studio franchises, adaptations, prequels, sequels and spin-offs, it's all about audience awareness and brand recognition — somehow making a din to get a new project on the mass audience's radar. It's just as hard to market a one-off theatrical movie via cinema trailers, billboards, television, bus and Internet ads as it is a single Movie of the Week (MOW) on TV. Broadcast networks, cable outlets and digital platforms work hard to develop original series that lure remote controls to click into their domain. Once they've identified, accessed and — hopefully — hooked these capricious viewers, TV outlets want to keep them sitting right there, week after week, committed to their programming. Thus advertising long term for branded groups of content (traditional scripted or reality series, limited series, anthologies, etc.) is easier than standalone programming.

This is yet another reason why high concept is so important for every genre and format, on every platform. The ability to re-market a loosely hung together genre "franchise" (sequels or prequels) familiar to the same target audience (maybe on the same channel, in the same time slot) — ideally year after year — are just some of the factors driving the resurgence in serial programming to flesh out a broadcast or cable outlet's annual schedule or digital platform's online inventory.

Limited, Mini, and Anthology Series

A limited series is defined as a show that is viewed in two or more episodes, totaling at least 150 minutes of run time, with a self-contained, non-recurring story, airing under the same title each season, with production team continuity. While a limited "event" series might be just a marketing ploy to try to make something seem more newsworthy and precious than it is, an **anthology** series is essentially a limited series — with a twist.

The primary difference between a limited ("event" or not) series versus a **mini**-series is that a limited (or anthology) series could come back season after season whereas a mini-series is closed-ended: meaning its story is completed in however many episodes its one and only "run" takes. The anthology or limited series audience comes to each new season with a set of expectations based on the branded title, genre, format and tone — but they are game to be surprised within each new framework. These series remain easier to market because the brand is established and the audience has been identified and engaged. The finite schedule of either limited or mini series allows television and digital outlets to attract *movie* stars such as Jessica Lange, Matthew McConaughey, Woody Harrelson and Billy Bob Thornton. By maintaining series options on this caliber of actors, this arrangement allows producers to project enhanced international value.

Many remember classic mini-series like *The Thornbirds*, *Roots* or *Shogun*. Younger generations are enjoying successful new miniseries like History's *Hatfields & McCoys*, Mark Burnett's *The Bible*, HBO's *Band of Brothers*, Ron Howard and Brian Grazier's *From the Earth to the Moon*, Spielberg's *Taken* and the 2016 *Roots* remake. All of these mini-series had a beginning, middle and end in their one, self-contained "season."

Whereas modern anthology series might stick with the same characters (and actors), worlds and themes for one season, then come back with a whole different story arc with different characters, the classic anthology series, *The Twilight Zone*, created by the brilliant Rod Serling, had unrelated stories in each episode. Other anthologies might use new actors as the existing characters (*Dr Who*), while others still might re-use actors as new characters in new settings with new plots, a bit like the television equivalent of a repertory theater company or even drama's answer to sketch comedy troupes. Ryan Murphy's wildly successful (and creepy) *American Horror Story* on FX is an excellent example of a modern anthology series. HBO's *True Detective* is another. FX spun the Coen Brothers' 1996 feature *Fargo* into a contemporary anthology series. Starz spun Steven Soderbergh's 2009 feature, *The Girlfriend Experience*, into an anthology series and *The White Queen* mini-series into a sequel mini-series, *The White Princess* (both adaptations of best sellers).

Reality Formats

In reality TV, a "format" can be the intellectual property asset that can be protected, sold and replicated in other territories — like the *Got Talent* franchise. Even though we all know most reality shows are scripted or at least extemporaneously improvised, they tend to fall into fairly identifiable format buckets, all sharing a variety of subgenres such as: adventure/survival, talent, lifestyle/social experiment, infotainment, romance, crime, makeover, courtroom, reality sitcoms — and of course: the celebrity variations of all the above. *Big Brother*, as an example, is an Endemol format that mixed a variety of reality subgenres (docusoap, competition, social experiment, vérité, etc.).

PRIMARY REALITY FORMATS
- Competition
- Game Show
- Reality
- Factual
- Docusoap

Identify Your Unscripted USP

Identify what is unique about your format in comparison to your competitors or other comparable shows (i.e. your **U**nique **S**elling **P**roposition (USP)). For example, there are lots of "shiny floor" talent shows but what sets *The Voice* apart from *X-Factor*, *Idol* and the *Got Talent* franchises are those spinning chairs — the sight-unseen element of making the voice literally stand on its own — and the judge's surprise reactions when they see from whence that "voice" emanates. Can you articulate the "it" factor that took *Got Talent* to 26 territories? Or *Idol* to 129 series in 42 territories with over 37 million viewers at its peak in the US?

What if you your reality idea were for a stand-up comedy competition? How is yours different than *Roast Battle* or *Last Comic Standing?* If you have a cooking competition show, how is yours different than *Chopped, MasterChef, Iron Chef, The Next Food Network Star?* How is *The Contender* different from *The Fighters?* Do some research. You need to do this anyway to develop and pitch your show and to ascertain who your prospects might be. Your market research can feed your creative development — and vice versa. You must know your field of formats inside and out, what worked for them — and why — and what may have been their demise or missed opportunities in order to pitch why yours will be similarly successful — or even better. Painful as they may be, read as many reviews and the whole way down those comments threads to see if there are any gems of insight therein. After all, that is your target audience, speaking their truth. Maybe.

If you've got a reality show concept, it's worth your while to literally reverse engineer show bibles for your comparable programs as part of your market research. *Do they start with a tease? End with a tag? Do they throw to a studio audience? Toss to a field reporter? Subject matter experts? Video confessionals? Do they shoot in a standing set? Is it in a studio or on location? Is it a news desk? Kitchen? Living room? Conference room? Workshop? Store? Do they use comedic or animated bumpers? Do they incorporate the home audience? How do they integrate their online community?*

REVERSE ENGINEERING YOUR FORMAT

We developed an extreme baking show, *3D Cakes*,[6] along the lines of *Ace of Cakes* — a Scottish *Cake Boss* meets *Project Runway* — with some exotic animals thrown in. We literally watched every baking and culinary show we could find. From the Food Network, TLC, Bravo and WE, we analyzed episodes of *Bakery Boss*, *Last Cake Standing, Ultimate Cake Off, Kitchen Boss, Cupcake Wars, Amazing Wedding Cakes, DC Cupcakes*, and of course: anything with the wonderful Alton Brown! The list goes on and on (and on and on!) *What is it with people's obsession with pictures of food?!*

We also studied every variation of "build" shows we could find. As divergent as *Orange County Choppers, Tiny House Nation, Face Off, Extreme Home Makeovers* and *Redwood Kings* are, we researched how the creative collaborative process was best cinematically captured and emotionally tracked from client concept meeting through to the tribulations of executing the creative vision to the dramatic unveiling in a variety of different milieus.

We also analyzed workplace reality shows like *The Apprentice, Pawn Stars, American Pickers, Deadliest Catch, Ice Road Truckers, Brandi & Jarrod: Married to the Job*, etc. While this research might seem all over the place, they actually have trends and themes that unify them — and truly informed not only our investor presentation — but the refinement of our show and finding its place.

Let's say you have a game show idea. What kind of game show is it? Competition? Elimination? Let's say you want to stage a studio trivia game show. Do some trade research. You might want to study: *Are You Smarter Than a Fifth Grader? Who Wants to Be a Millionaire? Deal or No Deal, One Versus 100,* and any others that you actually enjoy. Take notes. With a stopwatch in your hand. *How many contestants are there? How do they get them? Are they prescreened? Pulled out of the audience? Do we get video backstory on them? Or just playful banter with the host? How is the studio or home audience engaged? How many episodes are shot in a day?*

I worked on an ultra low-budget reality talk show (*Lifestyle Magazine* for Faith for Today TV) and we literally shot five, half-hour episodes a day (a whole season in three days!) to keep the costs of the studio rental to a minimum.

Is your show just an excuse for you to travel to spas and ski resorts around the world? Or is it something other people would actually want to watch? Is it universal enough to warrant exportation? Alternately, could it be localized? Is the format solid enough to be licensed to other countries to replicate? What are innovative ways you could extend the brand? And monetize via ancillary marketing?

Think about how your reality concept could be tailored to other audiences and nationalities. Sometimes the format can be replicated almost exactly "as is" as evidenced by Ant and Dec's successful UK live variety show, *Saturday Night Takeaway,* which came across the pond fairly intact as its American incarnation as Neil Patrick Harris' *Best Time Ever.* Or take an idea that's already been proven — and collide it with a new twist. Look at how successful *MasterChef Junior* has been or *The Dog Whisperer.*

Emerging territories in their reality TV infancy welcome production expertise of proven commodities. This might mean you will need to partner with an established ShowRunner or a ProdCo with the experience to deliver, week after week, on time and at budget. Their involvement will not only drive up the value of the format rights (Endemol and FremantleMedia are the kings in this arena) but they might be the difference between your getting 100 percent of nothing versus a much smaller percentage of a much more significant monetary amount — a consistent piece of a profitable show that's on the air for over a decade.

Protect Your Reality Format

You cannot copyright an idea or a title but you can copyright the expression or execution of an idea (or trademark a title). As a conceptual analogy: you could copyright a photo but not the creative idea behind it. In other words, you couldn't stop someone from restaging and replicating the image.[7] Still, that is one of the many challenges reality TV producers must contend with on a daily basis: *How do they share their idea with prospective partners — yet protect their concept from being stolen?*

You can ask professionals to sign NDAs.[8] While this might be common in Silicon Valley or maybe even on Wall Street, creative Hollywood executives — especially successful ones — are inundated by forklifts full of unsolicited ideas that they fly swat away upon approach. You don't want to give them yet another excuse to trigger their knee-jerk "No" reaction. I am sure there are plenty who will disagree with me on this,[9] but if you ask someone in the position to make your dreams come true to sign an NDA before hearing your pitch (reality, especially), they'll just say: "Pass. Next?" And remember you as either a neophyte or litigious — or both (neither of which is good). This is not because they want the freedom to steal (the rare unethical people who *will* steal it will ignore the NDA they agreed to sign anyway), but because they are insanely busy and ideas must be executed to be delivered and they've already got truckloads in development. Besides, it's much cheaper to just buy a worthwhile idea than to litigate over it for years.

There are — of course — exceptions to every rule. And crooks in every business, in every country. *Always trust your gut.* And do what you can to protect yourself. Do due diligence on your prospective partners. Figure out creative and multiple ways to indisputably chronicle, date-stamp and paper-trail the distinctive features and elements that you conceived of first, in order to protect your efforts and assets. Too many up-and-comers spend an inordinate amount of creative energy stressing their imaginations to belabor all that they don't want to have happen. Put all that time and energy into 50 new ideas!

To do any of this, first, you have to make your idea tangible. Get it on the page. Work out the kinks. This is a fantastic development exercise beyond just its legal applications. Create a bible or a "look book" with the set design, floor plan, series logo, wardrobe, theme song concepts — whatever you've got — and register this treatment or pitch package with the WGA. You could even dummy up a hypothetical pilot "script" to register with the US Copyright office for just $55.

🎵 HOT TIP!

Q: What do you do when you don't have an actual screenplay to copyright?

- You could register your treatment, one sheet or pitch package with the WGA: www.wgawregistry.org/registration.asp.
- You could write a hypothetical reality pilot "as if" it was shot (to demonstrate an example of a potential execution of your idea) and register *that* with the US Copyright office: http://copyright.gov/eco.

Let's say, for example, you have an idea for a competition show. You could literally script imaginary contestants — demographic avatars, if you will — of the types of talent you might solicit or that the show would try to highlight and draft a sample scenario they might find themselves in to demonstrate how the actual gameplay would unfold. Maybe even shoot a proof-of-concept pilot.

If your protectable, brandable, intellectual property can be registered or copyrighted, it can be protected. Whether these documents will hold up in court is an entirely different matter, but it will at least serve as an undeniable time and date stamped, third party confirmation, clearly articulating what your ideas were — and when you had them. It might be enough for arbitration or reverse intimidation. If nothing else, much like a business plan, it is priceless for you to go through the exercise of penciling out all this research and walking through every element of your show on paper. Even if no one ever reads it, it will dramatically refine and clarify your concept and empower your pitches.

If you've got money to burn and just one high-concept title idea, trademark your catchy title or prototype ancillary merchandising. Or simply register the domain name (URLs are far more in my budget!). If your due diligence on both your project and your prospects was truly exemplary, why would they bother try to do your show without you? But: Creator Beware. Follow-up with thank you's, calling out everyone who was in the room by name — and add the attachment — to further paper trail your provenance.

NOTES

1 Controversial often satirical comedy that makes fun of serious, disturbing or taboo subjects (also dark comedy).
2 R-rated (i.e. using profanity and sexual references).
3 See Black Comedy above.
4 Modern term for "blue" (in this context).
5 A parody of a documentary.
6 To download this (redacted) investor presentation or pitch package, please visit: www.Heather Hale.com/3DCakes.
7 This was taken to fascinating extremes in *Tim's Vermeer,* a documentary directed by Teller about an inventor (Tim Jenison) who strove to replicate a masterpiece by seventeenth-century Dutch Master Johannes Vermeer.
8 Non Disclosure Agreement (i.e. a confidentiality agreement).
9 You can write your own book. ;)

Know Your Target Audience(s)

20

BUT MY FILM/TV SHOW IS FOR EVERYONE . . .

Hardly. If you have movie stars in a big budget, studio tentpole, then . . . maybe. Maybe. But for the vast majority of independent filmmakers and content creators, one of the most important elements (at least to financial success) is identifying who your project will appeal to — and figuring out not just *where* to find them — but *how* to *engage* them.

You must know your target audience inside and out. Maybe there's more than one core or affinity audience you're targeting? You must know as much about them as you do about your characters and their world. Where and when are your prospective viewers online? What else do they like to watch? Where, when, how and with whom? How, when and where do they share their thoughts and opinions? On Facebook? Twitter? Instagram? Vine? Pinterest? SnapChat? LinkedIn? Tumbler? Google+? With customized memes? User uploaded videos? The generational studies of which age groups and genders predominantly use which social media platforms — why — and how — and what for — can be fascinating study as you delineate your target audiences and approach strategies.

DEMOGRAPHICS

Studios, brands and advertisers tend to segment their programming and marketing via age and gender, simplifying the expansive, eclectic marketplace into a reduction sauce of key "demos"[1] of men and women, young and old. In broadcast television parlance, the "key demographic" can refer to the group of viewers that is the most desirable to the vast majority of advertisers or to a specific advertiser. This varies by network, programming type, and time slot, but a default standard has long been 18–49-year-olds. Skewing a little older: 34–54 is another sweet spot.

Industry thinking has historically been that the younger you can attract a consumer, the less likely they will have already developed brand allegiance to a competitor and the greater longevity you'll have to enjoy them as a customer. This theory banks on the perception that consumers are too lazy to change brands once they're in the habit of buying a particular products. But if history has shown us anything, it's that you can't rely on stasis.

At the other end of the age spectrum, ad execs erroneously assumed senior citizens were set in their ways but pensioners have proven just as likely to switch brands as their younger counterparts — and the theory that spending drops as people age has also proven bogus: the two groups' buying rates are comparable.

Kids grow up faster than ever before (15 is the new 20) as we try to look and feel younger longer (50 is the new 30). But the truth is that the key demographic of 25–54 ignores 58 percent of the population. Increasingly significant: almost half the world's under-25 population is multicultural, which is too often ignored by homogenized programming. These underserved markets present opportunities for forward-thinking independent innovators.

Almost all advertising skews affluent, both due to the aspirational nature of media in general but also due to the advertisers' expectation that the wealthy would have more discretionary income to buy their wares.

FOUR-QUADRANT FILM

Males over 25	Females over 25
Males under 25	Females under 25

Many Hollywood studio films (especially Disney and the tentpole blockbuster hopefuls) shoot for what is known in the industry as the "four-quadrant film," meaning: they are designed to attract the whole family, three generations, ideally equally gender-balanced. While hugely profitable when they do hit, they can bankrupt a studio when they miss (and sometimes even their vendors[2] — in spite of being wildly successful). They are big risks. This is why so many studios cross-collateralize this risk, diversifying it across otherwise would-be "competitors" and stack the odds in their favor with A-list stars, best-selling source material or huge special effects. This is also why the limited studio movies continue to spiral towards the lowest common denominator, often empowering the adolescent boy in the family to drive a disproportionate share of the media spend decisions.

It's also another reason why so many feel unrepresented onscreen. But the readers of this book are the motor of the media revolution representing a broader spectrum of demographics on screen. The advent of the Internet has proven to be a leveling force around the world — from private homes through media to politics — and back home again. The escalation of the feedback loop has compelled seemingly monolithic, impervious entities to be more responsive to the social media communication circuit, further pushing towards a more egalitarian storytelling future.

PSYCHOGRAPHICS

Psychographics is the study of personality, values, opinions, attitudes, interests and lifestyles. Sometimes called IOA factors (for Interests, Attitudes and Opinions), psychographic variables can be much more relevant and actionable than demographic variables (such as age and gender), behavioral variables (brand loyalty, usage rates) or firmographic characteristics (industry, function, etc.).

Every business must know and understand its core customers. Manufacturers want consumers to love their products and services — and tell their friends. As an entrepreneurial content creator, you're a brand — especially internally, within the business — but you also want to be recognizable to your ultimate paying audience. You want (and need) to generate **W**ord **of M**outh (WOM), to establish your merit.

Most independents don't have the luxury of millions of dollars to buy television, billboard, bus and newspaper ads or have the fame or power to access the talk show circuit. It's unrealistic to think we can compete with these resources to make a blip on the radar when most of us can't even afford a seat at this deep-pocketed gambling table. Thus, we have to play a different — smarter, more resourceful — game. Maybe even create an entirely new board and make up rules as we go.

Where do your prospective ticket or DVD buyers or TV or VOD viewers hang out? Are they graffiti artists? Parkour enthusiasts? Vegans? American Muscle Car fans? Cosplayers? EMTs? Family and friends who've lost someone to cancer? Eldercare givers needing a laugh? Preppers? What do they buy? What do they need?

The better you analyze and understand your target audiences, the more you can quantify and track their psychographics (and empathize with them), the better positioned you'll be to authentically tap into their affinity groups, successfully crowdfund or DIY distribute. This is where psychographics trumps demographics. The better you know your audience, the more refined and successful your marketing can be, the more affordably and authentically you can reach them — and move them. Write for who you're really writing for. Shoot what they would appreciate and share. Create for "your people." Speak to your tribe.

BINGE WATCHING AND TIME SHIFTING

Watching programming when the viewer dictates (time shifting) or viewing more than two episodes of the same show in a single sitting (binge watching) are revolutionizing the modern television landscape. There are all sorts of statistics and studies suggesting that it takes four episodes for a first-time viewer to truly connect with and become a regular fan of a show. Not surprisingly, this aligns perfectly with the average binge-watching session. Full initial season contracts and multiple-episode release strategies have attracted both series creators and their prospective audiences alike. This responsiveness to both creator and consumer is driving the success of the leading OTT networks.

Home viewers have repeatedly watched DVDs and syndicated reruns in the past but now that brand new programming can be watched on demand, consumers can burn through in a day what has taken months to write, shoot and edit — and clamor within hours on social media for more! Some 61 percent of Netflix subscribers binge-watch shows every few weeks to "catch up." Whole seasons of many series are offered to captive audiences on long international flights. The traditional broadcast season runs for 35 weeks though most "full" series orders traditionally run only 22 episodes for broadcast and 13 for cable. While that is a grueling creative and physical schedule to maintain, even for the most high-energy and congenial writing teams, casts, and crews, it still leaves significant gaps in every year (for them to actually spend time with their "real" families!). And yet television programming executives must fill 24 one-hour (or 48 half-hour) boxes every day of the year, year after year, in an effort to appease (and effectively monetize) this insatiable appetite for content. While that is an incomprehensible duty and demand, it bodes well for those creating the supply.

NOTES

1 Short for demographics.
2 Visual effects studio Rhythm & Hues was bankrupt by the time *Life of Pi* won its Oscar.

Polish Your Pitch and Marketing Materials

21

GREAT TITLE

You never get a second chance to make a first impression.

What's in a name? Well, everything.

Your title is literally the first words actors, investors, sales agents, distributors and audiences will be exposed to. It defines every expectation. Ideally, it hooks everyone's curiosity and creates anticipation and desire.

In an ideal world, your title communicates genre, tone and theme. Maybe even protagonist and plot. That's a lot for a few words to express. *Do people get it right away? Is it memorable? Does it conjure the poster? The mood? The trailer? Opening scene or pilot episode? What will make it pop from a long list of VOD titles scrolling by on a screen? In a market catalog? Or on a poster at a multiplex theater?* The title might be the only thing a potential viewer will ever see, read or hear — no artwork, tagline, synopsis or trailer — just the words of that all important title — before making their buying decision. Make it great.

Short is good. Brevity allows enhanced design flexibility: it's clearer on smaller screens, stands out better on thumbnails, DVD covers — even posters and marquees. Your title is your promise of the premise to the audience. Think about how your title will look on artwork. Social media is crucial for marketing. Will your title fit in 140 characters on Twitter? What kind of Twitter #hashtag does it lend itself to? We're in an attention-deficit (or overload) world. Shorter is always better.

The SyFy channel's social media phenomenon, *Sharknado*, owed a great deal of its success simply to its high-concept, mash-up title that so clearly revealed the conflict and stakes — and teased its campy tone.

Source: Paul Bales/Asylum.

Alphabetical order might matter more in the future digital space. I often wonder if our title of *Witness Insecurity* was changed to *Absolute Killers* by the distributor to bump it up from a "W" to an "Ab" to get to the top of the Video On Demand (VOD) menu scroll.

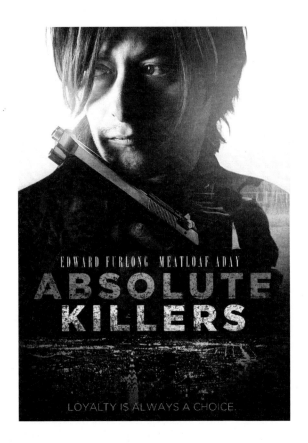

TERRIFIC LOGLINE

After titles, loglines are the next most important things you'll ever write — and you might not even get to have a say on your title — so get good at loglines! A logline is — without a doubt — the hardest thing you'll ever have to write.

And rewrite.

And rewrite.

And rewrite.

Professionally, at least. (Vows and eulogies probably trump loglines — but you get the idea.)

Loglines are rewritten constantly (see above). Every single word changes a hundred times to test every conceivable nuance until you nail it. Books, seminars, workshops, blogs, videos and panels galore cover loglines ad infinitum. I've done a few logline webinars, workshops and blogs myself, and my book, *Story$elling: How to Develop, Market, and Pitch Film & TV Projects*, includes a whole chapter on loglines, but for our purposes herein, let's just cut to the chase of the core elements. I will assume that you'll know that you need (give or take) something like this:

> *[Title]* **is a** *[format and genre]* **about** *[an interesting, proactive protagonist]*
> **who wants to/must** *[protagonist's goal]* **but** *[conflict = obstacles that get in
> the way/stakes if protagonist fails].*
>
> **Or**
>
> **When** *[the inciting event happens]*, *[our hero]*, **must** *[pursue the goal/drive
> the plot]* before *[stakes occur].*

If your protagonist is not proactively pursuing a plot-driven goal (i.e. a self-contained feature or episode), then maybe you have more of a character-driven or situational story that lends itself to serialized television programming (especially if the protagonist doesn't "solve" the problem or change the circumstances in 90 minutes to 2 hours of envisioned screen time). In which case, you'd need to adjust your logline (and maybe format?) accordingly.

If you have written a transformational character arc, make sure you point out your hero's flaw in your logline as it is key to your theme and plot points (her evolution). An ironic twist at the end of a logline is always good for extra credit — especially for comedies and thrillers (ditto for festival short film endings, FYI).

Always look for the source of conflict in the story. In an action-driven piece, it will be in the triangulation of the goal versus the stakes against the ticking clock. In a character-driven piece, the conflict will come from the situation she finds herself confronted by (i.e. the outer conflict catalyzing her inner growth). If you have created circumstances that accentuate a clearly defined central problem, perpetuating it from every angle or point of view but never actually solving it, then you might have come back full circle to a serialized TV show.

ADDITIVE TAGLINE

Ideally, your logline says it all. With an ironic twist to leave them laughing or worried — but curious to see how it turns out. Sometimes you have a great title but the tagline is what adds the ironic twist or gives a hint of the theme, plot, world, protagonist or antagonist. Taglines can be your "ba-dump-bump!" last word. Every word of your marketing ad copy should be intriguing.

SUCCINCT SYNOPSIS

Perhaps next hardest to write — at least for the original writer — or for the whole team to agree upon — is the synopsis: a summary of the film or TV show's storyline. There can be various iterations of this.

If you're pitching to a marquee-value actor to attach, their tweaked variation of the synopsis might highlight their role. If you're pitching to a director, the synopsis might focus on the cinematic potential of the storyworld. For an investor, scholarship, grant or potential product placement brand, the story beats might frame demographics, milieu, zeitgeist or other synergistic issues.

For a crowdfunding platform or public website, you might not want to ruin the consumers' future viewing experience with any spoilers whereas for a business-to-business synopsis, for a distributor or sales agent, they're going to need to know how it plays out, beat by beat — including how it ends — so they can ascertain if they can sell it and assess its marketability. For every part of this process: you gotta know your audience — and play to the room.

Writers and producers can debate until the cows come home about the various distinctions between synopses, treatments, beat sheets and outlines but suffice it to say that — like everything else in Hollywood or international mass or niche media — there's a wide spectrum of characteristics and uses for all these tools. Writing partners and directors might hammer out all the plot points and reversals in a "writers treatment" to make sure they're all on the same page before greenlighting the writing or rewriting of a script. Shorter outlines might be used by a writer to pitch their take to a director or producer to get an adaptation or remake assignment. Beat sheets are often used at various stages for department heads during the pre-production process — or even the writer for writing or rewriting.

In addition to your story synopsis with the familiar creative elements (plot, character and theme), you might also write a project synopsis that can be customized for different industry audiences. The project synopsis for an investor might just top note the project's unique creative and financial attributes and what production incentives and sweat equity deferrals you anticipate while your press release synopsis might tease the creative solutions to challenges to inspire reporters to dig deeper with interviews. Market presentations for distributors or sales agents might clarify which rights are available and show off clever social media marketing strategies. Ideally, you'll have a 1/2 page — 2-page synopsis that encapsulates your story[1] and that can be customized for a wide variety of purposes.

EXCELLENT SCRIPT

Nothing is more important than the script (or the high-concept TV format).
Period.
Full stop.
Let me reiterate: Nothing is more important than the script.[2]
There is so much to say on this topic that we couldn't even begin to skim the surface in this book. Bookstores, the Internet, and cottage industries of workshops, conferences and webinars are full of advice on every angle and element of screenwriting. For our purposes herein, suffice it to say that the script has to be brilliant. You are going to build a whole house of cards on this tiny little stack of paper. You will invest YEARS of your life. Your best creative energies and all your professional relationships and resources will get sucked into the vortex of this black hole. *Make sure it's worth it.* You owe it to yourself that your screenplay (or whatever literary material it is that you're pitching) is solid enough to warrant all the efforts that it catalyzes and will urgently and relentlessly demand from every aspect of your life.

Should I Bring Scripts to the Market?

Yes and no. As with everything else, there's a lot of debate on this (and every) issue but my personal advice would be to always be ready to respond to any interest immediately — in any way it could be requested. Have .pdfs at the ready to email. Maybe even have one bound print copy in your car or up in your hotel room (though I don't think I've handed out or snail-mailed a hard copy of a screenplay in a decade and a half!).

Tough as it is to get people to read back at home or in the office during normal business hours, when they're traveling, the last thing they want to do is carry on luggage full of one sheets — much less scripts! They'd much rather go to cocktail parties and see the sights and travel light. But, there is the off-chance that (if your pitch went fantastic and they're truly urgently intrigued — and time is of the essence), they *might* ask for a copy right then and there. Maybe they'll read it while sitting in their suite or on a layover heading home. You've worked this hard to heat the iron: be ready to strike when it gets hot! 300 pitches and six days from now, your best intentioned buyer might not even remember why they asked for it — or who you were — but be ready to deliver when asked — and get in their queue.

More likely than not, if *anyone* asks for a script, they'll ask for a copy to be sent to them to read when they get back home (or more likely, weeks later, it'll be assigned to a reader). Maybe you hand it to them on a cute flash drive trade show giveaway? Or email it right from your smartphone while standing there.

Of course, clear distributing the script in advance with your attorney or any partners or stake holders — but always be locked and loaded — and ready to fire. That's what you're there for, right? Ultimately everything you're doing at the market drives towards one goal: to get them to read — and fall in love with — your script (or pitch package/proposal) — and you!

"Send the Script" Edutainment Story: *The Courage to Love*

"SEND THE SCRIPT"

Here is an "in the trenches" story that I am embarrassed to share but I hope will edutain you.

In the last millennium, I was on the phone with Emily Gerson Saines, a Vice President of William Morris at the time, who repped Vanessa Williams. Incredibly long story wildly truncated: I had written an excellent five-page treatment that had made its way up through the food chain of gatekeepers to land on her desk. Truth be told: it was the first treatment I had ever written. I had just finished my first ever screenwriting class at UCLA. On writing treatments.

I had never actually written a script before.
Just this one treatment.
That was sitting — read — on the desk of this high-powered, triple letter[3] agent.
Gulp.

It was for a true-life biopic spec project originally entitled *Quadroon Ball*. It had piqued her interest.
She asked me to send the script.
In nine days.

Just to remind you (from a few sentences ago): I had never written a script. Or ever even started one.

As professionally as I could nervously bluff, I asked her "casually" (LOL!) Ahem . . . [throat clearing] "So . . . when you say . . . 'nine days . . .' . . . exactly . . . how 'firm' is that deadline . . . ?"

And (bless her heart), Ms. Saines said something that was instantly and forever seared into my professional memory: "*Oh. It's not a firm deadline at all. No. Not at all. I'm interested in your script. Vanessa Williams is interested in your script. I will be with Vanessa at Cannes in nine days. Where we will both be together. And interested in your script. At the same time. I don't know when the two of us will next be together again. And when we are: if we will still be interested in your script. But, no: it's not a firm deadline at all."*

Beat.

I swallowed, thanked her and — terrified — hung up. Before I allowed myself to second-guess myself, I dialed another number and promptly quit my mortgage banking job. Life had presented me one of those "all or nothing" moments and I knew I needed to drop everything and go for it. I bought and installed my brand new Final Draft software and typed "FADE IN," learning on the fly as I wrote the script in *eight* days (as I had to allow for an overnight FedEx to France).

Emily made her producing debut with my script.
Vanessa Williams starred.

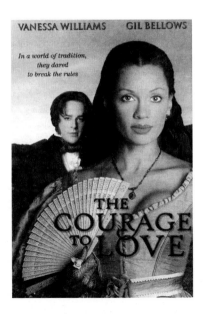

This was my first credit and put me on the map (sort of). I share this story not to boast but rather to inspire — and to drive home the point of how important a rock solid treatment can be — and how you have to be ready to deliver the script when asked.

To those who might think it impossible to write a first (much less marketable) script in just over a week: I had the benefit of three months' worth of historical research hammering out the time and place details; a terrific mentor, my first-ever screenwriting professor, Frank McAdams at UCLA, developing the plot and characters' story beats with me; a Bachelor's degree in creative writing and a background as a deadline-driven professional journalist.

But perhaps most importantly, I hope this story drives home the point that there will come times in your life where you must literally risk everything to capitalize on these precious, elusive opportunities that might otherwise fade away. The markets are where you can *create* these opportunities for yourself. There will be times when you get asked for literary or marketing materials — or a pitch — before you are ready. Do as much advance prep work as possible at all times because you never know when you'll be invited to step to the plate. Have your script, pitch and marketing materials as polished as possible and just do your best with the opportunities you create.

NOTES

1 Please visit www.HeatherHale.com/Samples/Synopses.
2 Feel free to stop reading right now to go work on your script.
3 Industry slang referencing the agencies that go by acronyms for their three names (i.e. CAA, WME, UTA, APA, etc.).

Develop Key Art

22

Key art is just that: the key image that serves as the fulcrum for the rest of the marketing campaign. Key art typically refers to a project's poster or "one sheet" — that one arresting image paired with the perfect title treatment that expresses the genre and tone of the project, often with a tagline hinting at an ironic, thematic plot twist.

Key art is usually associated with the 27" x 40" poster that hangs outside cinemaplexes to lure still-deciding viewers to buy tickets for their specific theater but this same artwork can be seen repurposed on everything from bus benches to billboards to newspaper and magazine ads to commercials. Entire exterior studio walls use key art to advertise their hottest TV shows. Key art unifies the hopefully recognizable marketing campaign all the way through to DVD packaging and VOD thumbnails to schwag.

KEY ART VERSUS CONCEPT ART

While key art teases the promise of the premise from the pitch through the marketing and advertising campaigns, it varies slightly from concept art, which shows the initial vision for the project from soft prep through to principal photography.

Concept art can include look books, storyboards, pre-visualization animations, headshots of hoped-for actors, or proposed locations. All of these elements visually express the potential of the project in business-to-business pitches — and increasingly, to the potential viewing pubic via crowdfunding and independent social media campaigns. Photo collages can reveal the cool factor of the surreal fantasy world conceived by the director or created by the production designer. Fabric swatches, composite masks and make-up, hair and wardrobe color schemes could show off the Glam Squad's creative contributions. TV show bibles could contain sketched blueprints of the standing sets. I'm always so impressed and humbled to see what each Department Head, working with their unique skill sets, media and means of expressing themselves, brings to the table to contribute to our collaborative vision. Done well, it improves your odds of success every step of the way.

In an undeniably visual medium, it's never too early to have either kind of art. Unfortunately, like so many aspects of the entertainment industry, key art, especially, has that notorious chicken-and-egg element to it. It is rare for a producer to be able to secure high-profile actors without pay-or-play-backed offers. A solid reputation, established relationships and a track record of solid credits can help — but not so much without distribution. Conversely, it is equally as difficult to ink distribution commitments without at least one marquee-value actor locked. Bringing it all full triangle: it's tough to secure equity development or production funds without distribution locked. It's an unending Escher-esque[1] triangle maze of catch-22s.[2] Key art is equally as challenging.

THE KEY ART FANTASY

In an ideal (i.e. well-financed) world, you'd be fully funded with A-list stars contracted, eager and available for special key art shoots — complete with hair, make-up and wardrobe — on the actual sets or vehicles of your storyworld. Time and logistical resources would be abundant and flexible, enabling you to design several key art choices with the winning concept obvious to the whole team. Also, in this fantasy scenario, you'd have your marketing plan all laid out before you even start principal photography, with all your project's production and marketing expenses fully line-itemed and safely deposited into your LLC's checking account. You'd synchronize your PR shots with your shoot days so you could easily cross-collateralize all your assets and resources — and . . . well . . . you get the idea. This is a great goal to for most independent content creators in the new millennium to shoot for! But the reality for the rest of us is . . .

The reality is that most independent producers are trying to raise money *before* they have any actors attached. And it's very difficult to come up with design concepts that express the story without showing any actors' faces — much less without any settings (because they haven't yet been secured — or, in some cases, even created). Thus, you might feel like you're stuck in a never-ending labyrinth. But, like most all things in our industry: good producers simply have to figure it out. We have to find a way to make it work. What follows are some clever and resourceful work-arounds.

The sooner you have key art — and the better it is — the more empowered all the players will be at each level and stage to disseminate your unified vision. With one HUGE caveat: cheesy, trashy key art can kill a project — at any phase. It instantly lowers the bar of quality expectations. *How can it not? It's all you've given them.* So, it's actually better to have no key art than bad, unprofessional key art.

Thus, in some cases, it's better that your impassioned verbal pitch leaves them envisioning in their mind's eye the highest caliber of production values they could achieve. Or what you might be able to better express with just words and conjured imagination: a great title, terrific logline, additive tagline, succinct synopsis and excellent script. That is, after all, the magic of storytelling.

Key art is that extra thousand words captured in a great image. A single visual composition that can be handed over to a pitchee who can then hand it up the ladder or share it laterally to all the greenlight powers-that-be so that everyone on the decision tree can "get it" in a nanosecond — hopefully accelerating that process. Every piece of the puzzle helps prospective partners get on board.

No one knows your project better than you. And likely, no one knows your specific target audience better, either. A distributor may know how to *market* better than you but not necessarily how to market your specific project to your subset of the tribe.

Taking the time, effort and minimal investment to create development key art serves the process the whole way down the line. Even if it gets thrown out, if it got you to the next level of the game, it's done its job.

If a distributor takes on your project, they will likely have the final say in how they market your project. Fair enough. It's their relationships, resources and expertise they bring to the table. *But what if you never get a distributor? And decide to self-distribute? And have to do it all yourself? Or what if you do get a distributor — and you hate what they come up with? And they deduct four times what you could've gotten great artwork you love for?*

It is possible the distributor will love the artwork you present — and will run with it (meaning no delay, no middlemen or add-on fees). It's also possible they'll come up with lots of brilliant options (it is their business after all and they've probably done exponentially more marketing campaigns than your whole team combined). Just be as proactive and collaborative as possible. Know what you're getting into, what the process, challenges, expenses and time frames are — and empower yourself, your team and your project in every foreseeable way.

While you're still in soft-prep, just as you are prudent to engage your intended sales agent and/or distributor in your casting wish lists (if your relationships and timing of the project workflow allow this — all covered in the next chapter), it might behoove you to garner their great insights on your developing key art, too. They know what sells — and how to sell each genre.

🔥 HOT TIP!

Ask them, if they don't do their key art in-house, for a recommendation or even a short list of their preferred vendors. Why not work with who they'll end up hiring anyway? That way, you can better control the budget and creative from the get-go but still incorporate your sales agent's or distributor's feedback and preferences early on in the process — or even facilitate and streamline their changes downstream. This could prove to accelerate a much more mutually satisfying and effective marketing campaign while controlling expenses and the expression of your ideas.

Just as a logline handed to ten different writers would result in ten wildly different scripts — varying not just in character development, dialogue, plot and storytelling devices — but even in genre, tone, theme and possibly even format; so, too, could every film be marketed a hundred different ways. You should have a clear enough vision that you can confidently pick through the well-meaning advice you get throughout the development and packaging processes to continue to stay the course toward your vision and goals.

There is inevitably a finite limit to the resources you have at your disposal at each stage of the process. Whether "going to market" to you means hitting the industry's

B2B circuits or going direct to consumers (B2C), you want to maximize the assets and resources you have available to you. You have a concept. Perhaps a script. Maybe a little more: a series bible, a sizzle reel, an actor attachment. Maybe you have raised some private equity or you've gotten a brand, a location or a post-house to commit to partial sweat or deferred equity. Maybe you're pre-approved for tax credits or a grant. Maybe you have a little less: just a treatment and big ideas. Regardless: in your mind's eye, you know what you envision. Your goal is to communicate that as accurately and as persuasively as you can within the constraints of the resources available to you at each stage. Your goal is always to enroll others in your vision of the project and to empower them to pitch it consistently to engage other assets.

There are various phases when a project most benefits from key art. Who pays for it — and when — varies as much as anything else in show business. In the early stages of independent film, it's usually the producer — but it can also be the writer, director, star, novelist — or whoever has the most at stake (or perhaps who owns the intellectual property or life rights being developed) — or stands to benefit the most. Like so many entrepreneurial endeavors, it often simply comes down to who has the money or connections to get it done.

"Key art isn't always thought about, budgeted for or planned right from the get-go — but it should be," Bridget Jurgens, Managing Director of DOG & PONY Creative (my favorite key art company), explains. If you're having a hard time, especially in the early stages, getting your prospective buyers or financiers to visualize your concept, "effective key art can help them feel the movie." Seeing the film laid out in a professional way can help demonstrate its salability.

"Don't try to tell your whole story with the one image, just focus on communicating one simple idea: the genre and tone." As an example, *Twilight* could have been marketed simply as *Romeo and Juliet* with vampires but if you think about it too much: in *Romeo and Juliet*, they both die whereas in the *Twilight* franchise, they have a kid together. Don't get lost in the details. What that mash-up communicates is the tone and genre — the promise of the premise. Move on to the pitch before they get lost in the particulars of those references. These are just jumping off points. Key art is a first impression, a thumbnail sketch, a tease: one image (or a series of images) that communicates genre and tone — and sometimes theme.

PLACEHOLDER KEY ART

The placeholder key art used in the beginning stages of your project's business-to-business lifecycle, when you're soliciting funds, attachments, and distribution commitments, is just as critical as the final key art used to entice prospective audience members. At the lower ends of the budget scale, the original key art used for investor presentations may never be upgraded to what ultimately markets the project to the general public.

It's not that difficult — or expensive — to get professional, on-point, expressive placeholder art that can matriculate through the process until you have a marketing budget to re-do it at the scope and scale appropriate to the project (if ever necessary or feasible). This initial key art may be tossed out completely — but sometimes, it can be so well done, it can hold its own all the way through to the end-consumer. Or it might just serve to uphold your team's initial vision by influencing all the artwork to follow (only at a higher production caliber). Most marketing expenses come off the top of your sales revenue. So, since you're going to end up paying for it in the end anyway, why not front what you really want and start projecting yourself and your project the right way from the get-go?

Queen of Harts is an example of an ultra low-budget comedy feature I'm attached to direct that is a collision of two worlds: the LGBTQA[3] community and football. Our story follows a former high school football player who's now a famous, fabulous drag queen who has to return to his rural Midwest childhood home of Harts, where no one knows his celebrity alter ego (or even that he's gay) to settle his estranged father's estate. Thus, notice the two wildly different fonts in our title treatment:

Visit my website to see this title treatment in full color: the soft curvy tiara rhinestones sparkle, backlit with pink illumination, while the high school letterman's boxy block style is in football turf green, hinting at the campy, over-the-top fun, anchored in sports, dealing with male/female duality. We had virtually no budget and had to out-of-pocket everything personally. We had an excellent graphic arts student affordably explore some key art concepts with us that we used as placeholder images just to populate our investor package and website to give them an idea of the tone with an eye to getting more professional key art done after we were funded and ideally, reflecting the cast.

LOW-BUDGET KEY ART STRATEGIES

My greatest professional insights in researching and writing this book came from what I learned about key art from Bridget Jurgens and Jen Sparks, principals of DOG & PONY, an award-winning design agency. What they taught me about logos, posters, book covers, fonts and color schemes was a 180-degree learning curve for me. A flat line: forwards. As I shared what was so fascinating to me from these conversations, I was delighted to find 30-year veterans learning right alongside me. So, I've endeavored to distill the highlights of those many conversations and workflow iterations into the following section in the hopes that it will really add to the value you derive from this book.

As many ways as there are to tell a story, there are just as many ways to sell a movie. In terms of key art marketing, though, they typically fall into three major approaches:

- Actor
- Concept
- Tone

Of course, we always strive to have our key art firing on all three pistons — but what if you don't have a famous name or face? Or even any actors at all? Or your story is a little more complicated than an easily marketed high-concept logline? Maybe you'll be best served trying to capture just its tone or mood. This is one of the many reasons that horror films are the easiest to market. And again: why demographics are so important to this process. And how much a high concept helps (they're just *easier* to *market*).

TEASERS vs. PAYOFFS

If you're hitting the film or television markets with a project that is still in development, fundraising or pre-production, you'll most likely have teaser key art that communicates genre and tone but often won't have any actors' faces yet. These initial images with title treatment will likely be used across all your early marketing materials: your one sheet, as the cover to your 8" x 10" pitch package, on your project's website, crowdfunding campaigns and social media sites — or even as a 27" x 40" poster to get the buyers at the markets excited.

Teasers are for packaging and pre-sales. When your cast is attached — and maybe even after principal photography — a payoff theatrical poster is usually done — in response to the teasers — which is the one most consumers will likely see.

Even big studio blockbusters follow this pattern. Think of how many *Batman* assets are teased for a year or two in advance of each franchise entry: from the logo to the bat-signal, to his chin, his silhouette, wardrobe, car, weapons — don't forget the villain — teasing the audience from every angle, every step of the way, until finally the big reveal of the highly anticipated star in the mask. They move through their media assets in premeditated patterns. Of course, the scale and scope for low-budget independent projects is much smaller and shorter but the same principles apply.

What do you do if you have a project in prep with no actors yet? Or even a film in the can with no stars? How do you develop marketing materials if your budget has been completely spent on production before you've even finished post? What if the best market for your project is right around the corner? And you didn't know to take production stills during the shoot? This, sadly, is not an uncommon scenario.

One of DOG & PONY's independent clients, writer/actress, Heidi Haddad Kozak, put up her own money to have key art developed for her feature spec script, *Mary Jane Girls*. She explained:

> Everyone I asked, everywhere I read, always said: "Don't include any artwork with your script." But when I asked why, they said it was amateurish. But when I delved deeper, it was because the *artwork* was always amateurish. When I showed my professional key art to my friends — even those working at studios — they thought it was fabulous. It just comes down to: do it right or don't to it.

Heidi explains:

> My spec is about all the compromises we make to belong. It takes place in a small town in Texas in 1962 and revolves around these high school girls' clubs that were taken very seriously. The script could be made into two very different movies: it could be a very commercial studio project, a cross between *Mean Girls* and *The Help*; or it could go in a very different, darker, edgier indie direction, more along the lines of *The Virgin Suicides*. Either way, I kept visualizing this white sorority sweater, much like a letterman's jacket: it was this coveted symbol of belonging and status, it was so much a part of the world and theme.

So, without any attached actors' faces to show, DOG & PONY worked up two different variations for Heidi to use, depending on who she was pitching to.

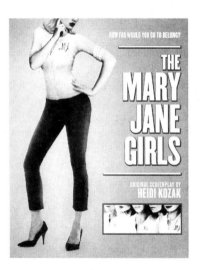 

What do you do? You have to reverse engineer your key art. Work with what you've got. You have to be flexible, realistic and creatively resourceful with the assets you do have available — or that you can create — quickly and cheaply — but well — in that elusive sweet spot.

Alexandra Boylan did just that — brilliantly — when she produced and starred in the low-budget, home invasion horror movie entitled *Home Sweet Home* (2013). Since they didn't do a marketing photo shoot prior, they had to rely on stock photography and screen grabs — which can really limit the key art designer's options (not to mention the quality of the finished product). But sometimes, that's all you have to work with.

So, without names or necessarily a high concept, they marketed the genre and tone of the film to speak to its clearly delineated audience. The blood splattered floor mat. The desolate landscape. The home off in the distance. The gal holding the ax: *Is she the aggressor? Or the victim?*

Interestingly, the house in the poster is from stock footage: it's not even in the film. Nor was her *Little Red Riding Hood*-reminiscent outfit even from the film's wardrobe. But they both serve the aesthetic well.

Alexandra's poster so clearly communicated the film's genre that when sales agent, Ryan Keller of Instrum International was flipping through DOG & PONY's portfolio at the AFM, considering their services for his own purposes, the poster they did for *Home Sweet Home* so jumped out at him that he asked Bridget Jurgens, Managing Director of DOG & PONY: "Do these people have sales agents yet?" Just based on the poster alone, he knew he could market their film. Their deal was launched off their key art alone: it pitched itself, which is, ultimately, key art's job.

Ryan explains:

They had their marketing materials ready to go. I didn't have to worry about the cost for new artwork, a new trailer or supplemental materials. They had a package ready for the market. They were ready to go. The filmmakers did a great job. I liked the female lead aspect to it. They gave her a weapon and made it look like a bad ass horror film when their film was really more thriller than horror. They made it look dark and gloomy when the film is actually brightly colored and a lot takes place in this vast open space in the desert — but you would never get that from the poster. You wonder: *is that girl about to wreak havoc? Is it a revenge story?*

Ryan knew he could find a domestic distributor for it and that it would work well in home video because its key art would

look good on a shelf. It set itself apart from other horror films. Normally, you have this damsel in distress. Usually, with a masked killer. But *Home Sweet Home* stood out as a strong female with a weapon. It promised suspense.

Instrum was, indeed, able to secure a domestic distributor, Image Entertainment. And while the poster was eventually re-done, notice how clearly their initial concept held:

This anecdote also serves to demonstrate not only the significance of great visuals and concepts but of picking your vendor partners well. Imagine getting your sales agent and distributor off your poster vendor — because they are hustling and networking at the same markets. Choose your collaborators carefully — with an eye to everyone on the team sharing the same interests — and faith in the project — and you.

KEY ART BEFORE ACTORS ARE ATTACHED

In the low-budget arena, teaser posters are often used to facilitate early stage fundraising, packaging and business-to-business pre-sales while payoff posters are typically used for consumer marketing. Often the distinction being that at the start of your film's marketing and pre-production lifecycle, you might not even know who your actors are, so stock photos can be used with the models' faces either not visible or heavily in shadow. They can then be swapped out with images of your actual actors and the high-light of your payoff poster. But sometimes, you can't even find stock art that will work.

In the case of *Billy Club* (2013), Writer, Producer, Director, Drew Rosas' killer antagonist — an umpire wielding a baseball bat with a retractable bayonet blade — was not something he was simply going to "go online and find in stock images." Thus — as a placeholder until they shot the film, they came up with a simple teaser image of items they could acquire or find stock footage of to tweak: a simple baseball that they could use computer graphics to wrap with the texture of human skin (eew) and splatter with blood. Framed by its tagline and title treatment, you get the idea: it's a creepy, baseball-themed horror flick. This is the conceptual teaser.

Drew and his team studied the marketing materials of relevant boogie man slasher comps such as *Nightmare on Elm Street*, *Texas Chainsaw Massacre*, *Friday the 13th*, among others and came up with conceptual drawings and instructions for the photographer (such as: low angle, backlit, ominous, menacing) for a relatively inexpensive key art photo shoot. Because of the mask, they didn't even need to use the actual actor.

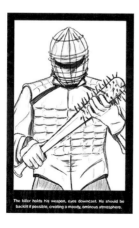

With these photos from the shoot to work with, DOG & PONY were able to create several versions of the payoff posters based on the reference boards.

You can see they tested different horror-baseball themed taglines but the fonts, color schemes and tone are all clearly unified. While you may dictate the specific shots you're looking for, your photographer will likely have some really incredible ideas of her own to add to the mix. Always be open to the input of the creative pros around you. You hired them precisely because they have expertise in fields outside your own core skill set — let them help you.

Billy Club successfully raised $15,000 on Kickstarter in 2011 but again: it was actually their poster that got them distribution. Back at the AFM, another sales agent (who was also a baseball fan) saw this in DOG & PONY's poster catalog and recognized how professionally executed the concepts were via their key art and Bridget and Jen graciously connected them.

Again: the more active and connected your team members are — the better for all of you. You want professionals engaged in the business because their overlapping spheres of influence can only serve to catalyze yours. If your concepts can be communicated quickly, professionally and especially visually, they serve as your proxy to pitch your projects for you to extend your reach and enable your fans and champions to capitalize on the confluence of opportunities that these events offer — even if you're not even there.

▶ HOT TIP!

You can find stock photography all over the Internet. One way of finding royalty-free shots you can modify and use freely can be found via a simple Google Images search:
Go to www.Google.com:

- In the upper right hand corner, click on "Images."
- Type in the keyword of what you're searching for and hit enter.
- In the right-hand corner, you'll see a little wheel.

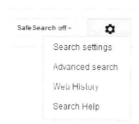

- Drop that menu down and select "Advanced Search."
- The last option, right above the "Advanced Search" button, is a "usage rights" drop down menu.
- Select "Free to use, share or modify, even commercially" — and hit search.

Another case study to illustrate how indie filmmakers can create effective key art before they have their cast attached is the faith-based film, *Catching Faith* (2015). Alexandra Boylan, pleased with the great job Instrum had done with her last film, *Home Sweet Home* (above), returned to them for her next project.

It's interesting to point out that while sales agents might get a bad rap as "middlemen" and not every distributor is right for every project or platform, a solid relationship with a great sales agent might prove to be the one constant between many films, saving you from having to recreate the wheel project-by-project. That time, energy and momentum can be precious, allowing you each to focus on what you do best: you on producing content, them on selling it and staying up-to-date on the marketplace and all its players.

Instrum even assisted Alexandra, now a known and trusted resource: "We'll get the money if you make it happen," they told her. Alexandra explains: "The process just gets faster once you have sales reps in place. *Home Sweet Home* was three years from concept to selling the film. *Catching Faith* was one year from the first conversation to distribution." Wow. That's something to shoot for!

Alexandra used what she learned on her first film to allow the film's key art to evolve as her next film was packaged. In their teasers, the actors' faces were obscured in shadows.

But as soon as all the cast was locked, they could easily Photoshop their faces in to the final payoff poster, keeping the images unified to stay familiar to their sales prospects.

From a sales and marketing perspective, you want your marquee-value actor featured prominently in the artwork and trailer just as, ideally, they are also front and center in the first five minutes of the film. Of course, story might dictate otherwise, but these are the push and pull creative versus marketing forces that must be reconciled into a mutually satisfying compromise.

Even if you haven't even started shooting yet, a full-sized teaser poster empowers sales agents and distributors to intrigue other territories and platforms at the various markets. With floors and pavilions wallpapered with the best key art from the most professional designers from all around the world, you simply can't skimp on this sales tool. These same images can be used early on to entice crowd donors and equity investors and every single person who can help move the project along.

Sometimes sales agents or distributors will be willing to front the key art expense so they can drive and control that process. While that may be a Godsend for many broke-at-the-finish-line producers, don't kid yourself: these expenses will ultimately be deducted from your revenue, so you're paying for it one way or the other. Far better for you to line item it upfront — plan and budget for it accordingly — and get the chance to at least express your vision. Even if it changes, it should be because you signed on with a team you trust will take it to the next level.

Distributors usually take what the sales agents offer, so your key art (and all the variations you created) will likely stay with your film through its entire marketing cycle everywhere it goes — right through to the foreign ad translations and cinema posters in other countries. Having some alternates empowers your sales agents internationally. As an example: Bill Engval is a famous comedian in the United States (especially beloved in the Midwest). Sales agents would use him as a star to sell *Catching Faith* to domestic buyers at the AFM. But humor is culturally — and language — specific. If buyers or viewers don't know what a "redneck" is, or have any frame of reference for his American blue-collar comedy, they won't be able to identify with him or appreciate his brand of humor, so his marquee value diminishes the further away from the bible belt he is marketed. That's no reflection on his acting ability in any given film, just his "star power." Thus for Cannes, the EFM and other markets around the world, where he might be a less familiar face or name, sellers might opt instead to use one of the two teasers that focus more on the concept of football or faith.

Ideally, your sales agents and distributors are as transparent to you as you are to your equity investors. Key art should be broken out as a line-itemed expense. *Where and how is all the marketing and advertising money spent?* Most designers' rate sheets list a minimum of three conceptual compositions. Producers rarely order more. Distributors typically use that as a starting place, likely ordering two to four times that, typically spending two to ten (to a hundred) times what a producer might spend on key art. Thus, if you can nip this in the bud with a concept that nails it straight out of the gate, you have saved money in the long run and the all-precious time now and empowered yourself with a priceless marketing tool few independent producers afford themselves the luxury of on the front end.

Even if they like the key art you provided, big companies like Lionsgate will likely re-do your art. They took your project on because they felt they could sell it — and they want to sell it to as many different markets, platforms and outlets as possible — and they know how to do that better than almost anyone. But the art you initially invested in may be why they were attracted to your project in the first place: you raised the bar on your project above the din of the marketplace and persuaded them there were at least a few ways of selling it. If you can get to this coveted position, then your investment will have undeniably done its job and paid for itself.

⚡ HOT TIP!

Have the work done at the 27" x 40" poster size because it is always easier to downsize than to blow graphics up. And if you need it, you'll have it.

About half the time, the 27" x 40" poster will simply be reduced for the DVD and VOD packaging but often, Walmart (Asda), Costco, Carrefour, Tesco, RT-Mart, RedBox, Best Buy, Target and the like have their own marketing criteria of what they will allow — or what does well — on their retail shelf space and the distributors must accommodate their specific mandates often on a case-by-case basis.

In addition to the all-important copyright, consider at least starting placeholder key art and a marketing plan as investments in your intellectual property assets. Bridget Jurgens explains:

> If you were selling your home, your Realtor might encourage you to spend some money to update your kitchen. You may not want to do that but that might be the difference of your getting the highest selling price — or even selling your home at all.

As with casting insights, bring your sales agents on as early as possible in the key art process. Solicit their opinions on your marketing and sales strategies. "Posters are typically made two different ways," Bridget explains. "Preferably, key art designers are brought on early where they have more freedom in terms of creativity and assets. But great key art can also be reverse-engineered after the film is in the can, too."

But their resources will be far more limited. Forethought is everything. Put as much time and effort into soft-prepping your full-cycle marketing campaign as you do your script development, financing scenarios, cast wish lists, shoot locations and potential product placement partners. This blind spot is one of the reasons so many independent films fail: they don't work backwards from target audience marketing or distribution realities.

It's tough for writers and directors, especially, to see how distorted their project might become. To accept that the sales machine might not actually care what their film actually *is* versus what they want viewers to think the movie *might* be (that might compel a buying decision). Bridget explained it's not uncommon for posters and DVD covers to have explosions, vehicles, weapons or locations that aren't even in the actual film. "People forget. They're not holding your key art in front of them while they're watching the film." The sales and marketing job is to sell tickets, discs and downloads, to get butts in the seats. Your job — once you have the audience — is to make them forget everything else and get lost in your entertainment.

Seasonal and competitive forces can often impact key art marketing strategies as well. "If the market is flooded with horror films," Bridget continues, "sales teams might market a hack and slash film as more of a thriller. Or vice versa. A thriller with very little blood that's coming out around Halloween might be made to look more like a slasher film" to capitalize on seasonal interest. It's all about Mo (Momentum).

International buyers speak a wide variety of native tongues: every language in the world, quite literally. Those who are fluent in your film's language as a second (or fifth) tongue won't catch every cultural nuance, reference or colloquialism. The more your story can be visually expressed, the less will get lost in translation.

 One last case study demonstrates how effectively key art can be used across multiple platforms, especially on a low budget. Sky Soleil's coming-of-age drama, *The Elevator*, is about a troubled teen addict who finds hope through a recovery program. Inspired by his own true life story, it is a low budget project still in the development stages, so he didn't have a lot to work with other than the concept expressing uplifting hope, doors opening and blue skies ahead. Look at what a professional image beautiful, cohesive key art can project.

DOG & PONY resized all of Sky's key art for Facebook and Twitter. His WordPress website designer used all these assets to create a beautiful, mobile-optimized website and these images were used all the way through to unify their crowdfunding page. A very high-end (appearing) suite across the board was thus accomplished at indie prices because all the assets were synchronized and seamlessly cross-collateralized.

The key art process is much like what you'd find at an ad agency. Your designer ought to read the script to have the big picture and thus comprehend all your project-specific references. You have to let go of (or at least take a few steps back from) what the film is actually about and zoom your focus in on how it could best be marketed.

Pitching media is all about the visual experience. *What do you want your prospects to imagine on the screen of their mind's eye? What expectations do you want to create?* Well-designed, high-quality key art doesn't just tease your project or demonstrate various ways it could be sold, it gives potential partners a glimpse into your professionalism, what you might be like to work with and the caliber of project you might deliver.

One of the biggest catch-22s in our business is the need to project the image you want the world to perceive in order to attract the production funds, distribution and paying fan base — but without the money, stars or numbers accrued, it's hard to project that image. Professional key art helps you do both.

Another irony is that you need these types of materials to attract savvy investors but prudent investors don't want to invest their money with producers who waste money. Your ability to show how resourceful you've been — and the caliber of the deliverables — puts a feather in your cap, increasing investors' and prospective partners' faith in you that you can actually do on the screen what you pulled off on the page with the resources you were able to cobble together at the time. It's further evidence of your filmmaking (selling and networking) skills.

RAW ASSETS

"The number one mistake independent producers make," Bridget explains,

> is not getting the digital raw stills. That's your very best asset. Sure, we can use screen grabs and stock photography but digital raw stills are always best. Screen grabs from 4K footage are fine for digital images but not high enough resolution for print. If you blow up an actor's face from a screen grab to the size of a poster, it will pixelate. It might be fine for a small inset on the back of a DVD but certainly not the cover. The number one comment we get back from Walmart or Red Box when we try to use screen grabs is to "make the photo sharper." But the edges of screen grabs will always be soft, so you can't make them sharper. You want your images to pop off the page.

Your photographer might think it takes up too much hard drive space or will take a month to upload to a site but make sure your photographer knows that you expect — *and contract her for* — the raw files. "If you shoot raw," Bridget explains,

> the creative director has the freedom to go back and adjust the settings on the camera. Try to shoot as close to what you envision as possible, though, because it's hard to go from extremes (such as changing bright sunlight to nighttime in a club or a rainy, gloomy setting).

Make the investment in a brand new extra external hard drive dedicated specifically for this purpose and have your photographer hand it to you or ship it to you —

and burn backups to DVDs. It's worth it. Period. Ditto your own personal external backup of all the film's raw dailies but that's a lesson for another day (or book!).[5]

The earlier and more crystal clear your sales strategy is planned, the better you can align all your efforts to securing the right assets at the right times. The more assets you have, the more options you'll have. When conceiving their posters, filmmakers often picture a keynote scene from their proposed movie: perhaps the first kiss or the cute meet from a RomCom or a spectacular stunt or a thematic moment reflecting the image system of a drama. It's rare, however, that a unit photographer can capture the right angles — perfectly lit — while your crew is actually shooting principal photography.

You're far better served to recreate the scene purely for marketing purposes. "High resolution stills from on-set and/or unit photography are great," Bridget clarifies, "but the best option is almost always a well-planned special photo shoot during the early days of principal photography, with your actors in make-up and wardrobe, against a white or black backdrop." If your schedule and logistics can endure the extra time, schedule a shoot on the set or at the location on the pre-light or strike days. This will give your set photographer some creative freedom (without her interrupting or being hamstrung by principal photography) and you'll save the precious time and money later by front-loading your investment while so many of your assets are conveniently aggregated. Your marketing campaign will be immeasurably improved.

🎬 HOT TIP!

Have your still photographer shoot — and deliver — *everything* raw (not "just" high resolution .tiffs or .jpgs).

For key art stills, shoot in the highest quality stills mode:

Raw Camera File Extension Examples:

Canon	=	.crs, .crw
Nikon	=	.nef, .nes
Pentax	=	.pef
Olympus	=	.orf
Adobe	=	.dng

Only pull frames from video shot with a DSLR as a worst-case resort.

As with all things, the earlier you start, the better. Plan your key art photo shoot right alongside your director's shot list. Coordinate the elements you anticipate needing for your social media calendar. Leave yourself some room in the budget and enough lead time to get these critical assets — poster, one sheet, postcard, pitch package and website — written, designed, programmed and/or printed in time for the first market or festival in your plan.

While studios easily spend six months and half a million dollars on this process, even on a micro budget, you should set aside a *minimum* of $500–$5,000 — and a couple

..onths prep time (if not four!) — to showcase your project in its best light. Of course, you're working hard on writing, budgeting, scheduling, shooting, editing and finishing, but don't skip marketing. Studios can spend 1/3 to 1/2 of a film's budget on marketing and advertising — often even matching the entire production budget. You can at least eek out 1 percent–10 percent. Do it right.

KEY ART COMPS

Think about the *comp*arable ("comp") films you like — or that your film is like (or you wish it were more like). Study your genre. What similarities can you discern about the key art or the trailers (which we will discuss in a moment) of the breakout box office hits or critically acclaimed festival darlings of your genre? What do they have in common? List and analyze these elements. Notice any trends. Brainstorm taglines. What is it *you* like (or don't like) about their marketing campaigns? What is similar — or different — from your film? This is a great exercise to do at any stage — and repeatedly — throughout the entire development and marketing processes. Success leaves clues. Follow the breadcrumbs.

🎵 HOT TIP!

Check out: http://impawards.com/designers/index.html for award-winning movie and television poster designers near you.

Not only is this a handy resource to price and compare styles and portfolios of vetted artists and design agencies all around the world (broken down by global territory) but it's a terrific, convenient brainstorming resource. If your project overlaps with the sensibility of a particular director, for example, you can click a button to sort and organize her entire career's key art side-by-side.

You can also search by genre to study the color palettes, layouts, and other elements used to communicate concepts that might be most effective — or to catalog and eliminate the tropes to come up with something entirely original. Use this tool to research and brainstorm tagline ideas.

Perhaps you have a project that would be great for (*insert proposed actress' name here*) and you want to see what elements are common among her hits. Just as a casting director can look at a table of upside-down headshots and instinctively grab the ones with the most life in their eyes, by studying hundreds of successful key art campaigns, you'll begin to develop a sense of what pops at the thumbnail size, which is, like it or not, part of our communal, digital future.

I studied this list and asked several sales agents, distributors and some professional peers off the LA Yahoo Producers Group for recommendations of great key art companies and that's how I originally found DOG & PONY Creative (great word of mouth).

FOCUS GROUPS AND GENDER PREFERENCES

 Pay attention to key art gender preferences and let your target audience dictate the best design. In the case of *Once Again*, a gritty, non-linear romance, where the protagonist goes back in time for a second chance at love and his rock 'n' roll dreams, we were surprised to discover an almost 50/50 clean gender break between our two favorites. Women almost unanimously preferred what we referred to as our "Yin/Yang" version that had almost a Harlequin romance novel feel to it whereas men gravitated towards the "Drums" iteration.

Art is subjective. Personal tastes matter. Design (even if only in stick figures and words) what your ideal poster might look like. Collaborate with a team that can help you achieve that goal. Ideally, you'll find the sweet spot between your personal preferences, what best suits the actual film, what might most resonate with the sensibilities of your target audience, what your graphic design pros encourage versus warn against, and what meets the goals of your sales team's strategies.

KEY ART CREATIVE BRIEF

DOG & PONY have generously shared with all of us a great gift: their feature film creative brief (the same principals apply to TV projects and books, just adjust the terminology). Please visit www.HeatherHale.com/KeyArt/CreativeBrief to download DOG & PONY's five-page Key Art Creative Brief.

I hope it is as instrumental a creative brainstorming tool as it has been to my teams: to help you refine not only your own key art tastes but your ability to articulate your pitch through comps and images to achieve consistency across all your marketing deliverables.

Even if you can't afford to do key art or aren't at a point in the process where you're ready for it yet, I have found having everyone on my core team complete this form independently — even just as an exercise — then discuss it — was invaluable to getting us all on the same page, speaking the same language. It helps to suss out really key differences we hadn't realized were there in terms of how we each saw the project, enabling us to better align our shared vision. Priceless.

As always, with creative artrepreneurs,[6] there's the delicate balance between champagne visions on beer budgets. You can't always afford to hire the best stills photographer and do professional shoot — even if you had all your talent attached. But figure out a way to squeeze key art out of your budget and into your schedule.

Yes, of course, you can have a relative or art school intern do your artwork but . . . having gone down that route myself too many times, let me just reiterate the age old warning that is so true: "You get what you pay for." But sometimes a friend or a student helping you out as a favor is a grand gift.

GOOD, FAST, CHEAP: PICK TWO

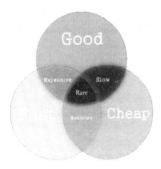

As independent producers, we are perpetually juggling conflicting demands and priorities — always a day late and a dollar short — but this doesn't always have to be so. The classic project management triangle represents the three constraints that seem to be forever at odds with one another: cost, time and quality.

You want something done fast and cheap? Odds are, it won't be all that good. You want it good and cheap? Are you willing to endure relentless delays? Fast and good? Pull out the pocketbook.

This symbiotic triad often forces you to choose which two to optimize, often at the expense of the third. Achieving all three simultaneously seems forever elusive — but it's possible. You simply have to do your best to assess — issue by issue — what's most important at any given time, within a scope realistic to your project.

My dad always used to say that startups always cost twice as much and take four times as long as you originally plan. Every one of your projects are essentially startup businesses — over and over again: brand new products, new R&D, new ~~Vulture Capitalists~~ (*I'm sorry — did I type that out loud?*) — I mean "angels".

You can simply never have enough time to plan and get ahead of all the things you must juggle, so start everything as soon as possible (i.e. right now!) and hope your diligent advance planning will shave time and expenses and improve the quality.

FACEBOOK AND TWITTER BANNERS AND AVATARS

You can resize your key art and change the layout to professionally unify your social media presence. Convert your poster to Facebook and Twitter Banners and Avatars (the little thumbnail "profile picture" that shows up when you comment as your project/team). The compositions for both are slightly different (with the avatar insert on the left of the banner) and their specifications constantly change, so it's good to get professional help. DOG & PONY did all these for us and as always: I think they did a great job! It's a great way to affordably raise the bar on your projects.

Twitter Banner:

Avatar:

ONE SHEETS

Historically, the one sheet referred to the 27" x 40" lobby posters used in theaters. This hand painted artwork from the 1900s and classic movie posters were shipped folded until the 1980s when they began rolling them in tubes. These are now collectors' items. But in the modern marketplace, a one sheet typically refers to an 8.5" x 11" (or an A4 or sometimes postcard-sized) piece of glossy, usually hard stock paper that sales agents create to sell your film to distributors. You'll see them in racks all over the market floors. They are great precursors to study, especially if you can collect those that would be considered comps for your project and compare the elements.

You can also make them up yourself — even just printed in color (ideally) on regular (or better) paper. A good one sheet will have your fantastic key art, title treatment and tagline on the front, ideally with any stars front and center, and, depending on the design, the logline or short synopsis, possibly cast, director, writer, producer and any notable credits, run time, language, etc. Some of this might spill to the back with a few great production stills (if you've got them), maybe market or festival screening dates, times and locations, award laurels, review snippets, social media and crowdfunding links — and don't forget contact info!

🔥 HOT TIP!

Bulk print one side in color then customize the backs for the different events you hit.

MARKET CATALOG

Usually you need a sales agent to get into the market catalog but if you've got the money, you can rent a booth and/or take out an ad in the catalog and market right alongside them. Some smaller production companies co-op booths or suites, or just rent a small table or share a page in the catalog to gain screening access. There are all sorts of ways of being resourceful to get on the map and in the game. Money always helps. Your key art in the market catalog — and in the online directory — can be indispensable.

VIDEO

In "the old days" (the twentieth century), it was sufficient to come into a room with cardboard stand-up storyboards and a nicely bound look book, even a bulletin board of 3" x 5" cards beating out the storylines with some location photos and actor headshots, cobbling together the overall concept, but today, the boom in home movie making software has blown those expectations out of the water. Four-year-olds can edit movies at home. We are in the media business. Moving pictures. Like it or not, the bar has been raised exponentially on what is expected from us in our presentations.

Multi-media is the name of the game. If you can deliver impressive, engaging written presentations and verbal pitches, that's terrific. But the more your content can pop off the page, emulating the viewing experience, especially in your business-to-business presentations, the better. "Having tape" is almost a prerequisite in pitching reality/non-fiction television but filmmakers have been using short films for years as an expression of their feature ideas as well.

If you've got tape, they almost expect you to come in with at least some of it to convey the tone, feel and mood of the pivotal moments and highlight at least the type of talent you envision.

Time is of the essence. The more you can boil down your idea and convert your vision to contagious passion in your prospective partners, the more likely you'll be able to lure their resources your way to make it happen. Regardless of what stage of development you're at in the process, there are a more video tools everyday to help you.

Trailers

If you're hitting a film market looking for distribution for a completed film, or a TV market to pitch a completed television series, then you'll have existing footage. When you hit the market, have your trailer or sizzle reel already available online as well as queued up on your local, internal storage of your smart phone or tablet so that you can quickly press play if anyone you're pitching to is willing to take a look (and not be held hostage by the possibly maxed-out wireless capacity of the event!). Make sure all your marketing materials have your project's trailer's URL, be it Cinando, Vimeo or You-Tube — or all of them (and passwords, if necessary).

If you don't have a trailer done yet, it's probably the most important multi-media-marketing piece you'll create. What a logline is to the script, TV show or format, the trailer is to the movie or television program. Just as the world of key art has its own award-winners, so, too, is there high art to feature film and TV trailers (and sizzle reels and commercials).

🎵 HOT TIP!

Check out:
www.goldentrailer.com/trailerhouse.php#trailerhouses for the best of the best trailer houses around the world. Use this free resource to study the best trailers around the world from your format or genre. *What elements or characteristics do they all share? What sets the winner apart from the nominees — and the rest of the marketplace?*

Write an A/V script for what your trailer ought to contain. Usually in a two-column format with **A**udio (voiceover narration, the actual dialogue from the clips, source or new music, sound effects, etc.) in one column and **V**ideo (the storytelling visuals you're depicting) in the other. Sometimes roughed out time codes are added as cues to assist your editor (or yourself) in assembling the rough cut. *What are the beats? What moments, images or lines of dialogue reveal your concept, characters and plot? What are the pivotal moments? Can you extract the plot point decisions in an intriguing way that deliver for your genre or format?* Look for the most emotional (exciting, funny, scary, sad) moments.

Even if you're still at the script stage, just like completing the key art creative brief, writing an A/V script for your would-be trailer or even storyboarding what its commercial might look like can prove to be a fertile exercise to improve your screenplay or format. As you look for "trailer moments," you might realize they don't yet exist on the page — but ought to! Your rewrite might be reinvigorated as you dig deep to enhance the marketability and cinematic qualities of your underlying literary material, especially in context with the best of the best of its genre and format.

Screeners

You'll hear all sorts of debate as to whether to give out screeners or links to your movie or full episodes. A lot of this debate is actually more about showing it to a distributor prior to your having a *festival* premiere, the fear being that you might be diluting the impact of distributors seeing a project before it's ready versus watching it in a far better environment (hopefully) in front of a live audience. Obviously, the latter is preferential, but we're talking here about pitching *product* to *sales agents* at a *market*. Product that may have already had its festival premiere or might not ever have one. Or, if successful at the market, might have a festival premiere in the future as part of a designed campaign in concert with the new partners you acquire at the market.

A festival campaign will almost always precede or trump your market run if for no other reason than prestige and fun (and the perception of exclusivity). Moreover, simply by virtue of the mass of projects screened at markets versus the curated selections shown at festivals, you're bound to get more consumer coverage at a festival but more sales traction at a market.

Don't handicap your market sales efforts with precious festival pedigree promotional thinking — they are two totally different worlds. Not to mention: sales agents are not (usually) distributors, so you haven't really blown your first impression with your ultimate buyers anyway — you're just initiating the sales process with the brokers in between — and they are used to seeing works in progress.

So, bring screeners to markets (that's what you're going for). Have them available on Cinando, YouTube, Vimeo, your website. Make sure your title and contact information is printed on the screener disc or flash drive as well as on any paper sleeves or color

For *3D Cakes*, we had two years and three terabytes worth of existing, high-definition footage from the builds of some spectacular cakes and the celebrity event deliveries to reverse engineer into a high caliber sizzle reel. We also shot some new, far more intentional footage that focused on character interaction and emotional engagement throughout the creative collaborative process and the unveiling. With this and a beautiful pitch package, we got a written distribution commitment from Discovery.

Please visit www.HeatherHale.com/3DCakes for a spec Reality TV sizzle reel.

labels. Insert your business card. Attach your one sheet. It's a trade show, remember: piles of paper, stacks of one sheets, business cards and discs. Do everything you can to not get lost in the shuffle.

Sizzle Reels

A sizzle reel is a business-to-business video expression of a concept that teases your prospects with a glimpse of your vision, hopefully inspiring them to want to see more. Just as the primary goal of a logline, tagline, one sheet, synopsis or pitch is to get someone to actually read the script or look at your pitch package, and the function of trailers and key art is to get the audience to buy tickets or digital downloads; reels are to establish your credibility to business professionals and for them to see the promise of your project. Their purpose being to inspire them to watch the whole movie or an episode, hear the pitch for your show or look at your proposal with enhanced confidence in your ability to execute.

Sell the *Sizzle* Not the Steak

Sizzle reels can be 30 seconds to 3 minutes — even up to 7 minutes — but shorter is almost always better. Somewhere between 30 seconds and 1 minute 45 seconds is a great range to shoot for. They should emulate the viewing and emotional experience of the larger piece they reflect. In other words: if it's a comedy, it should be funny. If it's a fast-paced action piece, it should be thrilling. If it's a reality show about people sharing their problems, we need to care about these people and see their engaging personalities in emotion — not just when they look their best.

Talent Reels

While a sizzle reel highlights the project, a talent reel focuses on the proposed stars, subject matter experts or hosts. A wonderful asset, especially for an unscripted sales kit, these video snapshots capture your reality talent in their domain, living out loud, being authentic in their own milieus, teasing the interaction that the circumstances promise, paired with on location interview sound bytes. Again, shorter is better (30 seconds) but it's not uncommon for these to run the length of a sample segment (7 minutes, one-third of a half-hour show).

Ditto if you are on-screen talent trying to get on some radars as a potential future host or guestpert. Show off your assets, your strengths. *What is it that we can count on from you? Hard-hitting psychoanalysis? Are you a fun medium that we'll enjoy watching as you chat up ghosts? Are you a cat whisperer? An entrepreneur who really knows houses, restaurants, make-up effects?* Deliver. The talent reel gives us just a taste of what we can look forward to.

For a feature, a director's reel, clips of your attached actors, even key Department Heads who excel in the skill sets most relevant to your project will be key (i.e. special effects for sci-fi; stunts or fight choreography for action; period costume, make-up, set dressing or locations for a historical biopic) to illustrate the caliber of talent of your production team.

Presentation Tape/Completed Scenes

If you've got a film that's just started principal photography by the time a market rolls around, you might not have enough diverse footage for a trailer — but you're beyond just paper — so you want to capitalize on all you've got thus far. Distributors and sales agents are open to seeing completed scenes. This gives them a sense of the production value and talent currently unfolding. Sometimes this can add excitement to the pitch: that it's unveiling and still rolling even as we're meeting. This can add not only a sense of exclusivity, but a sense of urgency to take advantage of the opportunity presented during this sneak peak before it is available to the entire marketplace.

Even completed films will often add some complete scenes or sequences in addition to their trailer on a DVD leave-behind to particularly interested leads. If your short film is your first act, that would be useful here. A TV show might illustrate one completed segment, or one storyline, or a full round of play of a game show. These could be up to 20 minutes. It's all about what will show off your content in its best light with the resources you have or can cobble together. Never have footage that is longer than it needs to be. They'll click off as soon as they've decided. No need to waste resources on what they won't likely see. Give them just enough to express interest and take the next step in the sales cycle — never one second of marginal footage that might make them second-guess their initial interest.

Proof of Concept Pilot

Some independent producers go to the full extent of shooting a whole pilot to express their concept. If sold, this might be completely re-shot with a whole new cast at a much higher budget but — like placeholder key art — it helps the powers that be envision its potential sufficient to overcome their reservations and objections — and commit to the next phase of its development — or a series order.

CAUTIONARY TALE: A PAINFUL LESSON

I have served as a judge for a great many film and TV festivals, webseries and screenwriting contests. At one television pitch contest in Hollywood, I vividly remember a gal brilliantly verbally pitching a comedy project. We were all hooked, laughing at all the right beats, communally relishing her delivery. She was a panel favorite.

Then she showed us the footage they had spent a quarter of a million dollars and months to shoot and edit.

It ruined the energy in the room. All our highest hopes were dashed. The actors, crew and locations were nowhere near as good as what her material deserved or what her pitch had effectively conjured in our minds' eyes. We all envisioned a much higher caliber of production value and comedic timing. Since we were the second-round judges and she was clearly going on to the finals, — and it broke my heart to be the one to tell her, I knew she needed to hear the constructive and well-meaning truth — she had to hide that expensive exercise and never let anyone see that footage again — it was killing her prospects. To her disappointment and frustration, the rest of the judging panel agreed.

She was far better served to move forward just based on the strength of her material and verbal pitch alone — and she went on to do admirably in the finals without the injurious footage.

Unless you've got stars in your back pocket or money to burn or you can pull this off fairly cheaply and easily with your own pre-existing resources and assets, test pilots are usually reserved for a network's production division to jump through its own distribution arm's hoops. They are not usually part of the indie playbook.

Rip-O-Matics

With all the new breakthroughs in technology this millennium, independent producers — especially for features — are increasingly creating what are called rip-o-matics, essentially "ripping off" scenes from blockbuster movies and classic TV shows to patchwork together a make-shift, mash-up trailer to illustrate their storylines. This can beat the short film approach because it can show the whole scope of the storyline versus just the set up or first act. And suddenly, you have the benefit of A-list stars, epic landscapes, stunts, special and visual effects you could never have afforded, because you're just "borrowing" them to express the concept.

But . . . Isn't that Illegal?

It is illegal to use copyrighted material without permission. Period. And yes, virtually everything in most of these "rip-o-matics" (thus the name) is copyrighted, so you could be exposed to civil liability from using clips of other people's movie or music. But, as an independent producer, if you are using these mash-ups in a private pitch meeting to demonstrate how an idea can be visually communicated, and are not posting this footage anywhere public (on social media or crowdfunding sites), and are just limiting your use to one-on-one pitch meetings at the markets (or maybe on a password protected website for your prospective investors), then your cobbling together these moving images to express your idea isn't wildly different than last millennium's strategy of cutting similar pictures out of a magazine and pasting them into a cardboard collage. You are not selling this mash-up for profit nor distributing it in anyway nor damaging anyone. It's a contemporary multi-media mix tape to express the emotions of the project — and your vision for what it could be (with the right budget and cast). It's a modern way to use pre-existing, relevant, accessible and available visuals to succinctly storyboard your ideas on a shoestring budget for a private, contained audience.

🎵 HOT TIP!

Google: "Rip-O-Matic" to see some great examples.
    Visit: www.HeatherHale.com/RipOMatic for links to samples such as:

- Joe Carnahan's director's pitch for *Daredevil* (PG-13 and NC-17 versions)
- Kevin Tancharoen's pitch to direct *The Hunger Games*
- *We Are Monsters*

Animatics

Some directors (with money, the right connections or skills) do full-blown animatics to express their vision. With the latest post-production software, you really can pull off editing, effects, music, sound design and titles for far less than what most production companies spend.

All these video expressions can, of course, be done for free or off favors from friends but I've seen production companies spend a quarter of a million dollars to execute a reality show concept that didn't get picked up. $500–$5,000 is not uncommon for independent producers. Even $50k, depending on the resources and confidence of the producing party in the project's prospects. We shot the whole script for a one-hour drama pilot proof of concept in two grueling days. It never went anywhere.

VISION STATEMENT

Sometimes you simply don't have the means to pull all that multi-media off. If there isn't yet footage available (or any good enough to share), you can "use your words" to illustrate the intended cinematic approach, the visual image systems and themes, the types of stunts or special effects, how you want the audience to feel, the kind of movie you intend to make through a director's (or even a producer's or team's) vision statement. A bit like a fine artist's statement, these impassioned write-ups can express your goals and intentions directly from your helmer(s) as part of your proposal.

> Please visit www.HeatherHale.com/VisionStatements for samples.

AWESOME VERBAL PITCH[7]

Have you ever raved about a movie or TV show that you absolutely loved — or even an exciting sporting event — to someone who hadn't yet seen it? Spoilers aside, your enthusiasm was probably contagious enough to make your listener want to see it, too (i.e. to take action).

You want to make whoever you're pitching to be genuinely excited to watch your film, trailer, sizzle reel — or to read your script or pitch package. Or at least feel that it sounds marketable enough to assign it to a gatekeeper to vet. Sure, in our fantasies, they write a million dollar check on the spot — but what are the real-world goals that can actually be accomplished during a market pitch meeting? Focus on that first milestone:

- *Primary Market Pitch Goal*: Elicit interest (entice a request for more information/ materials).
- *Secondary Market Pitch Goal*: Network (expand your relationships, enhance your reputation, open the doors for future, warmer communication).

Share Your Passion

For each and every pitch, your challenge is to translate whatever it was about the idea that got so under your skin that you were inspired — nay — compelled — to dedicate months to years of your life to express that premise. Share THAT! No one can give you that passion. You have to come with it authentically pre-loaded. If you don't truly believe in your project, everyone will see through your façade (and they won't be fooled by it either). Enthusiasm is contagious but desperate insecurity gets promptly quarantined.

Producers are typically better at pitching than screenwriters — but not always. While pitching is an instinctive art form, it's also a learnable craft. Those who are really good at it make it look easy — like Fred Astaire dancing — breezy and seamless. But it takes about as much practice, timing and finesse. But where do you even start?

At the beginning.

Pitch Perfect: Water Cooler 101

The first time an accomplished athlete is asked to give step-by-step instructions — be it a golf or baseball swing, shooting a basketball, throwing a football spiral, shot put or discus — it can often be clumsy and awkward even for Olympians to break down what they do instinctively in order to articulate the unique combination of moves. Their "coaching" may come across as disjointed. It may seem impossible to put all the pieces together and simultaneously do what they do in what looks like one fluid movement. But as the disparate pieces eventually jive — and everything falls naturally into place — it's pure grace. You, too, can achieve that with your pitch: invisible but flawless architecture that expresses authentic passion and results in genuine emotional engagement that inspires desired action.

Don't stress. Be like the duck, calm and oh-so-casual on the surface of the water (even if you're paddling frantically underneath!) Like the ballerina who, when she misses a step, smiles and continues on ever more confidently, we aren't quite sure if she screwed up or that was part of the choreography, don't let your facial expression belie your flub — continue with your performance. Lure us into your passion. That's where we all want to be. That's why we're all in this business. For those fleeting epiphanous moments of bliss where we are swept away by good storytelling.

NOTES

1 An artist known for his infinitely tessellated images (repeating optical illusion geometric patterns).
2 A frustrating dilemma with seemingly no way out due to mutually exclusive conditions.
3 Lesbian, Gay, Bi, Transgender, Queer and Allies.
4 Visit www.HeatherHale.com/KeyArt to see the full color versions of all of these posters (and more examples).
5 Send your indie film horror stories to me at Author@HeatherHale.com. Stories can be anonymized to protect industry reputations!
6 A word I made up: artist + entrepreneur.
7 My book Story$elling: How to Develop, Market, and Pitch Film & TV Projects (2018) covers pitching thoroughly.

What Goes Into a Pitch Package?

What goes into a pitch package depends on who you're pitching to. Maybe you're presenting an indie film to equity or angel investors. Or a documentary for grants or scholarships. Or a television program to an OTT network. Or even a whole slate for a possible international co-production partnership. Each of these scenarios is different. Based on your hit list targets and call to action goals, your package may or may not include all of the following material. You may not have all of it — or any clue as to what some of it is. That's okay: your learning process has to start somewhere, right? Might as well be right here, right now.

You may highlight certain elements, reposition the order and deliver it in a variety of formats. Maybe you give a one-on-one pitch over coffee with a sizzle reel on your iPhone. Maybe you snail mail a full-blown, full-color bound glossy business plan with a PPM[1] to your cousin on Wall Street. Maybe you put up a password-protected website for friends and family to support. Maybe you create a PowerPoint or Keynote presentation for a group presentation in a small rented ballroom, rec center or private home dinner. Maybe you simply share your screen on a web video conference call. It all depends on who you're pitching to, your resources, goals, access, timing, relationships — and the value of the outcome. You get the idea. Customize it. Make it work. What follows are the guts of what you might want to have lined up and polished to shine. Mileage may vary.

KEY ELEMENTS

- Executive summary
  - The five W's: Who, What, Where, When, Why (and How) customized top notes
- Project
  - great title
  - excellent logline
  - terrific tagline
  - fantastic key art
  - project synopsis
    - succinct and tone-expressing fictional story *or*
    - clear and intriguing TV format
  - Links to
    - trailer
    - sizzle reel
    - website

- social media profiles
  - IMDB, Variety Insight, Slated, etc.
- Letters of Interest or Intent (LOIs) for talent, equipment, services, locations, etc.
- Talent wish lists
- Distribution
  - targeted hit lists (*unless this is for a distributor*)
  - potential distribution strategies (probably not included to a distributor)
  - contracts (or LOIs on letterhead)
  - list of personal contacts as potential attachments/consultants/advisory board members
  - pre-sale forecasts or commitments
- Marketing: social media/crowdsourcing, event marketing and advertising campaign ideas
- Proof/source or use of funds (*are you proving you have or asking for money?*)
- Intellectual property: the copyrighted script or WGA registered show format.
- Source material (if relevant: underlying best seller, graphic novel, true life story, news articles, book reviews, video game, etc.)
- People
  - Who's involved at this point?
    - Don't feel the need to add a soul — sometimes "attachments" who don't really deliver the goods can just be a flock of albatrosses roosting around the project's neck.
    - Be very clear who you're legally obligated to versus who you just have circling the project as an option.
  - Production team
    - Director/producer/writer/DP/editor
    - Department heads or key crew members
    - Line producer, production designer, composer
    - If it's a period piece, maybe the costume designer
    - If it's a horror, maybe make-up and special effects
    - You get the idea — what matters to whom at this stage of the game?
      - A-list actors or directors (or well-respected, credible in the biz, high star power ranking pros)
      - famous race car driver/builder for a race film
      - famous Greenpeace captain for a seal-saving environmental/animal activist film
      - famous musicians for soundtrack possibilities, etc.
    - Photos can be nice if they're uniform, flattering or in action
    - Custom-written bios (specific to the project/undertaking) are great, resumes less so. In an interactive/dynamic presentation, the more full color or moving visuals, the better.
- Talent wish list targets
  Note: Tread carefully here so as not to mislead. If you're very clear these are your wish list ideas for key roles, they can be helpful illustrations — especially if you really think you can get them at those rates and terms through your relationships. Randomly listing the biggest stars will only undermine your credibility.
  - Targets:
    - photos (either the most recent or ones that most look like your character)
    - credit highlights (highest profile and/or most relevant to this project)
- The numbers/the plan
  - Film comps.
  - The budget:

- It could be just a ballpark figure, the top sheet or the full blown 50-page budget — again, depends on *who is asking*? (and is it any of their business?):
  - A product placement package might not ever mention the budget
  - If you're trying to get a high-profile star to consider the role without being deterred by the low budget, you might not want to even mention it (unless asked). Never lie. But no need to highlight a weakness (unless asked).
  - Investors — yes, of course, that's what it's all about. It's their money, how much you're asking for — and how you'll use it. Details, details, details. What are your numbers, where did you get them, how did you calculate them, what were your assumptions, etc. "Show your work."
  - Distributors — not necessarily:
    - If they are a BUYER or a VENDOR, it's none of their business what your true hard costs are as it *might* subconsciously influence their offer to you. What it cost you to make this film or where or how you cut corners and finagled deals or what your relationships favored you, none of that should have any bearing on your **sales price** (i.e. the market "value" of the film)
    - Partner (depends on the kind of partner):
      - *Sharing the risk* (i.e. putting up money?) — Sure, of course, show them all the skin in the game!
      - *Other partners*: it depends on when and how they come into the project and why they'd need to see the budget — how is it relevant to them? Does it hurt or help your case?
  - Revenue waterfall scenarios.
  - Any MOUs[2] or LOIs for distribution, talent, pre-sales, grants, tax incentives lottery placement, etc.
- P&A plan and budget
- If you know
  - estimated calendar (pre-production, principal photography, post production, release dates)
  - intended shoot location(s)
  - proposed tax credits

You have to give serious thought to WHO you're presenting your proposal to — and WHY:

- Are you seeking an attachment?
  - Are you wanting an A-list or high-profile actor to attach? (*That submission package ought to highlight that great "actor bait" role.*)
    Are you soliciting a high-level director? (*You might skew this proposal towards the visual potential, the intriguing promise of the premise or how uniquely the project redefines or blends its genre(s)).*
- Are you going after investors? *What kind of investors?*
- Some investors only look at the bottom line and will seriously just flip from spreadsheet to spreadsheet looking for a few key figures:
  - The waterfalls for ROIs of various revenue scenarios
  - Cash flow analysis: how — and when — their investment will be returned? Do they buy it?
  - Are your comps relevant and recent?
  - Are your formulas based on realistic numbers of screens, screen averages, weeks in theaters, exhibitor splits, expenses?
- Who are you targeting for the roles?
  - Are they strong enough to attract domestic distribution?
  - Can you legitimately get them?

- ○ Do they have any value abroad? Are they marquee value enough to deliver foreign box office? DVD/VOD?
- ○ Is your budget low enough that a great C-level ensemble cast and really savvy production strategies will mitigate most of the known risks and promise a worthwhile return? (i.e. Can you find a sweet spot where you might be able to bunt to get safely to first base instead of fouling out trying to hit that homerun?)
- Others look more at your team and your combined knowledge and expertise in a specific budget range and genre.
- Some are only interested in the story and the strength of the script — or its message (perhaps some political or social issues the project addresses that they feel very strongly about: homophobic bullying, gay marriage rights, animal rights, environmental activism, a particular disease, social or religious issue, etc.).
- Are you looking for a key product placement commitment or ancillary marketing joint venture (video game, merchandising tie in)? They're going to be looking at your distribution commitments or at least plans and social media marketing campaign.

There are myriad variations. Whether you slant the material differently, just verbally, or remove entire sections for certain submissions, just stay focused on who it's going to and what you want them to do as a result of reviewing your materials.

What's your call to action? What's insufficient to make a decision? How much will overwhelm? How much is just enough to trigger the next step? What — specifically — do you want them to do as a result of receiving your package or hearing your pitch?

- Do you want them to buy or option your script to produce it themselves?
- Do you want them to form an LLC with you to co-produce?
- Do you want them to offer you a distribution contract? Or just give you ballpark terms to start the discussion?
- Do you want them to invest private equity through a PPM?
- Are you asking for free or loaned product? Deferred labor? Equipment? Services? A location?
- Do you want them to sign a Letter of Intent?
  - ○ Will a Letter of Interest be sufficient?
  - ○ Will a letter on their (or their rep's) letterhead saying they've read the script/reviewed the package and are potentially interested be enough?
  - ○ Will a quote or email response work?

Be clear about what your expectations are — and what your end goal is. Make sure you're all on the same page. Remember: the biggest source of litigation is thwarted expectations. Be clear. Be firm.

Now that you've hopefully given some serious thought about who this proposal is going to and what exactly it is that you are "proposing," let's build your package around those actions you're trying to convince others to take.

CAST WISH LISTS

Cast matters. To some professionals, it's all that matters. It has to matter to you. In funding and marketing indie films, sometimes the journey makes it feel as if nothing else matters. And in some ways, it doesn't. In other ways, it's wildly skewed. But we are not here to make the business a fairer place. We are here to figure out how to work the markets and best navigate Hollywood, such as it is (or work around or outside of it).

"Directing is 90% casting."

~Elia Kazan? Billy Wyler? John Ford? John Huston?
Martin Ritt? Robert Altman?

(It's been attributed to them all).

It's disheartening because what should (and often is) the most fun part of direct-ing, selecting your palette of talent to conduct a creative symphony with, can often get bullied around by market forces and purse-string demands. At the independent film level, there are fewer choices and more concessions and compromises made. Even as a writer with a brilliant script you're so proud of, or as a producer with an impressive, professional package, you show up at the market with so much truly important work done and all anyone cares about is:

Them:	"Who's attached?"	Them:	"How much money have you
Us:	"Well, no one, yet . . .		raised?"
	That's why I'm here . . ."	Us:	"Well, none yet . . .
			That's why I'm here . . ."

I wish we lived in a world where we could cast exactly who we envision would be perfect for each role or give that great career break to whoever knocks it out of the park in their audition and have your gut instincts paid off by wonderful, award-winning performances. Unfortunately, directors don't always get to cast based on talent or preference.

We live in a world where actors are viewed as commodities — pieces of a much larger puzzle — almost like some Rube Goldberg Machine[3] where some other power-that-is gets to over-rule your heart's desire with what they're willing to fund or back. If you're spending someone else's million dollars (or even a tenth of that!), you owe it to your investors to at least try to get *one* marketable, monetizable name.

The highest profile cast you can get will help across the board. The challenge is, as "stars" get put on and off your shortlist — and you get jerked around waiting to hear back from anyone ('cause Hollywood's afraid to ever give a firm "No"), your project languishes on the vine. Here are some ideas . . .

Clever Attachment Strategies

In the "old days" (let's say the 1980s), you could cobble together a bunch of C- or D-level talent and go "straight to DVD" to make your money back — and then some! Many low-budget producers used to stunt cast cameo roles that they paid a dispro-portionate amount of the budget to as a one-day player, in maybe one to three scenes. They'd put this star's face on the poster or DVD cover. A misleading bait and switch, to be sure, but it was done all the time. The speed of social media today, however, makes this a much less effective strategy in our accelerated, opinionated economy.

Many filmmakers on strapped budgets think that if they can get an ensemble of solid TV actors, they should be in good stead. Not so much. It'd be great for the caliber of the production's overall performance (or the industry as a whole) if we could spread our casting budgets fairly across an equally talented ensemble but in terms of marketing, the industry tends to bank the bulk of their funds on one "name" actor. The cast may ultimately still be round out with all the other actors you envisioned, but they will likely have to work at scale (or the balance deferred) to make most low-budget projects financially feasible. It's unfair. But the industry (and life) are unfair.

Unless you only need an actor for a day or two, it is usually cheaper to contract them for the whole week because four days is more expensive than the five-day week (3½ days is the tipping point). In some circumstances, if they only work a few days in their second week, that can be prorated off a weekly rate.

SAG-AFTRA REAL WORLD DAILY/WEEKLY RATES

In the US, most mainstream film, television, new media and industrial projects work under the merged Screen Actors Guild-American Federation of Television and Radio Artists labor union contracts. As a ballpark point of reference only, here are the 2017 figures available when we went to print. Always check www.sagaftra. org for the most current figures, diversity incentives and fringes.

Table 23.1 SAG-AFTRA Real World Daily/Weekly Rates

SAG-AFTRA Agreement	Film's Budget Ceiling	Day Rate	Real World Day Rate	Weekly Rate	Real World Weekly Rate
Ultra Low Budget	$250,000	$125	$241 $336–$348		
Modified Low Budget	$700,000	$335	$645 $898–$931	$1,166	$1,982 $2,761–$2,860
Low Budget	$2,500,000	$630	$1,213 $1,690–$1,750	$2,190	$3,722 $5,185–$5,371
Basic Minimum		$933	$1,796 $2,502–$2,592	$3,239	$5,506 $7,670–$7,945

The top figure in the *Real World* daily/weekly rate columns above take into consideration that most principal photography shoot days are 12 hours (not 8, so that adds 4 hours of overtime each day at time and a half; you get an extra 4 hours of straight time on weekly contracts); and most actors have an agent (so that adds another 10 percent agency fee).

The second figure range below that accurately reflects the true bottom-line costs to a producer as, in addition to an actor's daily or weekly rate, you're also responsible for all the employer fringes:

- 17.3 percent = SAG-AFTRA's health, pension and welfare fund (HPW)
- 20–22 percent = Payroll fringes (FICA, federal and state unemployment, disability, medicare)
- 2–5 percent = Typical payroll company
  39.3–44.3 percent

When pitching, if you are financially backed, *the agent is required by law to present the offer to their client*. Thus, if you have 100 percent of a $200k budget raised, you're going to be taken much more seriously and actually get an answer than having 0 percent of a $3 million budget raised.

Schedule F

If a given star's face on your poster, DVD cover or VOD thumbnail is anticipated to actually help sell your film (and you're adhering to SAG-AFTRA minimums), it might be worth it to "Schedule F" one "name" actor. At our time of printing, that is currently a $65k flat fee (which is less rapacious when it's less than 10 percent of your budget). An agent's 10 percent commission on this amount isn't huge, obviously, but the closer you get to your shoot date, the more receptive high-profile actors (and their reps) will be if their schedule has suddenly opened up — and your project is ready to roll and they can make that money quickly and easily.

It's a catch-22. Or more like a catch-33 triad: it's nearly impossible to raise money or get distribution without cast — yet it's nearly impossible to get cast to attach without money or distribution. It's a constant shell game. You raise cast-contingent financing or distribution, or secure financing- or distribution-contingent cast. Baby steps. On a 100-mile journey.

Talent Agent Strategies

LA talent agents are by far the busiest, least accessible and least responsive, usually obsessed with getting their clients longer-term, better paying television gigs. Ultra low-budget independent films aren't often on their bottom line radars. You might have better luck with New York agents whose clients might be doing high-profile prestige Broadway gigs but might be more receptive to a film offer. UK agents tend to be the most polite, approachable and solicitous of all. Junior agents everywhere might still read themselves — and that's the toughest challenge of all: getting people to actually read.

Vetting Cast Wish Lists

Rather than just giving your cast wish list to an agent, if you can get them to read the script: engage their creativity. *Who do **they** see in the roles?* If you've done your homework, you already know who they have in their stable off IMDBPro or Variety Insight — but keep your ideas close to your chest — at least initially. You might be surprised that they come back with someone they rep that is a much bigger name than you thought you could possibly get or surprise you with some really cool and interesting options you hadn't considered. Maybe they've got someone hip-pocketed who hasn't publicly come over to their agency yet? You never know.

Run your top picks for each role past your International Sales Agent, too. Or the top few you intend to court first. It's a good way to get valuable information and prioritize who to go after first. But it's also a way to begin to engage their creative juices on a project you want them to consider — or at least start tracking.

List desired talent in spreadsheets for internal purposes. Look at the information from every angle possible to see if you can identify any insights. Add their IMDBPro ranking, their Variety VScore, *The Wrap*'s PowerScore. Average or weight or reconcile them. List their age.

❧ HOT TIP!

Plug the actors' birthdays into your spreadsheet software and input a formula that will automatically calculate their age as of "today" so that every time you open your master file, all the research you have done for any past project will help build a custom database of the actors you'd love to work with.

Delineate between your A-list shots in the dark without losing sight of your more realistic B-level or ultra low-budget realistic gets. Rank your preferences personally. Maybe coded with columns for the director's preferences versus the producer's (versus your spouse's all important two cents!). Don't forget to put in a column for your ISA's and CD's[4] opinions. What do you — as a team — ballpark their perceived marketability versus your preferred creative choices? Consider advice and suggestions from any relevant partners (investor's preferences, writer's vision, social media polls) and further refine your list looking for patterns and trends.

While all your lists might be wildly divergent, you might be surprised to find they all converge on one name. Or you may discover a cluster of potential options that are non-debatable on all fronts. Or interestingly, maybe your #1's are all over the place — but everyone agrees on #2 or #5. These might be the more prudent actors to go after because you might get shot down on your top choices anyway — and that could take months. It might serve your momentum to get a "Yes!" NOW on a B+ than to wait a year and a half to not get a "No" on your "A1" choice.

Continually refine your actor hit list. Then go after them. Try their agent, manager, anyone you know who's ever worked with them. I teach a whole series of classes on "Power Networking."[5] There are a ton of strategies to implement.

When you submit your pitch packages to talent agents of stars or actors you'd like to attach, look at the rest of their stable. Who else might be right for your other roles? Consider customizing just your cast wish list page to headshots of the talent they make commissions off of. It might really motivate the recipient of each submission.

You can swap this page out in your constantly evolving pitch package for each agent who reps a major star you want. You might be surprised at the depth of talent they have to offer. And how your traction accelerates when their commission goes from 10 percent on one actor to 10 percent on a dozen (not to mention, the grief relief factor of getting a significant percentage of their roster working!). That makes clients and bosses happy in addition to wallets.

Alternately, as suggested above: see who else among their stable they might recommend. They might have actors they're trying to lure from competitors or there might be some excellent talent among the other agents in their same firm that you hadn't even considered that they could assist you in securing. Or their spouse's or friend's clients. Another agent might come on board and help you package the project, becoming invested in its success. Maybe even a manager who wants to come on board as a producer. But be careful: you can become uncomfortably beholden to one agent who can then manipulate you, holding out the talent you really want as a bargaining chit[6] to force you to load your cast with actors you might not be interested in at all. It's a complicated, political dance card. But . . . unfortunately: you need a name.

The Next "Insert Star Name Here"

Jennifer Lawrence, Shailene Woodley and Ellen Page don't need your movie. But the *next* up-and-coming actor does. Pepper your cast wish list with actors who might be just on the cusp of breaking out — or ripe for a career resurgence. Quentin Tarantino's *Pulp Fiction* made John Travolta cool and hip again. *The Wrestler* rekindled Mickey Rourke's career (and arguably Marissa Tomei's, too). Risky independent films like *Rushmore*, *Lost in Translation* and *Moonrise Kingdom* continue to make us renew our appreciation for the depth and breadth of Bill Murray's acting skills beyond his comedic talents. Shane Black's fun 2005 *Kiss Kiss Bang Bang* (and *Ally McBeal* before that) helped put Robert Downey, Jr. squarely back on the map and helped launch him to the stratospheric blockbuster *Iron Man* franchise and fun *Tropic Thunder* romp. And the rest, as they say, is history.

If you're lucky enough to have a casting director, she'll know a lot of the inside scoop but you can (and should) do your own research, too. Who on your short list of actors is surprisingly "bubbling up" on the industry scoreboards? Dig. Maybe she's up to be the lead in the next graphic novel tentpole adaptation? Maybe she's got three pilots in the can? Any one of which could be a break out hit and if you could lock her up for her summer hiatus now, you'll be in great stead. Maybe she's in a low-budget darling gaining traction and attracting heat on the festival circuit? Elizabeth Olsen's admirable dramatic debut in the 2011 $3 million feature, *Martha Marcy May Marlene*, garnered 62 nominations and 22 wins. If you were paying attention to the Indie Spirit Awards in 2012, she might have long been on some of your short lists.

Pay attention to who the industry is paying attention to because that's who you're gonna turn around and sell right back to. Sometimes it's not just marquee value. Sometimes it can come down to just pure talent. Just by virtue of the caliber of cast, you will raise their expectations. Who are the Hollywood foreign press acknowledging with their Golden Globes? If distributors see names like David Morse, Lupita Nyong'o, Miles Teller, Edward James Olmos, Melissa Leo, Freddie Highmore and Catherine O'Hara, their confidence in the promise of the film's performances will automatically be enhanced.

Who's on the cover or inside *People* magazine? What about *Teen People*? *People en Español*? Who're the most popular actors in the territories your film is projected to do well in? Take a look at their awards shows and see who's most popular there.

Character Breakdowns

If you are fortunate enough to find yourself dealing with someone in a position to help you who not only *cares* who you creatively envision for the roles but is willing to contribute to the refinement of your cast wish list or help you figure out some alternates, they're going to need character breakdowns.

Character breakdowns are brief one-sentence to one-paragraph descriptions of the characters.

Actors scan them to see which roles they might want to audition for. Agents and managers peruse them to see who among their stable they should submit. Everyone in the project uses them as a jumping off point for their own character development. The Glam Squad tracks their "looks" from wardrobe to scars, bruises, tattoos and facial hair.

The production designer and art director contributing to what kind of a home or office they might occupy — and what it would be decorated with. The armorer and transportation department might reference them to suggest personality revealing weapons or vehicles.

You'll see breakdowns sent out by casting services that often give race or hair color. I'm always baffled by this. If Meryl Streep wanted to play your brunette . . . uhm . . . she could dye her hair. Wouldn't you be quick to whip out your word processing skills to change that one word? Or what if bald Patrick Stewart wanted the role. Why would you rule out actors you never even thought of? There are already enough stumbling blocks and hurdles in our business — don't add any inadvertent reasons for anyone to pass. Capture the essence of your characters in a thumbnail sketch so that the actors — regardless of race, age, height, physical abilities or differences, sexual orientation, etc. can be empowered to bring their artistic interpretation to light.

I try to write wildly specific yet very open, color-blind character descriptions — and, when possible: gender-neutral and age-vague. Obviously, the specificity of storytelling usually dictates the age and culture of your protagonist and antagonist, especially, be called out — but these roles are likely going to be attachments versus auditioned. These roles will be modified internally based on available options. For the rest of the cast that will actually audition, leave your options open.

The chef of the casting kitchen, a fantastic casting director will have lots of fun experimenting by mixing beloved comfort options with new, exotic additions in ways you might not ever have conceived of but you know "just work" when you are presented with their cast ideas. This also frees up the "playing field" for the best actor to nail it in the audition.

Please visit HeatherHale.com/Samples/CharacterBreakdowns for some samples.

 A TV series bible could have write-ups ranging from a sentence to several pages, for the leads, especially. In *Wife, My Fiancée & Me*, a spec sitcom I co-wrote with the hysterical Rob Foster, the three lead write-ups are longer. Kind of a *Three's Company* meets *Green Card*, we left the ethnicity of the "wife" character flexible but she has to be from a different culture where she's at risk (and afraid) of deportation. Without her expat culture, the comedy from our illegal marriage premise won't pay off. The supporting character descriptions are more what you might see in the traditionally circulated breakdowns but still, none of the descriptions dictate age, body type or ethnicity: they just give the actor an idea of the essence of the character they could embody with their vessel. Keep your options as wide open as possible (without diluting necessary areas of conflict or tension).

Tiered Proposed Cast Strategies

In spite of all the financial and marketing realities, indie directors still hope and dream to cast in keeping with their heart and mind's eye. Modulate your creative desires with what you can realistically accomplish. Find the intersection between all those best-case scenarios. Instead of compromises (where everyone ends up with what nobody ever wanted) — don't "settle": negotiate. Opt for concessions where the give and take is between all sorts of variables of differing values and significance.

Most packages feature big name stars. Tier a few proposed alternate scenarios. In addition to the cast list the ISAs can sell (that you'd be thrilled with any lucky breaks you're graced with), also maintain a list of "gettable" (i.e. more affordable/accessible) B-level actors. They might even be more motivated to help you promote the film as it'll be more important to them and their careers.

Ultimately, you'll end up with a patchwork of both. Leave room to be surprised by unknown talent. Don't be so set on your number one choice that you can't wrap your mind around anyone else in the role. Be wary of what the industry calls "temp love," an affliction usually in reference to filmmakers falling in love with the temporary tract an editor lays down as a placeholder until the composer scores and the music supervisor secures the rights to the key songs for the soundtrack. I'm sure the same occurs in key art, where you get so used to your original, holding-pattern image, that it's tough to appreciate a whole different approach. It happens with cast wish lists, too. The writer has envisioned actor A since they wrote "Fade In." The director has always wanted to work with actor B. The casting director is sure that actor C is just about to break out as a star. The producer has relationships to actor D while the ISA really wants actors X, Y and Z. And above all that: keep your options open to falling in love with an actor who surprises you all with a fresh, rich, surprising, layered interpretation. But never lose sight of the profit ball. It doesn't matter how great a job every member of your cast and crew does if no one ever sees it.

No one needs to see a sample yearbook page of all the usual fund- and distribution-attracting suspects' headshots we're all lining up and taking numbers to wait to hear back from. It changes from year to year but we all know who they are. And they make for laughably generic pitch packages. Don't do that. It insults everyone's intelligence and reveals your ignorance. Customize various approaches for whoever you're pitching to. If you're pitching to an actress' agent, show her as your only option for the lead with three different options for her love interest. If you're showing her prospective family tree, put her at the nucleus surrounded by her best apparent genetic matches. It might sound like a lot of work (and it is), but it's really only swapping out square images (how nice if all the headshots were of a uniform size!) and it's far less work than cold calling the next talent agent and starting from scratch again.

If you're making a Pay or Play Offer, you have to have a start date, rate and other terms of the contract worked out but when you're pitching for attachments at the pre-funded stage, sometimes the most you can get (or want) is some credible proof via a **Letter of Intent** (or Interest), maintaining flexibility for everyone. You don't want to be so eager that you attach an actor with zero foreign appeal who not only adds no value to your project — but worse, locks up the role, blocking out an actor who might've been an asset. Remember there is a difference between your wish list for *attachments* versus your actor wish list for *auditions*. A solid casting director — especially one you can afford and collaborate with who works in this budget, genre and target audience and/or who has worked with many on your attachment wish list — can be priceless.

Please visit www.HeatherHale.com/Samples/LOI for a sample LOI.

BIOS

Take the time to write polished biographies for all your Above the Line Players and Key Attachments. Sometimes we're the last piece of the pie we remember to market but these events establish long-term relationships. You'll end up in databases. They might copy and paste your bio into their smart phone contact managers and start tracking you. You want to proactively build relationships with the right caliber of professionals who share your sensibilities and work ethic. The time spent on this marketing copy will serve you well as it will be repurposed and updated throughout your career: for your business plan, investor presentations, your many websites and social media footprints, press kits, when you speak on panels, press releases, etc. Snippets will be lifted exactly as written for articles or to intro you on TV, radio and podcast interviews — so don't slop this together at the last minute.

Your bios should ideally all be about the same length (or again, tiered in relation to priority). They should be relevant to the project not only in life experience but also in tone. Don't regurgitate boilerplate from one project to the next. You've got all sorts of different facets. *What's relevant now? To this particular project? What earned you the right to tell this story? Why will you tell it better than anyone else?*

 On *My Wife, My Fiancée and Me*, we made a joke in my co-writer's bio that since there probably wasn't a statute of limitations on felonies, this wasn't ripped from his true life story, per se . . . but that he was "intimately involved in an eerily similar" Green Card marriage scenario. This established not only his first-hand expertise but honored the tone and provided a great ice-breaker.

 For *Malibu Wishes*, a sitcom billed as *Fawlty Towers Does Celebrity Rehab*, we acknowledged that my beloved (but sadly now late co-writer), was "no stranger to the rehab communities of Malibu." To establish his credibility in the art and economic milieus (one character is a Jim Cramer-like economic pundit while his love interest is a New Age shrink), we shared how he had "just patented the newest economic indicator" and that "his own successful contemporary fine art career was launched through art therapy." All of these little details are what make your ownership and resonance with the project stand out.

If you feel vain or awkward writing about yourself, hire a professional to do this critical copywriting for you. At worst, write one another's. But these blurbs will follow you, so make sure they are accurate and reflect you in an authentic style that you feel is professional and appropriate to your brand.

Please feel free to visit www.HeatherHale.com/Samples/Bios for sample bios.

EXECUTIVE SUMMARY

Like your logline that is so critical and rewritten a zillion times, or your one sheet that is done after all the creative has been polished, your Executive Summary is the last piece written of your business plan or pitch package. While this might seem counter intuitive, you are best served to wait until you have all the details worked out and can ad copy your overview, highlighting all the pertinent details. Every word, sentence, paragraph, page, table and image reflects your professionalism — and will follow you. How many times have you seen typos on the covers of self-published books? Does that inspire your confidence in the wordsmith within? Take your time. Do it right. Make sure it's accurate.

LET'S TALK ABOUT COMPS, MAN

WHAT'S A "COMP"?

"Comp" is short for *comp*arable. It means projects that came before yours that yours can be likened to either financially or creatively for comparative purposes.

If you have ever bought a house, then you have likely seen a real estate appraisal. Real estate appraisals compare the house you're contemplating buying (or the property you're soliciting a financier to loan you the money to buy) to as similar-as-possible homes, sold or listed for sale as recently as possible, as "competing" inventory to establish or defend its market value (hopefully at or above your negotiated purchase price). Ideally, these comparable homes should be as close to the same age, square footage and lot size, with similar quality of features as the subject property being scrutinized. These residential samplings should be in tight price and geographic ranges. Lenders analyze recent sales as indicators of current market performance as well as the amount of inventory currently available on the market (and the average number of days in the sales cycle for homes in that neighborhood to close) to project future supply and demand.

So, let's pretend you're buying a condo on the beach in Santa Monica. Your appraiser would survey all the escrows that closed, let's say, within the last month, ideally within less than a mile radius (or at least within the same subdivision or neighborhood) within a tight price point spread. As I'm sure you know, the property values, safety, and desirability of many cities can change dramatically just one street over. Certainly in a few miles. But if you're buying a ranch in say, Texas, the next closest homestead might be miles to acres, so the appraiser might need to broaden her search to focus on properties in the same school district or county. Homes in a historic district might not turn over for generations, so the most recent comp could be 20 years old. The appraiser must do her best to discriminate and contrast the most relevant representatives from the broadest swath of inventory she has access to.

Film and television comps are a lot like that. There are financial comps that you use not necessarily to project what your film will do but to average benchmarks of what films *like* yours (for whatever reason) have done recently to give a sense of that piece of the business pie. You might also use more extensive creative comps to illustrate historical genre trends, a bit like an antique provenance (which is a letter of authenticity that verifies the backstory of a valuable piece's origin, documents the chain of owners and provides supplemental research that might be of interest to prospective buyers). These films or television programs might be too old to realistically factor into your financial analysis but they can still serve as great touch points to orient your investor or other interested parties, especially to give a sense of your intended visual style or theme, to demonstrate the popularity and characteristics of the genre or its demographics — and highlight some of its relevant success stories.

Thus, the comps you need to research are precursors of what came before your project that will be used by an equity investor to dissect the assumptions you have made and/or for distributors or sales agents to see your opinion of where you think your project might fit in the marketplace (and if they agree).

Comps should not be used as templates to blue-sky[7] revenue projections externally but rather, they are far more valuable to reverse engineer internally what your realistic production budget actually *should be*. Comps also provide a microscope to help you identify the successful players in that specific sliver of the industry and help you build your hit list of potential partners to target. They can also be excellent case studies: everything from their key art, loglines and taglines to their social media and advertising campaigns to their distribution strategies.

RESEARCH RESOURCES

With industry subscription services like IMDBPro, Variety Insight, Baseline/Gracenote and a myriad free online tools such as BoxOfficeMojo.com, The-Numbers.com and pro.boxoffice.com, among others, the resources available today blow away what producers had just a decade ago. Use this information to truly pencil out prudent decisions.

CAUTIONARY TALE: PRICE POINT

 A screenwriting friend went off and made a million dollar sci-fi movie, sure that she could sell it to the Syfy Channel. When she brought it to me — in the can — during a four-year period during which I had access to a special NBC/IFTA independent development fund, she was chagrined to discover that their price point (at that time) for an independently produced MOW[8] was closer to a quarter of that. She was (understandably) crestfallen. And while my heart went out to her, we both knew: it was her own fault. Had she done *any* advance research to find out what the current market would bear for that type of programming versus what she willy-nilly[9] thought she needed to "execute her vision" — *before* executing it, she could've probably been far more judicious with the script; enforced massive production efficiencies; perhaps even gotten some skin-in-the-game equity deferral commitments from some of her stars and department heads; and backed into what the market would bear, turning that into a success instead of a really expensive "learning experience." Maybe she could have even pre-sold it to Syfy — which might have triggered a few international pre-sale commitments — and thus raised the budget back up to what would facilitate her vision. Who knows? She will certainly know better next time. But for now, it's a vanity DVD collecting dust on her shelf in a huge worldwide cemetery of such well intentioned but ill-informed bursts of enthusiasm.

I get hired to write a lot of business plans and I'm always appalled when a client "just" wants me to "do it all." Sure, I'm happy to make money like the next worker bee but do they really want to walk into their meeting, slide my pretty document across the conference room table and just do the unrelated song and dance they were going to do anyway? You really need to *design your* strategy. Personally. Even if you get professional help (that's great! Hire me, please!), it is incumbent upon you to understand every single number and step — from script page to project management, schedule to budget. Work your way down those hypothetical rabbit holes and u-turn out of the dead-ends *on paper*. Play *Dig Dug*[10] with every possible scenario in the safety of your computer, journal and your imagination before you spend your or someone else's money — and a good chunk of your life — on untested theories. It doesn't guarantee you'll pick the right strategies, but you have far better odds of eliminating a lot of the least promising approaches and have a better feel for what you're up against going in — and adjusting as predicted warning signs pop up.

Shy of actually executing your plan and either failing or succeeding in the real world, the best return on your money and effort, the lowest risk, highest upside way for you to test if your plan will work is to walk through every possible scenario on paper. Using spreadsheets, flow charts, heck even just mind mapping in a notebook: envision your game plan. Visualize the phases and steps. Where are your foreseeable bottlenecks? Highest risk time periods? Is there a point of no return just like for your protagonist? What are the potential pitfalls you might have to overcome? It becomes glaringly obvious if you are aligning with the wrong people who bring nothing to your table. What do you really need? Do they really offer it?

Who's pitching it? You. You need to know these numbers, deal points, salient sales strengths backwards and forwards. Far better for you to be challenged by non-threatening, supportive team players who are only poking holes in your plan to make you reassess and defend it from every angle than fall flat and get a rejection from a precious contact you worked hard to earn the right just to pitch to. Before you risk any real money, embarrassment, time, precious resources, jeopardize professional relationships or career traction, shore it up for the big leagues. Customize your presentations to their wants and needs just as you practice and hone your creative pitches.

Some of my best business plans no one ever read: they just empowered the client to make — and close — an amazing pitch. Consider these master's theses, Spring training to get ready for the major leagues, staged readings for your live premiere. How many years of training come down to moments of excellence judged in split seconds? This is your Olympic training, gearing all your preparation and resources toward that one golden-ring opportunity.

Even if you have a slate business plan, keep it compartmentalized enough to easily extract the individual project proposals in segments that can be presented one-by-one or as a mini-slate directly relevant to opportunities or parties in a position to do something with specific assets or to the tastes and sensibilities ascertained about a specific equity investor. Nothing else in your overall plan is their business (or quite frankly, likely of interest to them).

See www.HeatherHale/3DCakes for a customized (and anonymized) equity investor proposal for a reality TV show done as a time buy.[11]

Now that you've done your homework, in your business plan or pitch package, describe who (specifically) your audience is and how (exactly) you're going to get your material to them. And how is everyone involved going to make money off that? And when? Sounds ridiculously obvious but you'd be amazed how many so-called business plans skip these all-important elements. What the investor is most interested in: *When and how will I get my capital back and see a profit?*

Cautionary Tale: Don't Be Sloppy

This is hard to believe but painfully true: I can't tell you how many business plans I've received myself where I can actually recognize the original plan it came from — and flip to pages where I suspect they didn't even bother to correct the typos from the decade-old source document that's been making the rounds. Yeah, it's that bad. It's that obvious. Don't be sloppy.

Cautionary Tale: Don't Be Lazy

What about cloned "budgets?" How many times have we read on industry Internet groups: "Anyone got a million dollar budget I could use? My investor is asking for one." Wow. Just . . . wow. Yet, it happens. Every day. I'm not kidding. That's a bit like asking a room full of doctors: "Anyone got a diagnosis for me? Or a prescription? I'm ready to run with it!" "Sure. Here. Have at it! And good luck!" No wonder most independent films don't make money. But there's no excuse for any of that nonsense anymore. There is too much information out there and too many resources. Don't be lazy.

Spell out your Social Media Plan. Demonstrate that you have started to do the heavy lifting — and it's working. And what you're asking for is just to catch some wind beneath your wings to blow it up. Whether you write a business plan or not (and I, of course, highly recommend that you do — and rewrite it constantly — whether or not you ever show it to anyone) — or just create pitch decks[12] from it, you should think about these key questions:

> **For Each Project:**
> **What are you doing?**
> **Why?**
>
> **For Each Market:**
> **Why are you going?**
> **What are you trying to accomplish?**

Before you attend a market or a festival, or truly, before you even shoot one second of video, maybe even before you write one page of your screenplay: think your business venture through from beginning to end. I know that sounds like blowing all the fun pixie dust off the magic of movies and creativity but this is show *business*. *Business* is the transaction of goods and services, usually for *money*. It's what most people are going to the markets for. Your plan should "pencil out" every which way. And, if it's for profit: it should make money. It's all about risk mitigation — proving you can do what you say you can do.

If, for your own self-expression, you want to journal or do performance art or staged readings of your slam poetry, there are 99-seat theaters around the world far more appropriate as a forum for your self-examination and revelation. But if you're creating content for profit, to build a career, change the world or leave a legacy: you need a plan.

Analyze Your Comps

Once you've selected a dozen — even up to 50 — comps, you want to narrow it down to about 5, let's say. Really consider how well these films or projects did domestically and abroad. What were the most successful territories for them? *Did the feature comedies do surprisingly well in the Netherlands? Did the one-hour crime dramas notably excel in Germany?* Were there overlapping elements across their key art? Where do their target audiences converge? Diverge? If it's a television project, what other like formats are there out there for what you're proposing? How, where and why were they successful? Can you figure that out? (because you're gonna be asked). If you're working up statistics for a feature film: how many screens did all or the best comps launch on? Peak at? Average? How many weeks did they last in the theaters? What were their per screen averages?

Throw out aberrations that will skew your numbers. Average or consider the mode[13] of the most recent, accurate comps. This won't illuminate a crystal ball but it will empower you to sit opposite an investor with a straight face, having earned the confidence to know what you're talking about (at least on this project). She doesn't have to *accept* your selections or assumptions — but that's on her to suss out. You will have made a reasonably defended case. Nobody knows anything. You can only do the very best you can with the resources available to you (the same ones available to all of us — including your investors). But, odds are, throughout this process, you will have made an infinite number of tiny adjustments along the way based on insights you gleaned that will have inevitably sharpened your ax.

 MODIFIED LOW BUDGET MUSIC COMPS

A bit like the Texas ranchland or historic home, there weren't a slew of recent $700k films that got distribution for us to compare and contrast for *Once Again*, our SAG Modified Low Budget, non-linear rock'n roll romance. There was a dearth of "comps" in our rural low budget arena. But we did manage to find one very close at $1 million, *Once*, a $150k musical romance that did great and two others under $3.3 million — as close as we could reasonably get.

See HeatherHale.com/OnceAgain.

Whiplash was especially relevant because like our film, its protagonist is a drummer — with that same sort of *Black Swan* artistic obsession. *Blue Valentine* was a relevant non-linear example while *Winter's Bone* had the dark, gritty, drug and death elements. And they were mostly within six years of when we were pitching it.

We used their number of screens and weeks in the theater to make best guess estimates for our own projected performance. We also pointed out the critical acclaim so many of these films enjoyed. Not that we will necessarily be in their league but it shows prestige films can come from our range. And all their distributors and sales agents became the obvious starting point for our hit list as they have a proven track record in helping to create festival darlings, heat and momentum and demonstrated expertise with the exact type of film we're working on.

This information reveals clues. Really think about it. Sleep on it. Talk about it. Who were the financiers, sales agents, domestic and international distributors, television outlets? Does any entity stand out as a leader of this pack to help you refine your hit list ever further? These comps are as much for you and your plan as for your investors. Whether anyone ever reads your plan or not, *you* need to *have written* it. And by that I mean: you need to have made your mistakes *in erasable pencil* or in editable software.

Business plans, budgets, schedules, proposals, to me, are all living, breathing documents that can be just as creative and fascinating as the screenplays, key art, finished films and television shows they represent. Just as a screenplay or film or episode is never ever truly done, you should constantly be evolving your thinking and honing in closer to the sweet spot. On paper at least.

SCHEDULE

I'm forever amazed when someone says they have a budget but not a schedule. *How is that possible?* You have to break the script down into how many shoot days you're gonna need, a day out of days (for how many days each) for how many actors and extras you need to cast and ballpark how many pages you're going to shoot per day before you can even begin to get an estimate. How many vehicles, animals, stunts, special effects shots are there? Does the project require any major or unique equipment like cranes, process trailers, drones, honey wagons, portable toilets, parking, tables, chairs, utensils and shade tarps for the moveable feast of catered cast and crew meals? How many cameras will you need? And what kind? What size grip truck? What's on it? How deep is your crew? Are you union or non-union? Which unions? Under which union contracts? Can you estimate your shot ratio? How much storage space and processing power will you need in video village? In post? Do you need a DIT?[14] How much raw footage will your editor have to bin and plow through to make initial selections? All of this impacts your labor and equipment costs.

Either they haven't a clue how their script would translate to a schedule or a budget — or they simply picked a number out of a hat. Maybe that's all the producer's got. That's her credit card limit or what she's saved or sold her house for — and they are simply going to make the film for what they've got. So be it. Or, maybe she's analyzed the comps and decided that's what the budget *should* be — so they have to reverse engineer the script to make it work — and schedule *that*.

There are books, videos and classes galore on how to schedule or budget a film or TV show but that's beyond the scope of this book. But let's say you've tagged your script and used your breakdown sheets to board a ballpark schedule. Even if it's gonna change a zillion times between now and when you're actually in prep — and probably even during principal — there are a lot of uses for this deliverable beyond its primary production purpose.

I like to include schedules in my pitch packages or proposals to give the investors and collaborator a visual representation of our chronological plan and the anticipated sequence of events — kind of like a Gantt chart for our product and workflow to establish realistic expectations. But I don't use the old-school strip board version of the horizontal or vertical striped computer print outs or screen grabs. Unless you're in the business or actually physically producing this project, those schedules can be hard to read for the uninitiated and actually don't really mean much unless you're caught up in the minutia of the everyday because it's all constantly changing moving parts anyway. Far more relevant for an investor, brand or community is to put your schedule into an easily understandable context.

SHOOT SCHEDULES

Shoot schedules can be unpredictable and malleable, like a symphony of maestro'd logistics. Thus, until the actual dates are locked, I typically just put ballpark week numbers or estimated quarter so I don't have to keep re-doing these packages every time there's a change. I also try to give a sense of the *type* of activities that will be going on, where and why rather than assuming they have any reference for all that's involved. Sometimes this really engages their curiosity. If they are a real estate investor or a dentist exploring this asset class for the first time, they will appreciate being respectfully oriented and included. If they're a pro, they can quickly scan to see that you've got all your ducks in a reasonably ordered row.

Examples: www.HeatherHale.com/Samples/Schedules

CONTAINED LOCATION THRILLER

On *Absolute Killers*, we did a few things right. Way rural, about an hour outside of Charlotte, North Carolina, we shot this under-a-million-dollar feature thriller on two Red cameras. When people looked at our schedule, they'd scoff and say there was no way we were going to be able to shoot 25 locations in 18 days. But we did. Without any mid-day crew moves, which is a rule I always try to honor. We did this by rewriting the script to fit the locations we could secure and adjusting our central location dramatically to suit our needs. The investor, a doctor, and the author of the underlying self-published novel, bought a bank building that he intended to use as his future medical facilities after our shoot but allowed us free reign during pre-production and principal photography before he redecorated it and opened for business. We re-wrote the script to fit the location and we used every square inch of that property non-stop.

The story had several characters in the witness protection program. So, suddenly, one of them got a job in her new life at a bank. We figured we might as well use that long counter, storefront windows and big safe in the background for some shot. Why not? We dressed a couple rooms as our main characters' US Marshals' and District Attorney's offices. The conference room was overhauled to look like an investigation war room. We dressed one tiny room with vending machines to look like a police break room and the hallway to look like a prison hallway where we moved an expositional scene and had an inmate take a call on a jail payphone.

We actually built a police interrogation room in the middle of the bank lobby with a breakaway wall so we could do some cool camera moves through the double glass. Our production offices were all here along with our craft services. We ate under tents out in the big parking lot where we built our sets and parked our honey wagons and grip trucks. This contained proximity eliminated many hours of schlepping and loading and unloading equipment because we could simply lock it up overnight. It also allowed us to conveniently pre-light, set dress and strike sets on an almost constant rolling nature as so many sets were just a door or two apart. As we wrapped each set, our production offices and break space expanded. The stars of this creative efficiency were without a doubt, the Prop Tarts: Sara, Sophia, Jenny and Sean out of Burlington, North Carolina.

BUDGET

What's misleading is that usually the film "budget" that is distributed is almost always "just" the physical production budget (i.e. principal photography, pre- and post-production) — what used to be called the "master" (print) — the cost of getting the *film* into the can and ready to hand off to some other department to market and distribute. But that's obviously only half the picture — and battle — and true budget. Unfortunately, many independent producers don't bother to think beyond this 13.1-mile mark of their marathon.

It's an odd business to be in, indeed, where the world over knows your manufacturing costs — and ostensibly some version of your financial "success" — before even your first day on the market. Odd indeed. And what's even funnier is: no one's telling the truth about any number anywhere! And yet everyone obsesses over them constantly! Producers wring their hands in poverty when negotiating expenses with reps, crew or vendors, yet in the very next call, might inflate what's been spent to drive the perceived value up to potential buyers. It's all smoke and mirrors.

It's prudent for independent filmmakers to take a note from the studios who are, undeniably, marketing and distribution masters. Of course, shave your production budget down to the bone but, if possible, match those funds with an equal marketing and advertising budget, so people will actually be able see your finished product — and maybe you'll all make your money back and achieve the parallel goals of profit and praise. Many independent films don't even bother to set aside 10 percent for marketing or advertising. This will leave you vulnerable to any ambulance-chasing scavenger laying in wait for you, exhausted, at the production marathon finish line.

Try to budget — and protect — some sort of allocation to fund festival trips, money to hire a producer of marketing and distribution or a publicist or fund your own social media team. Yeah, sure, you can do it all yourself bucan you? Really? Wouldn't some help (or sleep or more expertise) be nice? Haven't you worked for free, figuring it out on the fly as you go along, long enough? Wouldn't it be nice to have some decent advice from someone who knows more than you? Who knows the ropes and is not incentivized to give you any kind of slanted advice? It's like the difference between having a commissioned financial services salesman pitch you on the insurance products he makes the most on versus a fee-based financial advisor who truly only has your best interests at heart because she's not making any hidden back-ends. She's just telling you what she'd do with your money if it were hers. Treat everyone's money like it was yours. Don't cut so many corners that you're just being frugal with the minutia expenses while being blind to the big picture.

Production Budget has Zero Correlation to Box Office

There is no perfect, magical budget number. You can't search the Internet for "the" budget to box office formula. *Budget has zero correlation to box office.* Any movie can be made for any budget. Literally. A special effects sci-fi project *could* get made (horrifically or terrifically) on a microbudget just as a top-heavy, bloated studio project could bankrupt a studio and still flop. Any movie. Any budget. Nothing to do with box office.

That said, there are sweet spots to shoot for as you reverse engineer the right price point for your film based on your comps. En vogue budgets vary like fashion styles but some repeating patterns have presented themselves through lots of independent feature film budgets and box office over the past 15 years. "No Man's Land" (where filmmakers who have gone before you have lost their shirts) seem to appear consistently in some budget brackets. Tread carefully in these places detailed below. Thar be dragons here .[15]

Table 23.2 Heather Hale Productions' Union Low-Budget Matrix

HHP Matrix of Overlapping Union Low-Budget Contracts

	Micro	Ultra Low	#2 Modified Low	#3 DIY Low	"Do-It-Yourself" (High)	#4 Low Budget	Studio
Budget ranges	0–$50K / $50k–$200k	< 250k / < $500k	< $700k / $700k–$1,050,000*	< $1.1 m / < $1.162m**	$1.03m+ / < $1.2m / < $1.5m / < $2.5m	$2.5m+ / > $2.6m / $2.6m+ / $3.75m / > $4.4m / $5.5m+ / < $7.5m / $7.5m+ / $9.9m	Sale or Co-Pro ↖
SAG	No to Micro Budget	ULB	SAG Modified Low Budget	SAG Low Budget		SAG Basic Agreement	
IATSE			IATSE Ultra Low Budget		IATSE ULB Tier 1	IATSE LB 2 / IATSE LB 3	
DGA		DGA Low Budget 1a	DGA Low Budget 1b	DGA Low Budget 2	DGA LB 3		
WGA		WGA Low Budget Deferred		WGA Low Budget	WGA Basic		

*Diversity in Casting Incentive; **Background Actor Incentive

SAG = Screen Actors Guild

DGA = Directors Guild

WGA = Writers Guild

IATSE = The International Association of Theatrical Stage Employees, Moving Picture Technicians, Artists and Allied Crafts of the United States, Its Territories and Canada, AFL-CIO, CLC

ULB = Ultra Low Budget

MLB = Modified Low Budget

LB = Low Budget

B = Basic Agreement

D = Deferred

There are also some "sweet spots": prudent intersections where variables converge and offer the highest market potential with the greatest risk containment. There seems to be a tipping point as projects crest the $1 million US threshold. It becomes false economy to keep shelling out cold hard cash to advertise, for marketing and promotions, prints (when even relevant anymore), DVD burning, jewel case, printing, shipping and handling expenses (all of which are disappearing with the digital distribution revolution), not to mention the oversight and management of all the middlemen. If you don't have name talent capable of sales-servicing that financial burden, your income may never surpass your expenses.

Of course, every project and release window is different. But many successful modern producers strive to stay safely in the "Do It Yourself (Low)" realm, where their worst case scenario risk can be covered by self-distributing online via your own website, crowdsourced screenings and clever festival event marketing to proactively team-promote a tightly budgeted project with a boutique distributor who will really work to create some festival pedigree and buzz and get it out there prudently. *Or* leap frog your budget up high enough (over $2.5m but under $9.9m) that you can afford the level of cast, production values (stunts, special effects) that would warrant the marketing spend to help you compete on the larger world stage.

Reason enough to perhaps leapfrog that and stay safely in the SAG Modified Low Budget of $700k. Or at least stay under the $1.16 million figure (if you max out all their diversified cast and background incentives).[16]

But once you cross that pivotal "just over a million" threshold, you enter the higher risk DIY territory where your expenses can compound much faster than your projected revenues. Of course this is all "just on paper" — but there are sufficient precedents. You might be best served to stay under that $1.162 million benchmark or leapfrog into their $2.5 million standard low-budget range where you'll have sufficient discretionary funds available to make some decent pay or play offers to attach name level talent that could build some precious momentum towards profit. If you're lucky, then, *maybe*, you can cover the exhibitors' 50 percent, your sales agents' 35 percent, all the fringes and fees, unions' residuals and royalties, IRS taxes . . . and — *remind me why we do this again?*

ULTRA, MODIFIED AND LOW-BUDGET SWEET SPOTS TO CONSIDER

$250,000	Three 6-day work weeks (18-day shoot)
$250k–$500k	*Can be dicey . . .*
<$700k	Five 5-day work weeks (25-day shoot) SAG MLB, IATSE ULB
	Optional: DGA 1a or 1b and/or WGA LB
$1.162m	Five 5-day work weeks (25-day shoot) SAG MLB (w/l), IATSE ULB
	Optional: DGA 1b (maybe 2), WGA LB
$1.163m–$2.49m	*Thar Be Dragons Here . . .*
$2.5m–$9.9m	SAG Basic, IATSE LB Tier 1, 2, or 3
	Optional: DGA LB 2, 3, or 4 or WGA LB

It may look like a shell game and producers get a terrible rap but what other industry changes all the rules on you mid-stream? The second your budget spend tips an arbitrary dollar amount because you hired one extra person, couldn't control the sun or even treated your cast and crew to a special reward meal for a hard day's work? But, them's the rules we must play by until something improves. We're a bit like Catherine Zeta Jones bending through that laser security maze in *Entrapment*. It's like a huge Rubik's Cube or game of Sudoku — and I don't know how anyone ever wins.

Another thing I find funny: Hollywood is one of the very few industries in the world where the Average Joe Casual Observer not only thinks he can do all our jobs better than we can — but worse — that it's completely appropriate — and that they are entitled to know — what your hard costs of manufacture, expenses, income and profit are. You'd never walk into someone's hair salon or auto-mechanic shop or restaurant or hedge fund office and say: "Open up your books! I wanna look under the hood!" But all day, every day, producers are asked — *by everyone!*: "What's your budget?" It's NOYB![17]

Independent producers are so accustomed to scraping by with so little and being so resourceful — for so long — calling in favors from all the friends who've called them in from us (because we have one another's backs and love what we do), that we forget to retroactively add back in our *years* of unpaid development, our sweat equity expertise.

Not to mention, when calculating a film's "gross," are we given credit for box office *plus* product placement? No. Are the studios' "wins" accurately calculated as their box office *minus* their marketing spend? Uhm . . . no. And since no one's sharing digital sales stats transparently, how are we to ever accurately gauge what a "success" or a "failure" online was? Much less predict one? Where's that level playing field? It's pretty much just an uneven minefield.

What about being credited for our fair market values with what our wages *should* have been? Or actually ever getting a check for that illusory but promised deferred pay? How nice would it be if we could build into our budgets the true research and development and manufacture costs of the content *before* the unions or middlemen got their hands in the pie? Ironically, half the time, the funds would actually be going directly to our union brethren who are chipping in with the favors anyway! But these systems put us unnecessarily at odds with one another. I don't understand — especially in America — why an independent business owner can't simply make — and keep — a fair deal with the people she wants to be in business with without having to reconcile four different, completely contradictory sets of contracts.

Please see www.HeatherHale.com/Samples/Budgets

~~Prints and~~ Advertising

As fewer and fewer movies are released on celluloid, the former industry standard requirement of and expenses for actual 35mm film prints has decreased dramatically — in some cases, it's now non-existent. In the old days (the 1980s), budgets used to allocate approximately $2,000 US for *each* film master. Multiply this by the number of theaters your film is screening in (2,000 used to be a benchmark for a wide release), add shipping and handling (and related delays), and you can quickly see what a significant impact so many cinemas switching to digital has had on producers' budgets.

Raging debates as to cinematic integrity aside, this advent also raises the stakes on piracy as that many more fingers have free and relatively sequestered access to the digital copies that are so quick and easy to replicate. Digital capture, post-production and distribution is porous and vulnerable to thievery from the very first shot through video village airwaves to the couriers who deliver DVDs and hard drives through your entire post-production workflow to any theater goer or employee with a smart-phone. These are all pressing issues but to keep us on topic: for most independent producers: there's almost no "**P**" in "**P&A**" anymore. Most independent films aren't factoring prints into their budgets anymore.

As to the "**A**": on average, studios typically spend an amount equal to their entire production budget on marketing and advertising: 50/50. Of course, this can vary from 50 percent to 150 percent — it's not uncommon for a hundred million dollar studio tent pole to spend easily that on marketing and advertising. Independents rarely have this luxury. Usually, we're lucky to have 10–15 percent of the budget allocated to marketing, advertising and distribution costs, expanding this (if possible) as a rolling commitment as a percentage off future revenues generated.

Think Outside the Schedule and Budget Box

I share this as fodder for your own projects. Is there a dilapidated hospital, high school or prison that you could rent — or even get the landlord to let you use for free, in exchange for a deferred equity position in the film or in trade for painting over the graffiti and fixing the broken windows? You could dress the various rooms as you need. Use the metal roll-up doors at the back to facilitate the loading and unloading off a raised truck. Even a long-vacant department or big box store or convention hall with wide-open space to build your own "studio" sets and high ceilings to hang lights off the trusses. Same thing with residential properties. You could offer the owners fair market value rent deferred. Reach out to your local Chamber of Commerce or City Managers to see what large properties with parking have been standing empty for far too long. Maybe they'll give you the contact information for a pro-business local who might see this as an opportunity to stimulate the local economy with jobs and meals and a little downtown excitement for the press?

SALES ESTIMATES

International Sales Agents will estimate what they think, based on the strong selling points of a project, might be the possible global revenue streams for a project. Back to Goldman's "Nobody knows anything": before you have any confirmed cast attached, no sales estimates can be "official" or even necessarily realistic. But, we work in an industry that is a huge game of telephone with a patchwork of educated guesses.

For examples, please visit: www.HeatherHale.com/Samples/SalesEstimates

PRE-SALES

While pre-sales are difficult to get under any circumstances, in order to secure sufficient funds to start or finish production, you might feel pressured (or that it's prudent) to sell off certain rights or territories at a discount to get the money in advance (which will be further discounted by any bank loaning gap financing with that as collateral). But a project without marquee-value stars is never less valuable than before it is finished. It is getting over that huge, seemingly insurmountable hurdle that creates quite the quandary for many filmmakers. When your film or project is finished — and let's say the project turned out better than anyone expected (except you, who had higher hopes), then you've already sold off your most likely candidates at fire sale rates and truly only managed to cap your upside. Liquidity is lovely — but not necessarily when it comes at such a price.

WATERFALLS

A "waterfall" is how the profits trickle down: a distribution hierarchy that delineates hypothetical corridors of who would get what, when and in what priority, based on various assumptions and variables.

Everything is an educated guess, based on proposed contracts and the track records of comps. Ideally, just like in math class, you should "show your work" and transparently disclose all calculations. For simple percentages, reflect these in an adjacent column so the numbers can be easily reworked if they have a different formula in mind.

A common waterfall scenario shows the investor(s) and producers splitting the net profits 50/50 after the investor recoups all her capital plus a 20 percent profit. Sometimes the back-end of A-list actors or deferrals of key department heads might be shown in here to be paid before or after the investor has received the return of their capital or incentive bump — or perhaps during, on a proportionate sliding scale. Every situation is different. This is just a simplified example.

While usually waterfalls show the same production budget across the board with different proposed box offices, some illustrate three different potential budget price points contemplated (for example: the ultra, modified and low budget sweet spots we've been discussing: $250,000, $700,000 and $1.162 million, respectively) or whatever the breakpoints are between $2.5 million and $9.9 million. Then, the varying domestic box office revenues can range accordingly.

Almost everyone will criticize your projected box office revenues. And everyone is entitled to their opinions or their statistics. But *nobody knows anything*. Do your due diligence research; explore different scenarios; ascertain trends or patterns that might serve as reasonable compasses. All the uncertainty is caveated and legalesed in boilerplate disclosures but it is incumbent upon every party to question and challenge every figure. Or don't invest.

PRODUCTION BUDGET HAS NO CORRELATION TO BOX OFFICE

There: I said it again. *Gigli* (2003) was one of the worst box office bombs in history. Reportedly, a $75.6 million budget (which may or may not include that much again in marketing, prints and advertising), grossed one-tenth that with just $7.2 million in international box office. At the time, if you remember, Jennifer Lopez and Ben Affleck, known jointly as "Bennifer," were two of the most successful media stars on the planet in the midst of one of the most publicized Hollywood romances of all time. It would be difficult to have "packaged" more white-hot chemistry, on- and off-camera charisma, name and face awareness, buzz, talent or "star power" anywhere in the world. And combined? *Fuggedaboudit.* And yet . . .? One of the biggest box office flops in history. This is, of course, in no way to slight either incredibly talented performer (they've both recovered just fine on all fronts, thank you very much), but it just goes to show you that even the most bankable assets, cobbled together in the most obvious of ways (playing opposite one another in a romance), are never a guaranteed predictor of actual performance.

Remember that sweet little Irish rock romance *Once*? One of our comps for *Once Again*, it grossed $9.4 million in the US alone. Off a $150,000 risk. With 21 award wins, including an Academy Award for Best Original song, that was a much more conservative, contained risk that no one knew would take off so.

For *Once Again*, we ran waterfall numbers at the 150, 339 and 567 screen mark with 16-, 31- and 45-week estimated theatrical runs — the lowest, average and highest of our comps — with slightly varying rental rates. We also projected our international and domestic distribution fees and fully disclosed all known expenses.

www.HeatherHale.com/Samples/Waterfalls

TV CASH FLOW ANALYSIS

TV is wildly different and far more opaque. Usually, from a creator's side, you're either getting a salary from some huge, vertically integrated conglomerate or a flat out option or purchase price. Or maybe, if you're as talented as Chuck Lorre, your income might fluctuate contingent on your ratings.

Analogous to 1980s infomercials, a new "client supplied programming" model reverse engineers syndication in advance, if that makes any sense. In other words, content creators fund (or find partners who fund) the production and buy the air time, preserving the ownership of the intellectual property, the rights, profits and future monetization opportunities to be wholly owned and controlled by the content creators (and their partners). Most television shows strive to be on the air for as long as possible: 100 episodes — a decade or more. But shows must *first get* on the air. This is a way to buy your way over that first hurdle. Staying on the air after that may be contingent upon the quality of the production but it can be a self-sustaining promotional vehicle that serves a variety of goals, products and brands.

THE DO's AND DON'Ts OF REALITY SHOW PITCH PROPOSALS

DO . . .

- **Know WHAT your show is.**
  - Is it a half-hour or an hour show?
  - If it's a competition program — what kind? Elimination? Build? Talent Search? Game Show? Social Experiment?

- **Know what your FORMAT is.**
  - This is what you are pitching in reality programming. This is your protectable asset.
  - Break it down: *What is it?* Register your treatment or outline with the WGA[18] or even work up a hypothetical pilot script and copyright that proposed execution of the idea.
- **Know your milieu.**
  - Is it Fashion? Health? Science? Foodie? Travel? Know your WORLD.
- **Know who your AUDIENCE is.**
  - What are your likely demographics? This is also your most obvious clue as to who your likely distributors or outlets might be.
- **Provide a snapshot of the project.**
  - Orient us with a quick overview. Frame our expectations immediately. So, we can be prepped to enjoy your passion!
- **Have at least a ballpark idea of the show's budget.**
  - Or at least what's realistic for your genre. Remember: *reality* is *profitable* because it is *cheap*.
- **Have a great sizzle reel.**
  - Thirty seconds to three minutes is ideal. As we've discussed: it is far better to have no sizzle reel than a cheesy one with marginal production values that could do more harm than good. If what I might imagine off your great pitch is better than what you actually got in the can . . .? Cut your losses and leave the clips at home — no matter what it cost to shoot.
- **If you claim to have a celebrity attached: have them attached.**
  - Even better, have *DE*-tachable "attachments."
  - If your show is contingent upon specific talent: should you bring them with you to pitch?
    - *Sometimes yes:* If they're "great in the room" and can sell the show better than anyone else — sure (especially if they are real creative and business partners with you).
    - *Sometimes no:* You don't want "your" talent pitching themselves instead of your show. The execs might be interested in your show — but not the talent that is sitting right in front of them — which inhibits the discussion of any other options on a *show* they'd otherwise be interested in.
    - If you are merely showing optional representatives of a "type" (a unique family, profession or lifestyle), then bring TAPE of candidates to express the possibilities and keep the discussion open and flexible.
- **Know your precursors.**
  - What is on the air right now that is comparable to the show that you have in mind in one way or another? How is yours different? How is yours better?
  - What elements does your idea share with successful, similar TV shows from the past? All the better if they are siblings from the network or cable channel you're pitching to — or even better: what they are currently competing against (and losing to).
  - Have a few great product-placement, sponsor, ShowRunner or Co-Pro candidates up your sleeve (even if only short list suggestions — and only if they ask).

DON'T . . .

- **Oversell with superlatives.**
  - This isn't your first-born.

- ○ Explain what your show could be (not the over-the-top ad copy of your wildest dreams of what the best in the business could do with a limitless budget and perfect conditions).
- **Tell them how to do their job.**
- **Be derisive of the industry.**
  - ○ If you think everything on TV right now is crap, then why would you aspire to write for it? And why would the people you're pitching to want to work with someone who thinks their entire business and its output is beneath them? Be smart. Be respectful. Be courteous. Sure, be creative and passionate just don't be rude or offensive. It never ceases to amaze me how people outside the industry can be so snide about it yet still pander to get into it. Or how bitter and jaded people who haven't even been burned yet can come across.
  - ○ Don't bring all your bitterness and past rejection into the room. Remember why you want to do this. You'll probably connect with the person on the other side of the desk who was at least initially inspired by the same reasons. Passion is an alluring commodity.
- **Over-encumber your project with a daisy chain of "attachments" that are just dead weight albatrosses.**
  - ○ Reality TV is popular because it is high concept, easy to market — and cheap to produce. Think: intriguing premises populated by unique characters in fascinating, unfamiliar worlds. Not top-heavy with delusional neophytes. Nor studio feature-level budgets, schedules, talent, logistics, locations or stunts.

NOTES

1 A **P**rivate **P**lacement **M**emorandum (PPM) is a legal document disclosing "just the facts" to prospective investors of the terms of the offering presented in the usually more persuasive, marketing-oriented business plan.
2 Memorandum of Understanding.
3 Google it. Okay: a silly, over-engineered contraption designed to perform a simple task (i.e. a complicated domino-like series of movements just to crack an egg).
4 CD = Casting Director
5 See: www.HeatherHale.com/PowerNetworking
6 An IOU (I owe you).
7 An investment term for making dubious, fiscally delusional projections.
8 Movie of the Week.
9 Haphazardly, randomly, without proper direction or planning.
10 A 1980s video game of gophers hitting dead ends and circling back up to the surface, trying to find their way.
11 See page 94.
12 A brief presentation, often in PowerPoint or keynote or on a website, usually to raise capital.
13 Mode = The number which appears the most often in a set of numbers.
14 **D**igital **I**maging **T**echnician is a relatively new position in the Camera Department born out of the shift from analog, celluloid film to digital video. This video engineer supports the Cinematographer with signal and image capture quality control, on-set color correction, ensuring sufficient back-ups with the right metadata, facilitating production workflow, etc.
15 A warning ancient mapmakers used, illustrated with dragons, to identify the threshold of the known lands and seas where they spilled into unexplored territories.
16 See: www.sagindie.org for more details and the latest updates.
17 None **o**f **y**our **b**usiness!
18 The **W**riters **G**uild of **A**merica is a labor union of writers who write movies, television, videogames, animation and new media content. Visit www.WGA.org for more information.

Gearing Up For Each Event

24

RESEARCH THE EVENT

This book serves as a survey of most of the key events, but visit their websites. Almost all of them have great "First Timer" orientation videos. Seeing the event in action — what the venue and weather are like, how business dressy or casual the attendees are — helps orient expectations. Many have terrific videos from past panel discussions that can offer wonderful education to get up to speed on the new issues they'll likely cover. The websites will typically have info on their hotel accommodations, early bird specials, FAQs,[1] tips and tricks — all invaluable directly from the source — to help tamp down nerves.

WHO ARE YOU LOOKING TO MEET?

This is why you're going, right? To meet people who can help you move your projects and career forward. Who do you need to meet? And why? What if you're not exactly sure who you need to meet? Let's take a look at all that.

RESEARCH YOUR PROSPECTS

The event websites will typically have all the speakers' bios and headshots posted, increasing in number and depth of detail as the event nears. Check them out. Copy and paste their photos and bios into your address book on your smartphone so you can recognize people onsite. Add the most relevant speakers to your hit list(s).

    If there is a pitch event, many of the catchers will be listed online as well — often with their mandates — revealing precisely what they're looking for — now. Add that to your contact database or spreadsheet. This can be priceless information especially to track year over year as you begin to build a portfolio of material and these relationships. In the future, you'll be able to search your own database with company names, credits or other keywords (genre, format, faith-based, etc.) and past delegates who might be new targets will come up as matches for new projects from the work you've done in the past.

    Don't proactively reach out to sales agents or producers who don't have a solid track record in the industry or in your genre or budget range. But some Googling, trades scouring, and study of company websites and especially bios (pay special attention to titles on credits) might reveal a brand new company you've never heard of this actually helmed by long-time industry veterans who will have solid established relationships.

RESEARCH THE OTHER ATTENDEES

Everyone from movie and television stars to studio CEOs, to print and software vendors, to union representatives attend these markets — but obviously not everyone is a prospect for your purposes. You need to weed out the masses to hone in on those who should actually be on your hit list.

As exciting as it is to run into Harvey Weinstein or Chuck Lorre, odds are, unless you already have a pre-existing relationship with them (or a very hot, high-profile property that their people are already interested in), the best you can probably hope for is a haphazard but successful meet and greet and maybe a memorable conversation (but not in a bad way!). Most attendees may be nice, lovely people (and hopefully many will become new friends — we all have plenty to learn from one another), but in terms of executing your precision networking efforts (what you paid to come to do), you want to focus on your bull's-eye targets — who you came to meet.

CREATE YOUR HIT LIST

The market profiles on each of the events' websites will detail which exhibitors have suites or booths. Not every production or distribution company will take space and sometimes the highest profile are in secluded bungalows or on discrete floors, requiring appointments to get past security — but most will be relatively accessible.

THREE MONTHS TO SIX WEEKS BEFORE THE EVENT: START DOING RESEARCH

Check out your event's website. It ought to have links to each of the company's respective websites. You can also use Cinando, the Film Catalogue, and of course IMDBPro, Variety Insight and Gracenote (formerly Baseline)'s Studio System. And there's always blessed Google.

STUDY EACH COMPANY'S WEBSITE

This might be a no-brainer but do you know how many people actually do this advance prep? (You'll be on the honor roll.)

Do you know any of their staff? Maybe not this year, but next year, you will. And every year thereafter, you'll know a few more — especially as they move up the ladder or shift and move from company to company or you see them at different events. The goal is to move from cold calling through luke-warm greeting to warm pitching to hot negotiating.

Do you know anyone they've worked with? Call them and get referrals — or even better — ask if they will reach out on your behalf and refer you to them in advance of the event.

What genres or budgets do they excel at? Do they have any recognizable titles? Any of your comps? Any other relevant credits? What are their breakout success stories? Where's the bulk of their inventory? Do you have something they've had success with? Or have an over-abundance of? Or need? What's the typical level of talent they have in their projects? The same as yours? Higher or lower? Do you see any actors you should add to your cast wish list? (especially if you're targeting an entity that's had past success with them).

Can you get your hands on last year's special market editions of the industry trades? Maybe borrow them from a friend who hit the market? See what they advertised last year. How did their films do? Google with specificity (names, titles, dates) to pull up past years' info.

Make notes of all of this. I use Excel spreadsheets, Evernote and my contact database but I've also used business card binder sheets organized by event. Any way that works for you — that you *will use* — that effectively captures all this information in a retrievable, manageable, maintainable system is great.

Look at their photos, pay attention to titles and contact info listed on the market websites and directories or on their company websites. You'll quickly see, for the bigger, more prominent companies and people, that they are often listed with the same "info@"-type email address (or that of a low-level coordinator accompanying them and facilitating their market schedules). That means they are not publicly sharing their *real* email addresses. That's fine. They've at least offered an appropriate, public starting place. But as you can imagine, the bigger the company, the more likely this will be a vortex of unsolicited, vetted, swatted away or ignored (I mean: fielded and delegated) queries. This is why so many in the industry pay for subscription services to streamline this process to get through or around the gatekeepers — and why it's critical that you hold onto their cards if they give them to you. Save those hard-to-get direct email addresses and cell phone numbers in your own records.

THE RIGHT TITLES FOR YOUR HIT LIST

Depending on the size of the company and your project's profile, you might be looking to meet anyone from coordinators on up to presidents, but you're most likely shooting for VPs, directors or managers with the words "development," "creative," "content," "programming," "production" and/or "acquisition," or your specific genre (comedy/drama) or type of programming (reality/original programming, etc.) in their titles. Depending on where you're at in your project's lifecycle, "marketing," "distribution" and "syndication" might also be reasonable candidates to add to your short list. Employees with titles indicating "legal affairs," "finance," "public relations," "affiliate relations" or "operations" might be irrelevant or premature. Everyone's great to chat with — but remember who your missiles are locked on.

I cover this extensively in my PowerNetworking series[2], but essentially: you may not know the exact names of the people you need to meet but you likely have an idea of which companies, affiliations and/or credits you want among your prospects. You can use those search parameters to scour the web. Scan their social media profiles. Google each person of interest's name. What do their public projections reveal to you? Do you get a sense of them? Do they own horses? So, they might be more interested in your equestrian project than someone who's not an equestrian. Are they a vegan animal rights activist? So maybe not the best bet for your marlin fishing comedy. Do they have a snarky, raunchy sense of humor? Maybe they're not the best candidate for your Christian melodrama. These are all things you can pick up from what they tweet and post. Go on to *The Wrap, Deadline, The Hollywood Reporter, Variety Insight,*

IMDBPro and search for them and their companies to find press releases and news articles announcing projects and personnel shifts.

FINDING THE RIGHT SALES AGENT FOR YOUR PROJECT

Target six to eight foreign sales agents who might be right for your project. Check their credits out on the IFTA website www.ifta-online.com under the members directory, which also links to their websites or Cinando. Perusing their online inventories and printed catalogs, take note of producers that have provided your prospect company similar content (i.e. the same genre, budget and cast level) and contact them directly to discuss their distribution experiences with them. If you are specific in the purpose of your call and your referral request, you might be surprised how candid their past customers will be. Did their past producers feel that their terms were fair — and honored?

As you narrow down your list for sales agents and distributors, do you have an entertainment attorney with distribution experience you can turn to? Perhaps you should be creating a hit list and getting referrals for trustworthy production or IP[3] attorneys, too.

It might surprise you to find out that the distributors and sales agents may be tracking you and your projects, too. Several exhibitors taking meetings have pre-printed organizer worksheets where they take detailed notes from their own prospect meetings. They track which market they met the independent producer at, what budget range and genres this new lead typically produces, whether their content was targeted for theatrical, video, PPV, free broadcast or VOD, current production status info, technical specifications, buying rights, and sub-rights available on current projects at the market, any festival activity or cinema play. So, it goes both ways.

Look for a distributor or a sales agent who believes in your content and whose company is a good fit. Ideally, this company's profile makes sense for and adds value to your project. You should be honored to find yourself in their slate — or at least feel like your project fits in their library or on their wall of posters.

If you are fortunate enough to have been accepted by of one the A-list festivals, you might be getting queries directly from sales agents. But if you will be premiering at a lower-tier festival, you will need to hustle to find a strong partner to represent your film. Do a market study (which, ideally, you should have already done to procure financing) to find similar or "comparable" titles in the marketplace and identify which sales agents sold those films. Use this information to filter the companies you approach.

SORT, RANK AND ORDER YOUR LIST

Divide your list into two groups: companies with offices in the city or region where you live or work — and those from everywhere else around the world. For the event, focus on the companies that aren't based near you. If you can't connect with a local professional during the event, it's much easier to follow-up with those in your hometown after the market has ended.

Further divide your list(s) by other factors such as the genres and budgets the companies represent. Do you have more than one project? You might want to make separate lists for each of your projects.

Create A, B, C and D priority lists for each project with, say, 10 companies on each list based on what you've learned from all this research. Tag keywords, rank and prioritize your personal preferences and instincts. Study the obvious candidates. Note if anyone from their firm is speaking during the event. That is, obviously, the day they will most likely be at the market as not everyone from every firm is there all day, every day. Consider these issues when creating your calendar. Make the highest and best use of what is sure to be a handful of very long, intense days.

PLAN AND PRIORITIZE YOUR MARKET GOALS AND SCHEDULE IN ADVANCE

Use your calendar to highlight the sessions that look of most interest to you either due to their content or presenters. Italicize or strike out those you could miss. It's helpful to keep them in your calendar because maybe the session on how to adapt your TV show to a video game is not of interest to you but it may be the reason one of your professional acquaintances signed up for the market and knowing what ballroom it is in in relation to the pavilion you'll be in will make finding a convenient lunch spot on a map that much easier from your smartphone onsite.

Copy and paste cell phone numbers and email addresses into your actual calendar appointments, so if you're running late, you don't have to dig but could give them a quick heads up or confirm en route. Of course, you never want to be late, but it can be hard to get from one venue to the next if you book yourself too tightly. Put the suite number in your calendar, too, so as you're hustling, you know where you're headed. You don't want to walk out of the twentieth floor elevator and go: *"Now what?"* And have to look for a directory.

It's probably not a bad idea to color code or somehow show your ranked priorities so you don't let your D meeting run late, potentially costing you an A meeting. You think you'll remember all these details "on the day" — but it's a lot to juggle. Of course, every meeting is important — and you never know where your career-making deal might come from — but just like the magic that can happen while shooting, the better your advance prep helps you stay on schedule, the better choices you can make on the fly. Your smartphone can be your first AD[4] with alarms, notes and reminders.

BADGE BUYING ADVICE

Almost every event has an early bird special to encourage advance commitment. With thousands of potential guests for any kind of event, it's nice to get a ballpark head count as early as possible to facilitate their venue arrangements. Plus, the earlier you book, the better pricing you'll get across the board. At least, the more options you'll have in terms of flights, accommodations, session or pitch requests.

Most unions, guilds and membership organizations will offer group discounts to their members. Ask around. Google for "Market + Discount Code" and see what comes up. Check out the event profiles for specific suggestions. Or use those message boards. Network!

BUSINESS CARDS

I know this is a no-brainer and should go without saying — but humor me: I can't tell you how many people end up at markets either having forgotten to bring their business cards or running out halfway through the market. It is so simple. But then, we all know we're supposed to eat fresh vegetables and get physical activity every day — but how many of us do it? *Everyday*? No one questions this wisdom but life gets busy and speeds up and sometimes we forget to do the most basic steps. So you have to set up structures to help you adhere to your best laid plan and honor your best intentions.

Bring twice as many business cards as you think you could possibly need. Then double that. And pack them in advance while you're thinking about it. Like cash when you travel: put them everywhere. Put a fresh clean stack in your suitcase, some in your luggage, more in your purse or pocket. Tuck them in your sales packets. Have them everywhere you might reach for them so they're there when you need them (crisp and clean).

NOTES

1 Frequently Asked Questions.
2 Visit www.HeatherHale.com/PowerNetworking
3 Intellectual Property (content).
4 The first Assistant Director keeps the director (and whole cast and crew) on time and frees them to focus on the creative aspects of filmmaking.

Part VI
During
At the Market

Prudent Market Scheduling and Logistics

Set realistic expectations. Schedule enough time to get from session to meeting to screening to meal. Allow some breathing room for running into professional acquaintances. That's one of the biggest reasons so many attend these events: precisely for these chance encounters — so don't book yourself so tightly that you don't allow time for organic networking to occur onsite because your event-making deal is just as likely to come from an introduction during one of these random coffees or cocktails. Allow for these opportunities to unfold. Thus, another reason to have with you at all times your rankings and priorities of the commitments you're juggling — and everyone's contact info.

Earmark time to compose yourself before you go in to pitch. Don't race in only to have the pitch be over before you've caught your breath. Notice who else is in the room. *Have you walked in on someone else's meeting? What kind of an impression will you leave in your wake?* Adjust your energy accordingly. Go to the restroom if only to find a private mirror to check your teeth and straighten your collar so you can walk in collected and ready.

It's okay if you miss a session or screening: your meetings are what matter. Often, the sessions are recorded and will be up on the website afterwards. Yes, you paid for them but that education can be acquired listening in your car or on the treadmill after the event. It's also a terrific option for the markets you can't attend — especially streaming live to track what's making news on social media. And much as you might enjoy watching all the films or TV programs you have free reign access to, you can see all of those later, too. While you've got boots on the ground: stay focused on your end game: meeting people face-to-face. Focus on what you can't replicate on your own. *What matters right here, right now? What did you really come for?* The confluence of professionals you can interact with who can make a difference in your career that are all gathered together in one place and time. Watch movies and TV later. Watch or listen to panels on video or podcast later. Get out there and network while the live opportunities in the present moment abound. It's only for a handful of days — make the most of them.

🌰 HOT TIP!

Wear Comfortable Shoes! Be Kind to Your Feet!

Jenean Atwood Baynes, formerly NATPE's Director of Buyer Initiatives and now a private consultant with PH 10 Creative Consulting, offers this prudent advice: "Wear comfortable shoes. You will be strutting that market floor, sun up to sun down, with two inches of carpet between you and concrete: be kind to your feet."

Source: © Marché du Film.

REVIEW YOUR HIT LIST

Hopefully by now you've scheduled meetings with specific individuals from the companies on your hit list. On the last couple of days of the market, when things have slowed down a bit, try swinging by those that wouldn't schedule a meeting with you on the phone or via email to see if you can do a quick meet and greet "fly by" or even a very courteous hit and run pitch. If they are busy, it's still worth it to check out their one sheets and posters, get a sense of them in person and get a better feel for if they'd be a good fit for your project or not.

PAY ATTENTION TO BADGE CLUES

Early on, make a point of figuring out the color codes, symbols or stickers on the badges or even lanyard cues that the event coordinators have established as a subtle shorthand for their staff and security. There are lots of revolving teams and moving pieces at these events. You can empower yourself by learning the systems established to help the event staff so that with a quick badge glance, you, too, can ascertain who it is you're dealing with (or would like to be).

Sometimes these details aren't decided until badge printings are processed just days before the event. They will likely vary from event to event and even change every year but often, they remain consistent or are easy to figure out. They aren't rocket science. And you can always ask a volunteer or staff.

Buyers, exhibitors and regular attendees will all likely be grouped by three distinct colors. Producers in the special vetted programs, panelists, speakers, judges and other VIP guests may have little stickers or insignias on their badges, ribbons or even different colored lanyards. Full-time event staff, interns and volunteers are all distinguished similarly. Sometimes full-time staff will have permanent engraved badges while volunteers, student interns, caterers and the A/V team might all wear event t-shirts.

Source: Courtesy SWPix and NATPE.

🎏 HOT TIP!

Read It, Write It, Say It, Hear It — Remember It!

Name Memory Trick: If you read their name off their badge or business card while saying it aloud (say, while meeting them for the first time: "It's nice to meet you, Bill"), it will help you remember it. Even if you only make a mental note as you scan their badge, reading their name, title and company will help anchor those associations in your brain. Handwrite and type it in your notes afterwards when you follow up with a post card or email. Even as you take another glance at their photo in the catalog or online, read it aloud as you write it down.

Pay attention to how those you want to meet (or might need help from) are identified. Keep a watchful eye out for your prospects and focus your networking efforts in their directions to make the highest and best use of your market investment.

Don't Ignore Your Own Badge . . .

If the badges have headshots, don't be vain and use a decade-old photo that no longer resembles you. Help people recognize you — especially if these photos are also posted in event databases that attendees will research in advance, during and after. Don't have them looking to meet your younger sister — or daughter. Help them find — and remember — you. Don't be that realtor who still uses the headshot on her posters and fliers from the day she got her license.

If you have multiple titles, use the one that is most relevant to your goals for your attendance at this specific market. If you're an actress attached to other people's projects, a casting director and a producer on what you're pitching now, focus on what you bought the badge for: to sell what you have a controlling interest in — not to get cast or hired for other gigs. That may happen naturally — and that's great! But pay attention to projecting a focused mission on what you came to pitch. You might not be taken as seriously as an actress as you will a producing peer, but once they've gotten to know you, you might still get audition opportunities on their projects.

Flip your badge right side up and keep it out and visible at all times. If you add a jacket, sweater, blazer or scarf, pull out your badge and make sure it's always readable. Not only will it make access everywhere seamless (as security won't be stalling you at the door as you try to catch up with someone you want to meet), but it will help people who think they might know you not embarrass themselves by allowing them to sneak a peek at your name and company as a memory trigger. Help them network with you. Be accessible. Let them see who you are, your title and company. The badges provide a convenient ice-breaking frame of reference for all parties. So: play fair. If they can't see your badge, they might think you're sneaking in on someone else's registration, which isn't the kind of first impression you want to make.

ICE-BREAKING WARDROBE

What I'm about to say might seem silly to many but I've taught PowerNetworking classes for a couple of decades now and while these topics make people laugh and giggle nervously — it is usually these tips and tricks that people write to thank me for later because these strategies paid off.

My dad and I owned a mortgage company together. He encouraged us to wear name tags or t-shirts with our company logo when we weren't dressed professionally. I felt ridiculous at first but eventually, I got used to "my uniform" as I called it and people coming up to me in the grocery store line asking me: "Where are rates at right now?" — always ending with them asking for my card. It worked. It's what I now call "ice-breaking wardrobe." Put yourself out there. And facilitate it for your cast and crew. Of course you can have t-shirts made with your key art and your film's URL. But it can also be as simple as a nice polo shirt from your country club or favorite vacation spot. Or, if you're going casual, a windbreaker from your favorite sports team — if it's relevant to your project, even better. Consciously think what might trigger conversation in an area where you'd have something directly relevant to contribute.

For the course of the event, for each day or outfit, it's a good idea to identify two pockets — one for outgoing business cards and one for incoming. Or have a business card holder where yours are on top and those you collect are in the back. Keep these in chronological order, one after another as you meet them — and paperclip or rubber band each day's (or half days') stack together. Ideally, you'll go through the stack each night — or at each break is even better — and process what needs to be done, adding your own first impressions, instincts, reminders to yourself, other leads or projects that might also be of interest to this prospect. Keeping them in chronological order will help with your memory later if you can't remember who someone was but you remember you met them after the panel discussion but before the cocktail party, they'll be in your stack between the other people you met according to your calendar.

ICE-BREAKING PROPS

Props. Same deal as wardrobe. If you're going to a market or festival that you've been to before, consider bringing last year's bag as your carry-on. Or if you're going to an event for the first time, bring a water bottle or a hat with a logo that identifies you're in the industry (TV Land, IFP, Miramax, Paramount, etc.).

Be creative. Wear your favorite turquoise jewelry that you bought while location scouting your Indian project or those funky steampunk accessories that will allow you to seamlessly weave right into your time travel comedy if they comment on them.

I used to go to a tournament every year down in Cabo San Lucas. I'd wear an event t-shirt and/or baseball cap, carry the bag or water bottle and inevitably, even in the huge LAX, sitting at our terminal on the way down to Mexico, half a dozen strangers would broach conversations with me and by the time I reached my destination, I had a van full of new friends staying at the same hotel — any of whom could be potential investors for my Sports RomCom set at the tournament.

MARKET FIRST TIMERS: DON'T BE NERVOUS

Almost every market offers first timer orientation sessions at their events. Attend them. Meet other first timers. Network. They also usually provide advance prep and support materials on their websites. Take advantage of every resource you can find.

Even before the welcome party, NATPE's PRO Pitch 2015 included an advance walk-through tour of the venue for the vetted producers pitching in their embedded event, not just to calm nerves but also to give them a chance to get to know one another — and what badges to look for — before the larger event launched. This allowed all of the participants to have 100 acquaintances greeting them on the market floor.

The Cannes Producers Workshop targets industry newcomers and offers three different guided tours, coaching sessions, an opening cocktail party and wrap up session just for members of the program and invited guests. The AFM offers two "First Time Orientation" sessions. And so on.

Check the schedule and allocate time to hear what the hosts and sponsors of your specific event suggest and take advantage of the opportunity to identify, meet — and bond with — other newbies.

If you have specific questions that can't be answered off the event's website, reach out to the event producers via email or phone. Jenean Atwood Baynes shares:

> People would call NATPE all the time, year-round. If our market didn't make sense for them, I'd always be honest. It's not about the money. If it's not going to help them accomplish their goals for the stage they're at, I advise them what other great next steps to take instead. It's all about helping people capitalize on our market to achieve their dreams.

Taking Meetings at the Market

RESPECT THE EXHIBITOR'S SPACE AND TIME

Sales agents will be set up in stands on the Palais and apartments along the Croisette at Cannes, on the market floors and in suites at the AFM and NATPE, in the ballrooms and convention halls of all the various events. Showcasing the films and programming they're selling, these are their offices at the various markets. They are paying steep rent for this precious, temporary real estate. Where you might have paid $1,000 to be here, they probably paid upwards of $10,000 — or three to five times more. Respect that, for them: selling comes before buying.

There will be trailers playing, posters on the walls, people meeting — don't interrupt. Be respectful. Be patient. Don't get frustrated if they need to reschedule you. Be flexible. It does you no good to alienate them even if you feel "you're right." Take it in stride and adjust. Remember that the sales agents' priorities are connecting with as many different *buyers* (distributors) as possible, too. They are pitching a wide variety of projects, closing many deals. Licensing your content for the next market is way down on their list of priorities (if it's even on there at all!). So don't take it personally if they ask you to come back at the end of the market — that's honestly when they'll be the most receptive to you. They're only here for a few days, get in to see them when you can. They'll be much more receptive to hearing your pitch if you accommodate their fluctuating schedule. Besides, when they're your sales rep, would you want them cutting short a sales meeting that's going longer than expected (but great!) with a territory interested in distributing your project to hear the next pitch waiting at the door for the next market? Keep things in perspective.

BEFRIEND THE GATEKEEPERS

There will likely be a receptionist, coordinator, an intern — or even your prospect's boss (you never know who's watching the door while their peers are in meetings), so: be respectful to everyone. Always. Offer your card and try to schedule an appointment with your cold-call swing bys. Ask if they will be hearing development or acquisitions pitches during the last couple of days of the market. Be prepared right then and there for them to ask you to pitch your project. Be as succinct, professional and passionate as possible. Your elevator pitch: the title, genre, brief but intriguing logline. It may be what gets you on the books — or a pass right there.

Keep in mind that the sales and marketing kicks in for new projects a couple months before the market it launches at, so you're truly building relationships for the future by positioning yourself for the next market — and your career. No meeting is ever wasted — just like no audition is a waste of time. You just never know when or how it will pay off down the line.

ESTABLISH YOUR CREDIBILITY

What have you done? Have your previous films been distributed? By whom? Who's attached to your next project? Writer? Director? Producer? What have they done? Do you have any note-worthy cast confirmed? No one cares about your fantasy casting. They want letters of interest (though it can be priceless to hand your wish list over and have a savvy eye scan it and call out the duds and the surprise dealmakers). Do these fly-by market surveys every chance you get. This is priceless information from people in the trenches, marketing these commodities all day, every day. Let them know who you are — and the top notes of your project.

What's your budget? Is it realistic for its genre? The level of cast (if known)? How much financing do you already have in place? Do you have a one sheet? Teaser footage? A polished elevator pitch? Can you quickly adapt your pitch to your audience and their interest level? What makes your project different? Original? Commercial? How can you prove that you can deliver a quality product on time and on budget? Have you done that before?

DEFINE THE PURPOSE OF EACH MEETING

If it's just a meet and greet, establish that up front. Let them relax for a minute with no expectations. If you want to close a deal, get to the point. What kind of deal? What's the product? Many production companies, some sales agents, and even bond companies have access to investors, EPs, or have the funds or ability to raise the funds or direct you to capital looking for content.

NEGOTIATING

Remember in negotiating: the first one to offer a number loses. Also: the first documents you see from them will inevitably be boilerplate: their low-ball offer, heavily weighted in their favor. Nothing wrong with that. He who writes the contract, controls the deal. But that doesn't mean you have to accept it. Remember those previous clients you reached out to, to see what kind of a deal they got? How does this compare? Those interviews should have prepared you with the questions you should ask and the verbiage you should request.

If you agree to work with them (or possibly as part of their courtship), they will generate a list of territories with "ASK" and "TAKE" columns that details, respectively, what they hope to get for your film and the worst they'll accept from each region, usually inclusive (or breaking out) all the windows (theatrical, DVD, cable, etc.). They shoot to get 10 percent of the negotiated value advanced from each distributor, but like everything in the business, this can fluctuate wildly.

While also varying and changing constantly, a decent rule of thumb is that 70 percent of your budget should be covered by what is estimated to be generated by the foreign territories (i.e. $700k of a million dollar feature). The typical top nine territories (outside the U.S.) for independent films are the UK, Germany/Austria, France, Spain, Italy, Japan and Australia/New Zealand with Mexico and South Korea trailing.

Never reveal the budget to anyone unless you are required to do so or there is some upside to the disclosure. Never lie, of course, just never offer up proprietary information to anyone who hasn't earned the right (or has a need) to access those figures. What matters is what is the *value* of your film — not its cost. What's it worth to them to be in business with you and your movie?

Make sure all your technical and legal issues are locked down. You don't want to blow a deal because your paperwork isn't in order. Make sure you are fully compliant with all your union contracts, all your agreements are sorted and signed that you have your chain of title, copyrights, clearance reports, insurance and all the necessary deliverables clearly stipulated and situated (formats, textless, M&E, etc.). Deals and relationships can go sideways when expectations aren't clearly expressed or honored so just make sure both sides understand what's expected of them — and what the consequences are for non-performance.

A WORD OF CAUTION: BIFURCATING THE RIGHTS

In keeping with the changing times, greater access to information and audience, the increasing knowledge of independent producers and their desire to eliminate the attrition of profits to a daisy chain of middlemen through their opaque bookkeeping methods, it's an increasing practice of independent producers to try to bifurcate the rights. Meaning: ensure that they only license the rights to the entities that actually have expertise in those specific arenas. In other words, you want to seriously think twice about locking up all your film's international rights exclusively to a domestic or digital rep as they might be ill-equipped to maximize opportunities outside their wheelhouse. This is prudent. In theory. You certainly don't want any rights collecting dust ignored due to a lack of expertise or relevant relationships (or quite frankly, interest).

No one'll love your baby more than you do — or work harder for it or you than you will.

This is just more motivation for you to do extensive due diligence on your partners. A lot of independent film producers think they can do it all themselves — and *they may be able to* — but think long and hard about this: *do you really want to?* What I mean by that is would you rather spend the next five years of your life figuring out the various technical specifications of deliverables in each territory you manage to sell, dubbing, subtitling and translating key art and trailers and collecting monies due to you, spreadsheeting and allocating who gets what and when . . . or would you rather be making more movies or episodes?

It's great to know all the pieces of the puzzle just as it's helpful to have experience in every position on a film crew or sport team, but you can't do it all alone simultaneously, indefinitely. At some point (after you've gained priceless perspective and education): you have to figure out what your strengths are — and play to them. Sometimes our strengths are our former weaknesses that we worked so hard at they became our core competencies.

A WORD OF CAUTION: CHECK THOSE DEFINITIONS!

! Pay close attention to the definitions in your contracts. Some wildly unscrupulous sales agents will use the "Definition of Gross Receipts" to skim off the top. Meaning: you know those union deposits you are forced to put in the bank as a reserve to stay in compliance? Shaving away precious production capital to set it aside in a contingency savings account to cover a percentage of the residuals and royalties you *might owe* in the future? So, the unions rest easy . . .?

At the 2013 AFM, a producer friend and I accidentally (divinely) overhead a veteran sales agent teaching a wet-behind-the-ears newbie how they could actually take an unearned and nefarious "commission" off the top of the SAG payroll security deposit as they passed through the account they manage "on behalf" of their clients. Wait a minute . . . They are supposed to *earn* commissions off *sales* they *generate* — not take part of my *capital* I am forced to set aside in savings . . . just because . . . *they can*? Because they have *access* to my funds? She was advising him how if his verbiage contracted "all receipts," it empowered him to take a percentage of any monies that passed through this account — regardless of how they got there or what they were earmarked for. Wow. Just . . . wow. Fiduciary *ought* to go both ways. This is why you must do due diligence on your prospective partners.

WHAT TO LEAVE BEHIND (IF ANYTHING)

Just by looking at the size of Part V Before: Preparation, it's easy to see that the lion's share occurs in advance. Maybe your prospects have viewed and read everything you provided in advance. Great! Maybe they can't remember you from the 100 other pitches they've heard in the past few days and whatever material you submitted has long-since been lost in the shuffle and they are requesting information you already provided months ago — upon their request. Don't be surprised or ruffled by this. Don't make them wrong. It's a bit like loan underwriting: just provide it again.

Don't be offended if they don't accept your leave behinds. Imagine traveling internationally with an extra bag full of unsolicited DVDs and scripts. If they ask you to send it to them after the market, consider that a win. Ask when they would like it. Tonight? A couple weeks after the market? And follow their instructions. Some will watch or read during their down time in the suite or on the plane(s) home. Some might prefer to catch up with their own lives and close deals and truly won't look at anything new for three weeks — to three months. So ask. If you honor their wishes, you'll be at the top of their stack as fresh and new as opposed to stuck under a month-old pile of guilt nagging at them from their inbox. Follow their lead. Be ready for anything. Don't take anything personally.

Some professionals have the budget to put all their multimedia content on customized tradeshow giveaway schwag[1] such as flash drives. Ensure all your printed or electronic deliverables have contact information and links to your videos. You'd think this would go without saying (to put your film or TV show's URL on your marketing materials), but you'd be amazed how many people forget to do this — just like forgetting to bring business cards to the market. Make following up with you the easiest thing for them to do on their "To Do" list.

ALWAYS HAVE AN ANSWER FOR: "WHAT ELSE HAVE YOU GOT?"

While this is far more likely to happen in TV than the film world, where the churn is so much faster, it is possible that what you've got is similar to something they currently have in development — or worse, had a recent flop with. Again: don't take this personally. If they pass and ask you "What else have you got?" consider it a win because they are too busy to be gratuitous. They really do mean they are interested in what else you might have. So: have something. Ideally, something they might like.

If you're pitching to a firm that specializes in thrillers and they pass on your Trilateralist Commission thriller cause they have another conspiracy theory type project in the works, maybe your other political espionage thriller would be too close but your erotic thriller might be perfect. Or maybe, they're flush with thrillers and your magical realism musical might be something fresh and new to them (provided they've done either or both in the past).

If you're pitching to the EVP of Programming and Original Movies for the Syfy Channel, maybe he's willing to hear any good feature or one-hour drama pitches you may have that have a really strong science element or some sort of creature or force. Hopefully, you've done your homework and have a very good idea of what might appeal to them.

POST-MEETING HOUSEKEEPING

Do what the sales agents do: make yourself a meeting book. Bring along an event-specific notebook with either a small stapler, business card pockets or sleeves, or a business card scanning application. When you get business cards from the people you meet, write notes on the back or in your app while it's fresh in your mind or organize a whole collection of cards in acrylic sleeves for each event or staple their card to a fresh new page for dated conversation logs. Jot down the contents of your conversations on the back of each card or in your notebook as soon as you can. Note any action to be taken (i.e. send the screener, teaser, script on Monday; follow-up in three weeks, (with that date) etc.) — then do it.

Send thank you emails, cards or post cards with your key art to cement each relationship with a subtle project or action reminder as soon as possible. I often keep logo or tone-appropriate blank cards stamped and ready to go in my car or carry on so I can literally do them on the plane ride home or, better, in my hotel room or during any alone time while I detail my notes and create a tickler file of follow-ups. Doing this as you go is infinitely more efficient because it's much easier to recall the morning's four hours of interactions versus trying to remember 40 conversations after an intense week. Plus, your reading it, writing it, saying it aloud and hearing it will help cement their names and companies in your memory, which will make for warmer chance encounters during the rest of the event. It's like you're your own political aide, whispering your own memory.

NOTE

1 Promotional products given away free, typically at trade shows.

Part VII
After
Follow-Up

Gauging Success 27

It can be hard to gauge your success. A bit like an auditioning actress, if you prepared to the best of your abilities and resources and gave it your all, that's as good as anyone can do. Maybe you didn't sell what you came to — and came home empty handed — but if the doors are open for you to come back and you better understand what a couple dozen legit buyers are looking for — right now — then your research trip was worth the cost of education.

All the better if they asked "What else have you got?" and/or asked you to follow up with more materials. Deals don't always get closed during these intense events. Everyone shoots for that, of course, that's why everyone goes — but they also serve as fodder and momentum for the time in between — and the rest of the year — so don't lose sight of the fact that maybe your marathon isn't quite over yet. You could be following up on leads for months to come — and closing deals at the next market or very likely, between them.

DEAL OR NO DEAL?

But hopefully after all this effort, you'll ink a deal. Or several! Every deal is different and the terms are constantly changing. Hopefully this book has given you a lot of insights on the questions you should ask and what you should look for in a deal. If you did all the homework leading up to the event, you'll have already answered most of your own questions through your own due diligence. You'll have resolved most of your issues by getting referrals or sample contracts from other filmmakers and content creators, scouring the Internet, reassessing your product and its place and value in the marketplace and hopefully working with your entertainment attorney. If you didn't ink a deal, set new goals to convert each pass into a relationship, raise the bar on your material and hone your hit lists such that at the next market, you'll be a success story shared as a case study.

These business cycles repeat themselves. As you are following up — the industry is already gearing up for the next event in the cycle. Even if you don't hit the next market, you'll be on the radars of all the people you met face-to-face at the last one who — as part of their jobs — will now be following up with you — to see where you're at with your projects — and what you have new in the pipeline. So the effort can serve you for years to come.

YEAR-ROUND NETWORKING

Wait a couple weeks and follow up again. Know that many sales agents and distributors take time off after each market. Familiarize yourself with other nations' holidays. Many Europeans take a whole month off in the summer for vacation. Don't be too anxious if there's no immediate reply. Better to be patient and wait for a delayed "Yes" than push to get an immediate "No." Polite persistence will get you a long way.

Your registration secures you access to the market website and online community for a year. Use it. Cinando, myNATPE, MyAFM and most of the others have online portals and forums. These can be worth the price of admission if you use them consistently throughout the year. Admittedly, they are far more active the three months leading up to and two weeks after the event, but they can be priceless if you forgot someone's name or lost their contact information or the market made you shift your targets — or for your next project ten months later before your annual membership expires.

This is also why taking great notes during and after the event is key. Years later, it's great to do a quick search in your own database of how or where you met someone — and what they were interested in or that you talked about — to open your "Congratulations on your latest project" email with details to remind them that you met at the "XYZ market."

Throughout the year, as you read articles in the trades and people jump out at you as particularly insightful or the kind of people who might share your sensibilities or just be the kind of people you'd like to work with, create records in your contact management software with some sort of searchable code "WtWw" (Want to Work With) or "EFM2019" that you met or want to try to meet at specific markets. Track trivia tidbits you learn along the way (i.e. drank Merlot at the EFM; macrobiotic yogi; has three kids, two horses and a Saint Bernard; dad was in the secret service, owns a ranch and lots of guns; sister has Lupus, lived in Tanzania after college, etc.) — you never know what might be relevant to a project in the future.

Part VIII
Important Annual Ancillary Events

Markets and festivals are cogs in the entertainment industry machine that interlock with its annual awards shows and ancillary events that keep the business gears shifting. There are myriad promotional opportunities that can influence the prestige, circulation and market valuation of entertainment properties. The most globally significant events are top noted below, highlighting their market-like elements or promotional, educational or networking opportunities as well as any unique missions the venues cater to to provide you with a quick, orienting overview of these overlapping landscapes.

Top Ten Market-Like Film Festivals 28

Film festivals can be incredible launching pads for films of all kinds but especially independents. Prudently strategized, if you have all your social media gears synchronized, with material that attracts good reviews and buzz, this ecosystem can function as an annual cascading distribution platform, creating momentum as you market direct to the consuming crowd.

There are over 3,000 festivals each year around the world, ranging from the high-profile to genre-specific (i.e. Scream Fest horror festivals) to format-specific (i.e. WebFests and docs). Filmmakers, moviegoers and business insiders debate which festivals are the most important for myriad reasons. Cannes, Toronto, Sundance, Venice are often neck-and-neck internationally with Tribeca and SXSW definitely competing with the middle two for most significant in North America. The prominence of each ebbs and flows based on their ability to attract that year's best world premieres and discover the buzziest dark horse gems. Curating programming that attracts media-vocal crowds doesn't hurt either.

They each have their own, distinct personalities and are better bets for some kinds of films over others, at different points in a film's lifecycle or a given filmmaker's career. Some fests cater to their local, regional or affinity audiences while others cater to the industry. But one thing is certain: distributors attend festivals to gauge audience favorites and pick up critics' darlings. They offer a brilliant forum to engage your cinephile tribe and expand your fan base.

It might seem counter-intuitive, but sometimes working outside the Hollywood system can be one of the most robust ways to actually break *in* to the very industry you're circumnavigating. As the traditional avenues to distribution dissipate, festivals have emerged as an increasingly important exhibition venue.

There are books, websites, blogs and classes galore covering all the festivals. Chief among them: Chris Gore's original 1999 classic *The Ultimate Film Festival Survival Guide* (now in its fourth edition) and his *Film Threat* does a brilliant job surveying this landscape festival-by-festival while Rona Edwards' and Monika Skerbelis' *The Complete Filmmaker's Guide to Film Festivals*, published by Michael Wiese Productions, provides a step-by-step guide to launching your film on the festival circuit. Because this territory has been so ably covered, I will merely CliffsNotes[1] the festivals that have market-like components or characteristics as well as some of those that can significantly impact global market pedigree. Of course, for your own custom film-by-film plan, also integrate niche festivals that cater to your genre, location or other affinity elements.

FESTIVAL DE CANNES

Touched on in the Marché du Film section, the annual Cannes Film Festival is the "Who's Who of Everybody Who's Anybody" in the movie business (or at least anyone who's got anything in play right now). Like its sister market, you must be "accredited," it's not a "People's Fest," you have to be vetted in the industry to attend.

> If you've got a credit on IMDB, you're eligible for free Festival Accreditation!

While distinctly a pure festival, the overlap with its inextricably adjacent and concurrent market is palpable. Tuxes and real diamonds grace the red carpet, black-tie screenings. The iconic, hand-cut, 24k-gold Palme d'Or is the most prestigious prize awarded with a massive press corps second only to the Olympics' press contingent. The whole glitzy event is expensive, housing is hard to come by and pickpockets abound — but you're simultaneously a part of history — and history-making.

Badge color envy and fashionista snobbery abounds. You can get away with "just" a coat and tie for the midnight premieres in the Palais des Festivals and the Directors' Fortnight and Critics' Week, where the more casual dress codes align a little more with other festivals.

Cannes audiences are notorious for being incredibly vocal — either way. Enthusiastic standing ovations for films they love, loud boos for those that don't measure up. It's not unusual to hear a competing cacophony of both for "love it or hate it" entries.

If you are accredited for the market, you can attend all the festival screenings as your schedule may allow. A few events are open to the public. There's a line for their nightly screenings but this can be really fun — especially if you bring a picnic basket and a blanket.

> A cheaper badge can be scored via the Short Film Corner or you can sponsor the film of a filmmaker who cannot attend and attend on their behalf.

Two festival sections are available to the public: tickets to the competitive Critics' Week series are free, while, for a small fee, you can buy a ticket to the non-competitive Directors' Fortnight. Locals (with verifiable ID) can access the free Cannes Cinéphiles screenings held just outside of the festival.

> A few days into the festival, the security on the free local screenings relaxes.

Opportunities

L'Atelier invites the directors of 15 features from around the world, based on the quality of their project and their previous films, and connects them with international financing that might accelerate their production process.

From emerging countries, **La Fabrique des Cinémas du Monde** identifies ten up-and-coming directors working on their first or second feature and invites them to attend the festival along with their producers.

TORONTO INTERNATIONAL FILM FESTIVAL

A public festival, the Toronto International Film Festival has a much more diverse audience cross-section and a much more relaxed dress code. It is known for being one of the most receptive audiences to independent film. Jonathan Wolf, Managing Director of the American Film Market, observes:

> The Toronto audience is uniquely respectful of the artistic process. If you and I were walking along a museum and we stopped at a piece of art that didn't interest us, we would simply move along to the next piece of art. That's like the Toronto audience. They don't boo or hiss or complain and make a big deal out of it, they just move on to the next film. Thus, it's a much safer place for producers and distributors to premiere a film.

TIFF also accepts studio films, which many other film festivals do not. This helps attract bigger stars, larger audiences and more international buzz — possibly at the expense of some of the smaller indie fare that might get lost in the shuffle within such an impressive line-up. It attracts many high-profile foreign language films. About one-tenth of TIFF films are documentaries.

While not a market, per se (meaning there is no market floor with booths or suites), in addition to the public, over 5,000 industry professionals come from 1,800 acquisition outfits from 78 countries to buy and sell the over 1,200 films screened, giving it quite the market-like feel. Over 40 major film sales were announced at the last market and Toronto holds the record for the most expensive film sale to date: $12 million (US) for Chris Rock's *Top Five* (2014), which grossed $25 million.

Lots of business press coverage intermingles with critical reviews. Buyers are incredibly perceptive of public interest and many companies have large teams on the ground gauging the public's response to properties of interest.

TIFF is 11 days in September and also offers a four-day Kids TIFF event in mid-April and TIFF Next wave in mid-February for films by and targeted to teens. The pure size of TIFF's program and its positioning in the calendar make it a unique hybrid model between a traditional bricks-and-mortar marketplace and a public festival.

Opportunities

TIFF offers an annual **Filmmakers Bootcamp** where their press office helps you build a press strategy to tap into your audiences well before the festival to build buzz for your screenings well in advance of ticket sales. Obviously, this is a prudent "win-win" to attract buzz and heat to both their event and progeny as they actively support you by promoting your trailer on TIFF's social media channels.

Their **Midnight Madness** program is the perfect launch pad for genre titles. Colin Geddes, who heads the program, does a great job at whipping their audiences into a raucous frenzy before the screenings. This event reminds you what the collective experience of cinema is all about. These are often the first sales of the festival, largely attributed to the energy of these screenings.

Producers Lab Toronto is a co-production workshop that's produced in partnership with the European Film Promotion and the **Ontario Media Development Corporation (OMDC)**. The Producers Lab connects filmmakers from Europe, Ontario and other guest nations interested in finding partners for the development of co-productions. During the Festival, the OMDC also hosts an **International Film Financing Forum** which is available to experienced producers.

Market-Like Elements

TIFF hosts a **National Film Agency Pavilion**, which helps support over 20 export and trade bodies such as Telefilm Canada and uniFrance have a home base within the Festival Village to encourage the sales of their nation's content.

TIFF offers a **Territory Rights List**, which offers buyers information about which territories are sold for each film in the Festival. Sales agencies can market their screenings directly to registered professionals and there's a **Buyers Lounge** where deals can be privately discussed. The Press and Industry Screening Library enable industry professionals to catch up on festival titles on their own schedule.

Included in the registered delegates' festival passes are business-to-business subscriptions to **Cinando** and **Festival Scope**, which offer delegates critical streaming services following the festival and access to contact information for the global film industry.

> **www.festivalscope.com**
> Festival Scope is an online platform for film professionals involved in acquisitions, programming, international co-productions, film promotion and reviews which allows access to the programming of selected festivals around the world to be viewed on demand.

Private screenings in the TIFF Bell Lightbox cultural center can be hosted by the rights holders during the Festival. The **Delegate Guide and Search** is an in-house tool for registered attendees and the **Brokers Corner** is a concierge service that connects filmmakers with sales representatives and assists with decoding licensing contracts.

TIFF hosts a major Industry Conference over the first seven days of the Festival, which includes the pitching forum: **Telefilm Canada's Pitch This!** Their conference attracts over 10,000 attendees annually to hear the 280 speakers discuss new strategies for the development and creation of independent film through lightning talks, workshops, panels, keynotes and state of the industry talks.

Support for Canadian Films

Founded in 1989, **Film Circuit** is TIFF's successful film outreach program, bringing the best of Canadian and international films and artists to communities across the country. Encompassing over 180 groups in more than 160 communities across Canada, the Film

Circuit helps TIFF lead the world in building markets and audience for Canadian cinema. Film Circuit arranges print traffic, provides development support, researches and prepares film titles and availability lists, offers programming consulting, books guests and ensures cross-Film Circuit communication. Films screened on Film Circuit are event-based and generally classified as limited releases.

TIFF also offers Canadian filmmakers a year-round professional development program geared towards strengthening the domestic film industry and better connecting it with the international marketplace. **TIFF Studio** is a year-round accelerator program for mid-career producers. Eight producers have passed through monthly modules focused on the areas of Development, Collaboration and Team Building, Project Development, Festival Readiness, Financial Resourcefulness, Legal, Distribution and Marketing. Structured peer review and mentoring sessions see their projects through development. With Canadian and international guest speakers, TIFF Studio is a space for filmmakers to feel inspired, consolidate skills, exchange ideas and discuss challenges in a collaborative environment.

SUNDANCE FILM FESTIVAL

The United States' most important film festival, Sundance is the cradle of the American indie movement. The biggest festival for North American distribution with a pretty decent hit ratio, the second your film is publicized in a press release, sales agents will start calling. Significantly the first date in the distribution cycle, Sundance opens the indie film year in January in Park City, Utah.

Out of the over 4,000 feature films submitted from all around the world, only 113 were selected to screen at Sundance in 2017. Features pretty much have to be world premieres unless you luck out and are selected for the highly curated, out-of-competition Spotlight section.

While TIFF screens two and a half times as many films as Sundance, Sundance films do better on a domestic level — especially documentaries. Roughly one-third of Sundance films are documentaries, with a distribution ratio of almost twice that of TIFF. Sundance can also be credited with discovering the majority of the doc Oscar nominees over the past five years.

The Weinstein Company, Sony Pictures Classics and Lionsgate are regulars at Sundance along with all sorts of sales agents and distributors looking for new additions to their slate. *Fruitvale Station, Beasts of the Southern Wild, Swiss Army Man, Weiner* and *Whiplash* were notable recent acquisitions.

Opportunities

Online resources, live workshops and a network of allied organizations empower filmmakers navigating the changing independent film landscape. Institute alumni benefit from a wide array of digital distribution opportunities, promotion and consultation for crowdfunding campaigns and strategies for audience engagement.

SUNDANCE INSTITUTE LABS

An independent film vanguard since the 1970s, Robert Redford and his beloved Sundance established their Institute Lab Program in 1981. They have supported and championed emerging and leading independent filmmakers from over 60 countries for over

30 years. Embracing, encouraging, mentoring and incubating distinctive, singular voices and visions, the Institute has evolved to provide in-depth, year-round support to help the next generation of artists mine their unique and original foci to bring deeply resonant storytelling to engage worldwide audiences.

Fellows in the labs get to meet with creative advisors (screenwriters, directors and showrunners (for their episodic program)) and industry mentors (producers and studio/ network executives) and enjoy one-on-one creative story meetings, pitching sessions, group conversations and, for the episodic program, simulated Writer's Rooms.

Depending on the Lab, many of the Fellows receive customized, year-round support including: ongoing creative and strategic advice, year-round mentors, targeted introductions to ShowRunners, networks, agents and other creative and business professionals as well as opportunities to shadow working television writers, directors and producers and visits to the Writers' Rooms of shows currently in production.

With a mission to espouse freedom of expression, experimentation and risk-taking, the program has opened up and enriched a meaningful and vibrant dialogue across cultural and geographic boundaries. An international model for supporting artists around the world, their esteemed feature film program in Utah includes:

- Screenwriters Lab
- Directors Lab
- Creative Producing Lab and Fellowship

They also offer grants, fellowships and labs around the world. Check their website for the most up-to-date information: www.sundance.org/programs/feature-film.

🔥 HOT TIP!

Independent Screenwriter Fellowship

https://blcklst.com/cassian-elwes

In conjunction with the Black List, Producer Cassian Elwes (*Lee Daniels' The Butler*, *Dallas Buyers Club*, *Blue Valentine*) awards one writer an all expenses paid trip to the Sundance Film Festival and mentorship. The Black List chooses ten screenplays imbued with an independent spirit by unrepresented screenwriters and sends those on to Mr. Elwes for his consideration.

VENICE FILM FESTIVAL

The world's first film festival, founded in 1932 by the Venetian City Council, Venice ranks right alongside Cannes in attracting splashy premieres, star-studded parties and paparazzi galore. The Venice Film Festival is part of a series of separate events entitled "Venice Biennale", which includes art, architecture, dance music and a kids' carnival. Some of the globe's most important premieres, like *Brokeback Mountain* and *The Wrestler*, vie for their grand prize, the Golden Lion, for the best film screened at the festival.

BERLINALE (BERLIN INTERNATIONAL FILM FESTIVAL)

Source: Andrea Teich © Berlinale 2006.

As covered extensively in the EFM and Berlinale Co-Production Market sections, when industry pros reference "Berlin," they are often referring to this trifecta, lumping all three events together due to their seamless logistical and scheduling confluence.

From its Cold War roots in a now-united Berlin, the annual Berlinale is one of the world's most important film festivals. 2015 marked its 65th anniversary with more than 300,000 tickets sold and almost 20,000 industry professionals attracted from 124 countries, including 3,800 journalists from 80 countries. This same year, they were perhaps the first high-profile film festival to begin including top-quality TV series. They also have tracts for shorts, classic restorations and rediscovered films, docs, indigenous films — even culinary-oriented films that sync with a fun, social food truck event.

The Berlinale is an audience festival that shows approximately 400 films as part of its public program, the majority of which are world (or at least European) premieres. Like most major film festivals, they try to program a little bit of everything for all kinds of filmmakers and audiences. In addition to their international competition films, they have a **Panorama** section for independent or art house films by semi-established international filmmakers and a **Forum** and **Forum Expanded** for riskier, artier ventures from newer filmmakers. **Generation** caters to younger audiences while **Perspektive Deutsches Kino** presents the best German films. All non-English films in the festival are presented with English subtitles.

Your EFM market badge includes access to most Berlinale festival screenings (depending, of course, on capacity). Specific screening numbers for each screening are conveniently listed on the website as well as in the printed program. The EFM app will help immeasurably with keeping your calendar straight but Berlinale also has a website with the full festival program and a robust program planner that allows you to search for films by time, date, venue, country, title, people; view trailers and stills; read synopses; tag favorite films you want to keep track of and add screenings to your calendar or even buy tickets. If you would like additional guests to join you for the screenings (who don't have market credentials), they can either buy a festival badge (which ostensibly gets them into all the same festival screenings afforded by a market badge) and/or individual specific film tickets.

🔥 HOT TIP!

Berlinale Tickets

www.berlinale.de | programme My Programme Planner
   Half an hour before every screening starts, all leftover tickets are sold at 50 percent off at each box office. Students pay half price or a 2€ surcharge can get you tickets for any screening that is available at: www.eventim.de.

Berlinale Talents Market Hub

The Berlinale Talents Market Hub offers EFM badge holders first looks at 40 new films developed during the various Berlinale Talents project labs.

Source: Peter Himsel © Berlinale 2013.

This annual initiative enables 300 outstanding creatives from the fields of film and drama series from 78 countries to debut themselves and establish sustainable industry contacts with sales agents open to discovering new talent. This interactive laboratory teaches up-and-coming talent how the EFM works and introduces them to 150 veterans at the peak of their craft, willing to share their experiences and insights to help prepare them for their one-on-one meetings with emerging distributors in the convenient meeting place right in the gallery of the Martin-Gropius-Bau.

SXSW (SOUTH BY SOUTHWEST)

A play on the name of the Alfred Hitchcock film *North by Northwest*, the beloved South by Southwest staggers five overlapping events over nine days in mid-March. Originally, making its name showcasing new music in 1987, SXSW uniquely celebrates the "convergence" of all forms of entertainment and media. Their Film Conference and Festival runs for nine days concurrent with their Interactive Festival, which goes for five days, followed by their Music Festival and Conference that lasts six. Special programming throughout the events on overlapping topics allow any badge holder of one tract to mix and mingle with the other disciplines. Their website (www.sxsw.com) describes the event as "a nexus of discovery and collaborative energy," "SXSW celebrates the art and business of the possible," while their speakers "embody the DIY spirit, ingenuity and entrepreneurial drive."

A record number of 2,400 feature submissions were recently whittled down to 145. Music-oriented and/or interactive films might play particularly well here. Soundtrack-driven premiere or release parties with live music or clever interactive elements might be particularly warmly received here, capitalizing on the spirit, energy and community of the event. Austin, Texas is, indeed, a wonderful haven for creatives.

TRIBECA FILM FESTIVAL

The Tribeca Film Festival was founded in response to the tragic 9/11 attacks. As part of an effort to revitalize the Tribeca neighborhood of lower Manhattan, their mission is to redefine the film festival experience and enable the international film community and the general public to experience the power of film. The festival generates $600 million annually, drawing an estimated three million people to see the 1,500 screenings selected from 8,600 entries.

A unique feature of the Tribeca is Festival is its **Artists Awards** program in which emerging and renowned artists (sculptors, painters, etc.) celebrate filmmakers by providing original works of art that are given to the competition winners.

INTERNATIONAL FILM FESTIVAL ROTTERDAM

Essentially the first co-production market, CineMart is covered extensively in that section as embedded in the **International Film Festival Rotterdam** (IFFR). One of the largest audience- and industry-driven film festivals in the world, the IFFR celebrates 220 feature films from 60 countries over 12 festival days in late January in South Holland to an audience of over 287,000, with 2,400 of them film professionals.

Launched in 1972 to support the newly established art house cinema circuit in the Netherlands, the IFFR maintains its focus on innovative filmmaking by talented newcomers and established auteurs as well as on presenting diverse, cutting-edge media art.

The festival's Tiger Awards Competitions, Bright Future and Spectrum sections contain recent work only, many of which are world premieres, while its Signals section presents retrospectives and themed programs.

To participate in the famous Rotterdam Lab, which includes speed-dating pitches, panel discussions, networking lunches and cocktails, you must be nominated by one of their partner organizations.

SOFIA INTERNATIONAL FILM FESTIVAL

In 2015, the Sofia International Film Festival celebrated 100 years of Bulgarian Cinema with a special acknowledgment as one of UNESCO's Creative Cities of Film. Actually celebrating the twentieth anniversary of the festival and featured as one of *Variety*'s top 50 cinema festivals, more than 1,600 feature films and documentaries have been screened since 1997 with more than 1,000 distinguished guests. What started as a thematic music film festival now brings world cinema to Bulgarian viewers — and contemporary Bulgarian cinema to the rest of the world.

The Sofia Meetings and Balkan Screenings are covered in the Co-Production section.

PALM SPRINGS INTERNATIONAL FILM FESTIVAL

Due to its proximity to Los Angeles, Palm Springs is an easy, peaceful drive that attracts a surprising number of stars and heavy hitters, eager to escape the industry city for weekend getaways. Because of its savvy industry audience and focus from inception on international cinema, it is noted for screening the most foreign Oscar nominees. Prior to the festival's public opening, several of the foreign filmmakers convene to discuss strategies on funding, producing and promoting their movies.

One of the largest festivals in North America, it attracts around 135,000 people and lots of press to its star-studded gala awards which have included: Ben Affleck, Cate Blanchett, George Clooney, Daniel Day-Lewis, Leonardo DiCaprio, Clint Eastwood, Sean Penn, Brad Pitt, Natalie Portman, Charlize Theron and Kate Winslet to their spectacular desert scenery.

Palm Springs ShortFest and Market

The ShortFest is one of a handful of Oscar-qualifying festivals in the US, with its first place winners in live action, animation and Best of the Fest automatically qualifying for nomination consideration by the Academy Awards. Out of 3,000 entries from 82 countries, 320 shorts were recently screened for 400 filmmakers. With a concurrent market of 2,700 titles, the ShortFest Forums also provide master classes, panels, roundtables and networking.

NOTE

1 Study guides that consolidate and simplify lots of information. Canadian Coles Notes originated the concept (and licensed US rights).

Globally Significant, Pedigree-Building Film Festivals

There are a great many festivals that, while they might not rank in the "Top Ten" or have market-like elements, are significant on the global scene for creating awareness, traction and contributing to a film's perceived value in the marketplace. Several such key festivals follow below in alphabetical order.

AFI FEST

AFI FEST is Los Angeles' longest running international film festival. The only film festival in the United States to hold the prestigious FIAPF accreditation, assuring a high standard of quality and reliability for the international film community, AFI FEST has been bringing the best in world cinema to the film capital of the world since its launch as FILMEX in 1971.

Nightly red-carpet galas, special screenings, conversations and tributes, AFI FEST presents a program of new international cinema from filmmakers around the globe. The Academy of Motion Picture Arts and Sciences recognizes AFI FEST as a qualifying festival for both Short Film categories of the annual Academy Awards®.

While not officially affiliated, they are just a few freeways away from and concurrent with the American Film Market (the only market in the world not partnered with a film festival).

AUSTIN INTERNATIONAL FILM FESTIVAL

Where screenwriters are perhaps most honored, the Austin International Film Fest is one of the most fun, casual film festivals. Founded in 1993, the AFF champions storytelling language.

A wonderful community in a relaxed, walking town, the four days of panels and workshops and eight nights of films and parties often end in memory-making all-night hangouts at the Driskill Hotel lounge on 6th Street and the bar area in the Intercontinental Hotel on 7th and Congress, next to the Paramount theater. An inspiring, relaxing break, the AFF allows screenwriters, especially (and those who love or at least appreciate them), to connect and reinvigorate.

BANFF

The Banff Mountain Film Festival, held in conjunction with its Book Festival, in the fall in Alberta, Canada, takes its best 25 films out of the approximately 60 screened from the 300 submitted and tours them to 305 cities in 20 countries. Adventure sports, mountain culture and environmental films tend to do well here, especially climbing, skiing, snowboarding, kayaking, biking, mountain biking, BASE jumping, snow-kiting and speedriding.

BEIJING INTERNATIONAL FILM FESTIVAL

The Beijing International Film Festival is fairly new (launched in 2011) but has quickly become the largest in China's burgeoning film scene. Held in April, it is hosted by the Film Bureau of the General Administration of Press, Publication, Radio, Film and Television of China and the People's Government of Beijing Municipality's Bureau of Radio, Film and Television. A significant platform for the Chinese film industry and a major cultural event for Beijing, striving to establish itself as China's cultural center, this festival focuses on the development of China's film industry, including the Beijing Film Market.

BUENOS AIRES INTERNATIONAL INDEPENDENT FILM FESTIVAL (BAFICI)

For 11 days, every April since 1999, Argentina welcomes cinephiles to theaters in every district of their city. About 370,000 film fans enjoyed the 400 films at their 2015 event. Like most film festivals, they prefer to score worldwide premieres but will accept being the first showing in their country. They especially love risky, innovative, groundbreaking material and reserve separate awards for the best Argentinean features and shorts. There are, of course, several international competitions and thematic tracks as well as conferences, seminars and concerts. The Buenos Aries Lab (BAL) allows works in progress to compete for funding.

A popular cultural event, many of the city's film students and other film fans cram in as many films as possible during BAFICI. They'll take coffee and meal breaks to hobnob with other festivalgoers in and around the recently renovated Recoleta Village. The public is invited to vote for the People's Choice Award. Most films are shown in their original language with either English or Spanish subtitles and many are followed by cast and ATL[1] crew Q&A sessions. Tickets for the official selections sell out quickly. You can buy tickets in advance online.

BUSAN INTERNATIONAL FILM FESTIVAL

As covered briefly in Chapter 17, the Busan International Film Festival focuses on discovering Asian and specifically Korean cinema talent. They celebrated their twentieth anniversary in 2016 with 300 films (with 122 of them world premieres) from 69 countries on 34 screens in 5 theaters.

The Asian Cinema Fund offers financial support through feature length incubation, for post-production, documentaries and independent films in Asia.

CHAMPS-ÉLYSÉES FILM FESTIVAL INDUSTRY DAYS

While the Paris Co-Production Village is covered in the Co-Production section (Part IV), it is organized by Les Arcs European Film Festival but takes place during the Champs-Élysées Film Festival's Industry Days. For six days in June in Paris, this relatively new festival showcases its competition of American independent features and shorts as well as French shorts. Its out of competition selections includes French and American premieres and classics as well as themed curations. In addition to the Paris Co-Production Market, this festival also hosts the US in Progress program, a workshop for films in the final-editing stages competing to win promotion and post-production services.

HONG KONG INTERNATIONAL FILM FESTIVAL

The HKIFF is one of Asia's most reputable platforms for filmmakers, film professionals and filmgoers. Screening over 280 titles from more than 50 countries in 11 major cultural venues across the territory, the Festival is Hong Kong's largest cultural event. It reaches an audience of over 600,000, including the 5,000 business executives who are in concurrent attendance at the Hong Kong International Film & TV Market (FILMART) and over 500 members of the local and international press.

The Hong Kong International Film Festival Society (HKIFFS) is committed to the development of a vibrant film culture in Hong Kong and Asia. As such, the festival premieres the breadth of Chinese cinema and showcases Asian talents. Beyond just watching movies, festivalgoers are welcome to attend seminars hosted by leading filmmakers from around the world, visit film exhibitions and enjoy the parties.

LES ARCS EUROPEAN FILM FESTIVAL

In December in the French Alps, Les Arcs ski resort welcomes more than 130,000 visitors (including 800 industry professionals and 90 journalists) to watch 70 European films (including Turkey and Russia) to be screened in 114 screenings in the resort's 7 theaters. A total of 12 films compete for the Crystal Arrow while 10 European films are screened as previews and 8 classics are screened for young people. The event includes parties, special events, concerts and DJ receptions (that is, if you can get away from the amazing skiing). Les Arcs European Film Festival programs the Paris Co-Production Village (covered in the Co-Production section, Part IV) that is held during the Champs-Élysées Film Festival's Industry Days.

LOS ANGELES FILM FESTIVAL

In the heart of Hollywood, this festival attracts more than 90,000 people and showcases a variety of independent, feature, international, documentary, short films and music videos.

MUNICH FILM FESTIVAL

The largest summer festival in Germany, second in size and importance only to the Berlinale, the Munich Film Festival has been held since 1983. In late June, over 200 feature films and documentaries grace 18 screens for approximately 70,000 movie fans. The festival attracts 2,500 industry professionals and 600 members of the press and media. Honoring everything from classic and new German films, to no-budget emerging film-makers and retrospectives, to kinderfest for kids four and up, the line-up is quite eclectic and much less about the transactional buying and selling of films and far more about their discovery and enjoyment.

NEW YORK FILM FESTIVAL

Not exactly a "discovery" or even a "submission" festival, the NYFF is a highly curated event programmed by film critics and organized by NYC's Film Society of Lincoln Center. Selecting the most critically acclaimed films from international auteurs from the world's top film festivals and mixing them with some lesser known titles from emerging filmmakers, the NYFF's line-up of about 30 films is always hotly debated but represents each year's most intriguing cinematic offerings. Music and art events are coordinated, as are their touring screenings in Los Angeles, Las Vegas and Miami.

RAINDANCE

Held for 10 days at the end of September, the Raindance Film Festival screens about 100 feature films and 150 shorts and webseries in Piccadilly Circus in Central London. Immediately following that, in early October, they also host a three-day market that reveals industry-only first-cuts and works-in-progress from Latin America.

🎵 HOT TIP!

Raindance Masters Degree

Raindance offers an innovative, immersive post-graduate program that can be taken part-time, online, 80 percent of which can be customized to what you want to learn — including making your own independent film — resulting in your choice of a Master of Arts or a Master of Sciences, validated by Staffordshire University. For more info, visit: www.raindance. org/postgraduate.

SAN SEBASTIAN FILM FESTIVAL

Created in 1953, the San Sebastian Film Festival is one of the 14 competitive film festivals accredited by FIAPF.[2] Hosted in the Basque country of Spain in September, it has hosted such historical cinematic milestones as the international premiere of *Vertigo*, Woody Allen's *Melinda and Melinda* and the European premiere of *Star Wars*. Since its inception, the festival has welcomed luminaries such as: Alfred Hitchcock, Bette Davis, Gregory Peck, Elizabeth Taylor, Audrey Hepburn, Robert De Niro, Meryl Streep, Richard Gere, Michael Douglas, Catherine Zeta-Jones, Mel Gibson, Demi Moore, Naomi Watts, Brad Pitt and Roman Polanski. The festival was also key in the advancement of the professional careers of Francis Ford Coppola and Pedro Almodóvar. In spite of being one of the lowest budgeted festivals, it remains one of the most significant, especially among Spanish speaking countries.

SINGAPORE INTERNATIONAL FILM FESTIVAL

Focused on telling the stories of Asia, Southeast Asia and the world through the cinematic experience, 2017 was the twenty-seventh installment of the SGIFF. Late November, early December saw 12,000 festival attendees watch over 100 films from all around the world.

TELLURIDE FILM FESTIVAL

With well over a 40-year history, the Telluride Film Festival celebrates the four-day Labor Day summer weekend in this affluent Colorado ski town. Operated by the National Film Preserve, Telluride only accepts films for which it will be offered North American premiere rights. The festival honors three important cinematic figures each year, ranging from past and present famous and "deserves to be better known." Relying on audience loyalty, they screen both new and classic films but don't announce their line-up until the day before the festival begins. A bit like summer camp for cinephiles, it's hosted in a pricey resort town that can be tough to get to and doesn't offer a lot in terms of low-cost accommodations, though there are outdoor screenings and free showings of docs and special programs in a small local theater for those on a budget. This event is all about the movies but there is a Labor Day BBQ celebration.

TOKYO INTERNATIONAL FILM FESTIVAL

Established in 1985 and recently held during one week on October, the TIFF is the only Japanese festival accredited by the FIAPF. Their best film is awarded the Tokyo Sakura Grand Prix.

🎬 HOT TIP!

Many festivals now require that your first public debut be your world premiere with them. You can still enjoy cast-and-crew screenings or capitalize on works-in-progress co-production opportunities — but be careful: if you charge anything at the door or get significant press for a screening, your premiere status might be jeopardized and cost you your best festival opportunities.

NOTE

1 Above-the-Line (Pre-Production Creatives).
2 Fédération Internationale des Associations de Producteurs de Films; English: International Federation of Film Producers Associations.

Television festivals are growing rapidly. Studios, networks and television stars increasingly see the value of marketing their content in person to their affinity groups via these live events to build momentum, social media buzz — and community. Geographic regions capitalize on the opportunity to celebrate the medium while courting industry to discover the locations, amenities and production resources of their hubs. This is a constantly changing landscape but, below, a few of the most established and newer breakout players are highlighted.

ATX TELEVISION FESTIVAL

For four days every June in Austin, Texas, 150 panelists (98 percent of whom are not local to Texas) debate and celebrate the past, present and future of the medium of television through screenings, panel discussions and events.

BANFF WORLD MEDIA FESTIVAL

For 37 years, BANFFWMF has brought content creators from all around the globe to Canada in June. Some 150 development executives join producers and content creators, broadcasters and online publishers, and the full gamut of production service vendors, professional service providers, associations and policy developers to examine the critical issues confronting television and digital media.

CELTIC MEDIA FESTIVAL

Established in the UK in 1980, three days in March every year are spent honoring the best in film, television, radio and new media that promotes the languages and culture of the Celtic nations (Scotland, Ireland, Wales, Isle of Man, Cornwall, Brittany and Galicia) in 20 different categories.

EDINBURGH INTERNATIONAL TELEVISION FESTIVAL

Since 1976, the MacTaggart Lecture has been the centerpiece of the August UK event, delivered by Ted Turner, Rupert Murdoch and Kevin Spacey, among many others. The Gamechangers strand showcases the disruptors while Meet the Controllers provides insights from the major commissioning players. Through its charitable council, the festival offers two fully funded programs to nurture the next generation of talent. Started in 1990, the Network allows entry-level talent the opportunity to apply for free event accommodations and the opportunity to work alongside volunteering veterans while Ones to Watch is a bespoke mentorship program for those with 3–5 years professional TV experience. In 2015, 2,000 attendees from 22 countries enjoyed 60 sessions, screenings and master classes as well as speed-pitching matchmaking over three days.

FESPACO (THE FESTIVAL PANAFRICAIN DU CINÉMA ET DE LA TELEVISION DE OUAGADOUGOU)

Held in March in Burkina Faso, West Africa, the Panafrican Film and Television Festival is exclusively for African filmmakers and content creators. Opening night is held in the national stadium and the organization works year-round to promote African cinema and content to other international festivals.

FESTIVAL INTERNATIONAL DE PROGRAMMES AUDIOVISUELS

Established in 1987, FIPA is a six-day platform in France in January for the discovery and debate for both television professionals as well as the general public, connecting content creators directly with their audiences, including over 1,500 school children and students as well as a three-day core program of industry matchmaking and pitching. Approximately 130 programs in a range of genres are selected from over 1,200 entries from 70 countries to compete in 6 categories or screen in 3 competition sections.

FESTVAL SPAIN

Spanish radio and television networks share their new premieres and organize a jury of critics every September in the Basque city Vitoria Gasteiz.

ITVFEST (INDEPENDENT TELEVISION FESTIVAL)

The original public television (and webseries and short film) festival, ITVFest is held in the verdant Vermont mountains in September, where over 1,000 content creators, executives and audience members gather to relax and enjoy independent episodic content. IndieWire calls this event the "Sundance of Independent Television."

MONTE-CARLO TELEVISION FESTIVAL

Founded in 1961 by Prince Rainier III of Monaco who recognized television as a new art form that could bring cultures together and enhance their respective knowledge, the Monte-Carlo Television Festival is one of the finest festivals in the world (no doubt enhanced by its location). In addition to their prestigious Golden Nymph Award, among many others, for the past 11 years, the festival has paired with Eurodata TV Worldwide, a television ratings analysis firm, to give the International TV Audience Award to the drama, comedy and telenovela (soap opera) series that have achieved the most viewers across five continents.

NEW YORK TELEVISION FESTIVAL

A pioneer of the independent television movement, the NYTVF has been connecting artists with networks, studios, agencies, production companies, brands — and their fans for just over a decade and providing a year-round forum through their NYTVY 365 programming. The weeklong festival is held in the fall in Manhattan and most recently saw 115,000 attendees attend 704 free events screenings and panels. 1,027 traditional and online programs were selected from over 15,500 submissions. All Official Artists selected are comped badges and invited to participate in the **NYTVF Connect** collaborative industry networking environment which included 412 meetings, 20 development chats, 10 networking mixers, resulting in at least 20 guaranteed development deals.

SCAD'S ATVFEST

Georgia's film and television industry has grown to $6 billion annually, perhaps inspiring the Savannah College of Art and Design to host aTVFest to enable their student body to network with and be screened alongside work of professionals from around the world. 2016 marked the fourth year of their four-day event held in February in Atlanta. 2015 saw 6,000 attendees honor Terrence Howard with the Spotlight Award, Timothy Hutton with the Icon Award and the students of *How to Get Away with Murder* with the Rising Star Award.

SERIESFEST

In Denver, Colorado, the birthplace of cable television, the best new pilots and emerging television shows from established and emerging content creators are showcased at the Red Rocks Amphitheater in June. 2017 marked just their third year, which allows the general public sneak peeks usually reserved for the industry as well as the opportunity to watch a writer's life change as three scripts selected out of hundreds are brought to life via a table read and one is selected for a development deal to possibly get their pilot professionally produced.

VERCIÊNCIA BRAZIL

Since 1994, during the third week of October, the International Exhibition of Science on TV provides free admission to public screenings of television programs that convey science in an interesting and informative manner. Augmented by free, related public lectures, this non-profit, non-competitive event occurs simultaneously in multiple cities in Brazil, including Rio De Janeiro, São Paulo and Brasília.

International Documentary Festivals

31

HOT DOCS

Hot Docs Canadian International Documentary Festival is North America's largest documentary festival, conference and market. Founded in 1993 by the Documentary Organization of Canada (formerly the Canadian Independent Film Caucus), their 2017 market had a record attendance of 215,000 and attracted 2,000 delegates including documentary filmmakers, buyers, programmers, distributors and commissioning editors from around the world.

This festival presents a selection of more than 230 documentaries from Canada and around the globe. Fifty producers with the most compelling completed films and rough cuts have the chance to meet one-on-one with an impressive list of 190 distributors, sales agents, commissioning editors, financiers and festival programmers through the Hot Docs Forum, Distribution Rendezvous and Deal Maker meetings. Because of its unusual format, it's also a preeminent source of market intelligence for both buyers and sellers.

INTERNATIONAL DOCUMENTARY FESTIVAL AMSTERDAM

Please see this entry in the Co-Production section (Part IV, Chapter 17).

SUNNY SIDE OF THE DOC

Sunny Side operates international television markets focusing on specialist factual and documentary programming to promote co-production and sales relationships amongst production companies and broadcasters. Celebrating their twenty-fifth anniversary in 2014, the 2017 event in La Rochelle, France hosted over 2,000 delegates including 300 international decision makers and 500 exhibiting companies from 60 countries including delegations from Australia, South Africa, Brazil, China and South Korea presenting over 700 projects and programs.

Asian Side

Created in 2010, the first Asian Side of the Doc was held for four days in March of 2015 in Xiaman, China and has averaged 500 delegates from 40 countries.

Latin Side

The last Latin Side of the doc was held in November of 2012 in Mexico with 59 decision makers reviewing 102 registered projects including 16 pitched docs and 9 docs in progress.

In an industry of performers and marketeers, there is no end to the awards given by festivals, critics, unions and guilds. The key film and television awards can raise audience and industry awareness as well as professional pedigree and potentially translate into extended distribution windows and enhanced profits. A few of the major awards are highlighted below.

KEY FILM AWARDS

The Oscars (Academy Awards)

Hosted by the Academy of Motion Picture Arts and Sciences (AMPAS), a professional honorary organization of almost 6,000 motion picture professionals from around the globe (though most are based in the United States), the Academy Awards (now officially known as "The Oscars") is one of the most prestigious filmmaking awards in the world. Dedicated to the advancement of the arts and sciences of motion pictures, the Academy also annually awards the Governors Award for lifetime achievement in film, Scientific and Technical Awards to innovative professionals and companies, Student Academy Awards to filmmakers at the undergraduate and graduate levels, and up to five Nicholl Fellowships in Screenwriting to amateur screenwriters.

Film Independent's Spirit Awards

Film Independent's Spirit Awards was the first event to exclusively honor independent film. Its trophy, a bird sitting atop a pole with shoestrings wrapped around it, is a nod to the budgets that independent filmmakers must typically contend with. They celebrated their thirtieth anniversary in 2016.

Intentionally scheduled the day before the Oscars, they capitalize on all the talent already in town for the next day's more glamorous event. While more casual and relaxed, the Indie Spirit Awards is still quite the star-studded event. They are known for the great party they throw, traditionally on the beach in Santa Monica (but, of course, it's still Hollywood: so there's valet parking). They set up huge tents in the parking lot à la a traveling Cirque du Soleil performance. Broadcast on the Independent Film Channel and celeb-loving Bravo, winners are voted on by the non-profit Film Independent and Independent Feature Project Members. While the bulk of the membership is made up of independent filmmakers, true to the spirit of indie film, film lovers from the general public are welcome to join and vote, too (capitalizing on the free DVDs and screenings) and even volunteer to work the event as well.

🚦 HOT TIP!

An excellent career goal for an up-and-coming indie filmmaker is to shoot for the **Cassavettes Award** that honors the "Best Feature Made for under $500k (US)." This is the perfect "Get on the Grid" award that could set you apart. Professionals respect and track these winners as an early indicator of future potential.

German Film Awards (the Lola; Deutscher Filmpreis)

Named in honor of Marlene Dietrich's title role, the Lola Award is the highest honor of excellence awarded within the German cinematic landscape. From 1951 through 2004, it was juried by a political commission: the Federal Commissioner for Cultural and Media Affairs. In 2005, the members of the German Film Academy followed the American model for voting and have hosted the annual gala since 2006. With cash prizes of €3 million, it is the most highly endowed cultural award.

Asian Film Awards

Annually recognizing the excellence of professionals in the Asian film industry, the Asian Film Awards Academy organizes the Asian Film Awards. Recently relocated from Hong Kong to Macao, the red-carpet event attracts over 4,000 guests from around the world to celebrate the growing power of Asian cinema on the international film scene.

Hong Kong Film Awards

Founded in 1982 by the Hong Kong Film Awards Association, the event is currently in April and honors films commercially released in Hong Kong in the prior year that satisfy two of the following three criteria: the director is a Hong Kong resident, at least one of the film companies are registered in Hong Kong and/or at least six of the production crew are Hong Kong residents. Films that don't fit two of the above criteria (but are released in Hong Kong) are eligible for "Best Asian Film."

Spanish Film Awards (the Goya; Los Premios Goya)

Established in 1987 by Spanish Academy of Cinematic Art and Science, the Goya Awards are Spain's most significant annual film honors. The ceremony takes place at the end of January or beginning of February, awarding the previous year's films.

The MTV Movie Awards

Executively produced by Mark Burnett (*Survivor*, *The Bible*), nominees for these awards are selected by MTV executives and producers, allowing the winners to be decided online by the general public through a special link at movieawards.mtv.com. Of course, the show airs on MTV.

KEY TELEVISION AWARDS

The Emmys

What the Oscars are to film, the Emmys are to TV. There are actually several Emmy Awards ceremonies but the two that garner the most attention are the Prime Time and the Daytime Emmys. Other live (but not usually televised) events include awards for sports, news, business and financial reporting, documentaries, advancements in technology and engineering as well as regional awards for local, statewide and international programming as well as the College Emmys (which are a great way to break into the business if you're a student!).

The Emmy Awards are presented by three different entities, each of which administers their respective tract: the Academy of Television Arts & Sciences (ATAS), the National Academy of Television Arts & Sciences (NATAS) and the International Academy of Television Arts & Sciences (IATAS).

NATPE's Reality Breakthrough Awards

Reality television has grown exponentially in every direction. In an effort to shine a light on stand-out programming that managed to "break through the clutter" of their distinctive subgenres, in 2015, NATPE unveiled its first annual Reality Breakthrough Awards at a luncheon hosted by Howie Mandel. *Shark Tank* Producer and NATPE board member Phil Gurin spearheaded the blue ribbon panel of TV buyers, executives, agents and distributors who nominated unscripted programming that they felt represented the best in five categories (Competition, DocuSoap, Game Show, Reality and Factual) that they felt became a part of the cultural conversation and altered our expectations of what constitutes a reality program.

The Brandon Tartikoff Legacy Awards

Named in honor of Brandon Tartikoff, a beloved programmer whose imprint on the television industry will be forever felt, NATPE's Brandon Tartikoff Legacy Awards was inaugurated in 2004. A select handful of television executives are recognized every year, who exhibit extraordinary passion, leadership, independence and vision in the process of creating television programming and evoke Tartikoff's incredible spirit of generosity. One of the highest awards in television production and programming, his Legacy Awards are presented every year in a ceremony at the NATPE conference after a gala rooftop cocktail party overlooking the ocean.

Realscreen Awards

The Realscreen Awards honors non-fiction and factual entertainment excellence in a high-profile, global celebration presented at Realscreen West in Santa Monica in June.

BOTH FILM AND TV AWARDS SHOWS

British Academy Film and Television Awards (BAFTAs)

The British Academy of Film and Television Arts (BAFTA) is an independent charity made up of over 6,500 expert members from the UK and the US who annually recognize the best moving image work of any nationality seen on British film, television and gaming screens the preceding year.

The Britannia Awards

The Britannia Award is the highest accolade presented by BAFTA Los Angeles. It is a celebration of achievement honoring individuals and companies from the US, UK and beyond who have dedicated their careers or corporate missions to advancing the art forms of the moving image. Presented annually at the Britannia Awards gala dinner, peers and colleagues celebrate the work and accomplishments of the distinguished honorees who gather to celebrate the fruitful relationship between the UK and US industries. The first Britannia Award was presented in 1989 to Albert R. "Cubby" Broccoli, pioneer producer of the *James Bond* films. Since the gala's inception, the Britannia Awards ceremony has expanded to include multiple presentations celebrating living legends, rising British stars and internationally acclaimed colleagues.

Golden Globes

The Golden Globes is an American award that is voted on by the **H**ollywood **F**oreign **P**ress **A**ssociation (HFPA), a non-profit currently comprised of 93 international journalists based in Southern California who serve as "boots on the ground" conduits of entertainment industry news to all the outlets in their respective countries. Nearing its seventy-fifth anniversary, the Golden Globes recognize excellence in film and television, both domestic and foreign. Its trophy is a golden globe with a filmstrip encircling it.

 Every year, the daughter or son of a celebrity is named to assist with the high-profile event. Miss or Mr. Golden Globe Timeline: www.hfpa.org/missmr-golden-globe

The People's Choice Awards

The People's Choice Awards is a popular culture awards show voted on by the general public. Produced by Procter & Gamble and Reality TV producer, Mark Burnett (*Survivor*, *The Bible*), the People's Choice Award is broadcast in America on CBS and in Canada on Global.

TV Land Awards

Celebrating classic television that is no longer in current production, the TV Land Awards recognizes actors, series and producers. Aired since 2003 (save a two-year hiatus), the statuettes are given for a variety of categories that differ slightly from year to year but typically include: Future Classic, Pop Culture, Pioneer, Legend, Little Screen/Big Screen Star, Favorite Airborne Character, 100th Anniversary, Impact, Great TV Music Moments, Innovator, Lucille Ball Legacy of Laughter, Fun Favorite, Classic TV Housewives. Hosts have included: John Ritter (the inaugural year), Neil Patrick Harris (of course), Megan Mullally, Kelly Rippa, Vanessa L. Williams, Tim Allen, Brad Garrett, Cedric the Entertainer, Terry Crews, Jane Lynch and George Lopez.

Streamy Awards

The Streamy Awards celebrate the best in online video, bringing together YouTube stars to recognize online channels, series, shows, creators, producers, writers and personalities. Seven million views on YouTube, 2.8 million Vine loops in 24 hours and three worldwide trending topics on Twitter in 2014 led to 2015's five-year anniversary being broadcast live on VH1 from the historic Hollywood Palladium. 2016 saw it expand internationally to Streamys India. 2017 is set to air live on Twitter from Beverly Hills.

Razzies

Since 1980, the Golden Raspberry (RAZZIE®) Awards have publicly dishonored the Worst Achievements in Film. In categories as obvious as Worst Picture, Worst Actor/Actress to the Worst Prequel, Remake, Rip-Off or Sequel, Worst Screen Couple, Worst Screen Ensemble, the Razzie Awards are themselves a light-hearted parody of award shows in general (the Oscars in particular).

Like the Indie Spirit Awards, the Razzies are the day before the Oscars to capitalize on the stars being in town and available. Most (not surprisingly) don't show up to accept their awards but Director Paul Verhoeven was the first recipient to claim his award in person. He "won" for Worst Picture and Worst Director for *Showgirls* in 1995. Sandra Bullock (*All About Steve*, 2009), and Halle Berry (*Catwoman*, 2004) both famously braved the scene, too, to accept their public humiliation in person, garnering more fans in the process for having exhibited a sense of humor about themselves and their performances. J. David Shapiro won twice in a decade for the same film: *Battlefield Earth*: Worst Screenplay (2001) and Worst Picture of the Decade (2010). Adam Sandler recently shattered Eddie Murphy's record for the most nominations. Covered by all the major media, E! On-Line recently called the Razzies "the foremost authority on all things that suck on the big screen."[1]

EGOT

The polar opposite is the pinnacle of achievement in our industry: the EGOT. Considered the "grand slam" of show business, only 12–16 talents (depending on whether you count honorary awards or not), have achieved this esteemed apex on winning an **E**mmy (TV), a **G**rammy (Music), an **O**scar (film) and a **T**ony (Theater).

NOTE

1 www.razzies.com/1/post/2016/05/-the-razzies-own-your-bad.html.

Overlapping Industries' Events 33

CONSUMER ELECTRONICS SHOW (CES)

Ironically, not open to the public, the International Consumer Electronics Show (or more commonly referred to as just "CES"), is an internationally renowned electronics and technology trade show, representing the $292 billion U.S. consumer technology industry. Another massive, sprawling event, the annual show is held each January in the Las Vegas Convention Center in Nevada with 3,900 exhibitors attracting 170,000 industry professionals from 150 countries. Sponsored by the Consumer Electronics Association (the technology trade association), the show typically hosts previews of new products and technologies, a whole pavilion of startups and over 300 conference sessions. CES rose to prominence after its former rival show, COMDEX, was canceled. Many studios and brands take customized VIP tours of this event[1] to stay get ahead of the trends and get the jump on synergistic opportunities just bubbling up on the horizon.

CINEMACON (FORMERLY SHOWEST)

Known as ShoWest for 36 years, the official convention of the National Association of Theater Owners (NATO) marked its five-year anniversary as the newly rebranded "CinemaCon" in 2015. A star-studded extravaganza with a trade show, screenings and an awards ceremony, 2,300 theater owners, ranging from single-screen art-house theaters to 2,000+ screen chains, from 80 countries around the world, converge on the Colosseum, a premiere, state-of-the-art performance venue in Las Vegas, which boasts three levels of seating capacity of 4,200, which can accommodate the entire delegation under one roof at the same time for the same screening. Rounded out by 500 booths and 14 suites, all 6 major studios conduct one-on-one meetings behind closed doors at Caesars. With a significant increased focus on overseas markets, their Directors Forum has hosted Martin Scorsese, Ang Lee, Guillermo del Toro, Oliver Stone and Sam Raimi.
     They jointly make industry decisions on programming that serve the entire industry's interest. They are joined by the equipment manufacturer dealer trader group, the International Cinema Technology Association (ICTA), and their food, candy and beverage vendor alliance, the National Association of Conessionairs (NAC) as well as the full spectrum of ancillary professionals. Exhibition premier event, their official magazine is *Boxoffice*.

NAB

The **N**ational **A**ssociation of **B**roadcasters is the trade association for radio and television broadcasters. Referred to colloquially in the industry by its three-letter acronym, "NAB," their show of the same name is the world's largest annual conference and expo for professionals who create, manage and distribute entertainment across all platforms. A six-day event in Las Vegas, NAB is far more technical and political than many of the other content creation, financing and distribution-focused events covered in this book. The latest advances in streaming, engineering and content creation are highlighted at the convergence of media, entertainment and technology. If you're looking for hands-on experiences with the latest innovations (drones, Virtual Reality, 6K, etc.), NAB is the place to be (or send your DP,[2] editor, post-production supervisor, and D.I.T.![3]).

PROMAXBDA CONFERENCE

Promax was established in 1956 as a non-profit, full-service, membership-driven association for promotion and marketing professionals working in broadcast media. In 1997, The **B**roadcast **D**esign **A**ssociation (BDA), who had partnered with Promax for years on their annual conference, officially joined forces with Promax — and they jointly became PromaxBDA.

Their association represents more than 10,000 companies and individuals at every major media organization, marketing agency, research company, strategic and creative vendor and technology provider and is considered to be the leading global resource for education, community, creative inspiration and career development in the media and media marketing sectors. Entertainment marketing professionals include those in promotion, public relations, communications, design, interactive, media planning, media strategy, brand integration, sales support, affiliate marketing, creative services, traffic, on-air, off-air, research and brand strategy. Drawing from more than 65 countries, their conferences take place in Europe, Arabia, the United States, Asia, Australia, Africa, New Zealand, South America and the UK. PromaxBDA members drive audiences and ratings to the networks, stations and content brands through effective and creative marketing strategies.

US–CHINA FILM SUMMIT

Established in 2010 in an effort to unite the Hollywood and Chinese film industries, the Asia Society Southern California attracts about 400 top executives for one intensive day to discuss market trends and co-productions, topped off with a gala dinner. The 2016 event was held in November at UCLA.

THE WORLD ANIMATION AND VFX SUMMIT

Held at the California Yacht Club in beautiful Marina Del Rey in early November, the worldwide animation and VFX Summit connects studio executives, producers, agents, distributors and talent face-to-face in a warm and intimate coastal club environment. Meet the technology companies who are introducing the latest software and hardware to cut costs and streamline the international co-production process and hear from studio professionals how they make the blockbusters that set the bar for international distribution. Stay up-to-date online via their *Animation Magazine*.

MIDEM

The leading international business event for the music ecosystem. The same team that coordinates all the MIPs hosts Midem, the acronym for the **M**arché **I**nternational du **D**isque et de l'**E**dition **M**usicale. Right back at the Palais des Festivals in Cannes, this is where music makers, cutting-edge technologies, brands and talent come together under one roof to source, sell and sign new music, digital solutions and innovative ideas. This tradeshow is focused on the core music business (labels, publishers and rights societies), the technology sector (startups, developers and big tech companies), brands and the agencies that represent them for music+brand campaigns. Launched in 1967, thousands of musicians, producers, agents, managers, lawyers, executives, entrepreneurs and journalists from around the globe gather to hear new artists and live music being showcased night and day.

INTERNET AND TELEVISION EXPO
(INTX, FORMERLY THE CABLE SHOW)

A mash-up at the crossroads of entertainment, communications, technology and the Internet, the entire digital media ecosystem converges in May in Chicago including: network operators, content creators, online video providers, streaming and cloud services.

NOTES

1 One highly recommended CES VIP tour company is StoryTech (www.http://story-tech.com).
2 Director of Photography (also known as "cinematographer").
3 Digital Imaging Technician (digital camera crew department member).

Significant Consumer Events

COMIC-CON INTERNATIONAL: SAN DIEGO

Comic-Con is not "technically" a festival. It is a convention (its name gives that away). But it more than deserves inclusion in this book. Not because it is such a mammoth event (which, at 167,000 in attendance in recent years, is the largest show in North America — ten to a hundred times the size of most of the other events covered herein), but because it serves as such a terrific platform to raise project awareness, build community, buzz and momentum for science fiction, graphic novels and anime film and television projects. A favorite launch pad for studio graphic novel adaptations and sci-fi tentpole blockbuster hopefuls, it also provides an in-person forum to celebrate a shared love of these genres through screenings, panels, parties and awards. Sharing so many characteristics with markets and festivals, it is pop culture affinity marketing at its best.

Not surprisingly, Comic-Con originally started as a comic book convention. Manga,[1] anime,[2] collectible card games and video games have long been popular attractions. It has evolved to showcase film, television, animation and other comic book-spawned or science fiction, fantasy or horror-genre multimedia arts. The four-day event is typically held Thursday through Sunday during the summer at the San Diego Convention Center in Southern California. The Wednesday evening prior to the official opening of the event, there is usually a preview for professionals, exhibitors and select guests pre-registered for all four days. Comic-Con awards the **Will Eisner Comic Industry Awards**, which is the comic book world's version of the Oscars.

ENTERTAINMENT EXPO HONG KONG

Launched in 2005, Entertainment Expo Hong Kong is a consolidation of a whole slate of events for both the industry as well as the general public, some for education, some for promotion and plenty for pure entertainment.

NOTES

1 Japanese comic books, read right to left.
2 Animated manga.

Denouement[1]   35

Films and television programs of all genres, formats and budgets from around the globe churn in and out through the revolving doors of commerce, continent by continent, year after year. Many deals close at each venue during a given event while a great many are negotiated in the gaps in between. The ebb and flow of our industry's trade is in large measure dictated by this annual market activity.

Whether you are following traditional business practices or macheteing your own unique path, understanding the lay of the land (and its power grid) will help you better analyze which of your projects are best served where, when and why — and at what point during their respective lifecycles they might benefit most from a market presence. Staying apprised of these events — and attending a few here and there — keeps you in sync with the pulse of the *current* worldwide marketplace. Fusing your festival campaign(s) with your market strategies might enable you to innovate new ways to achieve your goals outside the establishment.

These events are a lot of fun. You learn a lot. You get to relax and enjoy some constructive downtime with your peers, when and where everyone isn't pressured to race back to beat the traffic to get back to work or pick up their kids. Markets are often in exotic tropical locations with epic views or gorgeous historical landmarks with stunning architecture in fascinating, energetic cities. Relax. Enjoy the scenery and company. Going to different markets will expand your cultural horizons and expose you to a far broader world than what is going on in the industry within your normal viewfinder. This annual injection of inspiration, education, fresh information, and camaraderie, not to mention the catalyzing force (to the creative class, especially) of arbitrary and cyclical deadlines for milestones and deliverables, cannot be underestimated. Check with your accountant to see if you can write the expenses off as legitimate business deductions.

The vast majority of business-to-business, country-to-country sales of entertainment properties are transacted via this annual, worldwide circuit of entertainment industry trade shows.

All the intimidating and overwhelming industry statistics aside, the myriad barriers to entry are being pulled apart brick by brick, like the Berlin Wall, as clever, indigenous storytellers from all parts of the globe wend their way over, through and around every obstacle the industry or technology can throw at them. I hope this book not only inspires you but helps us all figure out creative new ways to find our tribes, rally forces with one another who face similar challenges and at least empathize with others' experiences and world views.

Perhaps some light at the end of the tunnel: if you can extract yourself from the over-saturated mire that consistently gums up our system — both inside the business and the ubiquitous content that's omnipresently available to the consumer — there is wonderfully fresh air above the dregs. The "competition" up on the higher playing field is of a more discriminating, rewarding caliber. Thus, you are charged with making your project — whether it's a web series, short film, a TV format idea or "the little indie feature that could" — be the very best it can be, whatever it is — at any budget, on any platform. As unique as your voice is, you must find your place. Find your stride, your tribe, your pride. I hope this book has served as part subway, roadway, trailway, airway, off-road map and compass to help you fend for yourself and has inspired you to see — or create — potential new paths along the way — for all of us.

NOTE

1 The final scene of a movie or TV show that resolves all the storylines.

Index

Page numbers in italics refer to figures. Page numbers in bold refer to tables.

Egeda 129
EGOT 272
Egypt 46
E-IP *see* Entertainment-Intellectual Property
    (E-IP) Market
Elevator, The 180–1, *181*
Elwes, Cassian 252
Emmys 84, 149, 269, 272
Endemol 151, 153
Endemol USA 105
Engval, Bill 179
Entertainment Expo Hong Kong 276
Entertainment-Intellectual Property (E-IP)
    Market 127
Entrapment 217
ESPN 86
Esquire Network, The 85
Estonia 73, 127
E.T.: The Extra-Terrestrial 28
EU *see* European Union (EU)
EUR award 129
Eurimages Co-Production Development Award
    128
Eurodata TV Worldwide 264
Europa Distribution 131
Europe 23, 54, 55, 78, 79, 87, 97, 99, 105, 118,
    119, 128, 129, 130, 131, 244, 250, 259, 260,
    274
European Audiovisual Observatory 100
European Collecting Agency 36
European Commission 73, 130
European Documentary Network (EDN) 56
European Film Agency Directors group (EFAD)
    131
European Film Market (EFM) 14, 49, 50–7, 64,
    69, 70, 123, 125, 125, 179, 253–4, 255; app
    254; Drama Series Days 54, 125
European Film Promotion 250
European Union (EU) 100, 130, 131
Europe–Latin America Co-Production Forum
    129
Europe Sails with Latin America Mixer (EFM)
    46
events 223–8
Evernote 225
Everybody Loves Raymond 89
EVP 240
Excel spreadsheets 225
Executive Summary 207
Exhibitor(s) 6, 11, 13, 17, 32–34, 36, 46, 51, 53,
    63–66, 69, 73, 93, 103, 106, 115, 127, 197,
    216, 224, 226, 233, 236, 273, 276; AFM
    Exhibitor List 63; NATPE Exhibitor List
    106
Expo Hong Kong 72
Extreme Home Makeovers 152

Fabrique des Cinémas du Monde, la 248
Facebook 62, 181, 186
Face Off 152
Facts on Pacts (Variety) 29, *30*
Fairmont Miramar Hotel & Bungalows 60, 112,
    113
Faith for Today TV 153
Fantasia International Film Festival 45, 129
Fantastic Fanatics Mixer 46
Fargo 151
Far Side, The 88
Fast and the Furious 28
Fawlty Towers Does Celebrity Rehab 206
FCC 86–7
FDC *see* Film Development Fund (FDC)
Federal Commissioner for Cultural and Media
    Affairs 268
Federal Foundation for Culture 126
Fédération Internationale des Associations de
    Producteurs de Films (FIAPF) 128, 257,
    260, 261
Fédération Wallonie-Bruxelles 130
FESPACO *see* Festival panafricain du cinéma et
    de la télévision de Ouagadougou
Festival de Cannes 14, 39–49, 73, 97, 247, 248–9
Festival Internacional de Cine en Guadalajara
    45
Festival Internacional de Cine Panamá 45
Festival Internacional de Programmes
    Audiovisuels (FIPA) 263
Festival panafricain du cinéma et de la
    télévision de Ouagadougou (FESPACO)
    263
festivals, *vs.* markets 14–16
Festivals and Sales Agents Mixer 46
Festival Scope 250
Festival Spain 263
FIAPF *see* Fédération Internationale des
    Associations de Producteurs de Films
    (FIAPF)
Fighters, The 152
Film & Media Collecting Agency 36
FILMART *see* Hong Kong International Film &
    TV Market (FILMART)
FilmBuff 33
Film Bureau, General Administration of Press,
    Publication, Radio, Film and Television
    of China 258
Film Catalogue, The 62, 63–4, *63–4*, 65, 224
Film Circuit 250–1
Film Development Fund (FDC) 114
film distributors 33–4
Film Export UK 74
Film Factor Market 127, 128
film festivals 247–56, 257–61
Film Independent 267–8